NATURALISM AND THE FIRST-PERSON
PERSPECTIVE

NATURALISM AND THE
FIRST-PERSON PERSPECTIVE

Lynne Rudder Baker

OXFORD
UNIVERSITY PRESS

OXFORD

UNIVERSITY PRESS

Oxford University Press is a department of the University of Oxford.
It furthers the University's objective of excellence in research, scholarship,
and education by publishing worldwide.

Oxford   New York

Auckland   Cape Town   Dar es Salaam   Hong Kong   Karachi
Kuala Lumpur   Madrid   Melbourne   Mexico City   Nairobi
New Delhi   Shanghai   Taipei   Toronto

With offices in

Argentina   Austria   Brazil   Chile   Czech Republic   France   Greece
Guatemala   Hungary   Italy   Japan   Poland   Portugal   Singapore
South Korea   Switzerland   Thailand   Turkey   Ukraine   Vietnam

Published in the United States of America by
Oxford University Press
198 Madison Avenue, New York, NY 10016

Library of Congress Cataloging-in-Publication Data
Baker, Lynne Rudder, 1944–
Naturalism and the first-person perspective / Lynne Rudder Baker.
p. cm.
ISBN 978-0-19-991474-6 (pbk. : alk. paper)—ISBN 978-0-19-991472-2
(hardback : alk. paper)—ISBN 978-0-19-991473-9 (updf)   1. Naturalism.   2. Self
(Philosophy)   3. Perspective (Philosophy)   I. Title.
B828.2.B35 2013
146—dc23
2012030940

ISBN 978-0-19-991474-6
ISBN 978-0-19-991472-2

3 5 7 9 8 6 4
Printed in the United States of America
on acid-free paper

To my dear sister and friend, Catherine Rudder,
and to her partner, Helen Gibson

CONTENTS

PART II

AN ACCOUNT OF THE FIRST-PERSON
PERSPECTIVE

CONTENTS

ACKNOWLEDGMENTS

Gratitude is due especially to David Hershenov and his assistant Adam Taylor for reading and commenting on a draft of the whole manuscript. Also I thank Hilary Kornblith and members of our seminar on Naturalism and the First-Person Perspective, Phillip Bricker, Alex Rosenberg, Mario De Caro, Philip Kitcher, Sam Cowling, and the late Gareth B. Matthews for reading parts of drafts of chapters. I am also grateful to Peter Ohlin and Lucy Randall for their continuing help on this project. I apologize to anyone else left unmentioned who helped bring this project to fruition.

I also want to acknowledge the following for permission to use parts of articles I published:

For a part of Chapter 3 and a part of Chapter 4:
- The University of Illinois Press, "Does Naturalism Rest on a Mistake?" *American Philosophical Quarterly* 48(2): 161–73, 2011.

For a part of Chapter 4:
- Ontos Verlag, "Naturalism and the First-Person Perspective," *How Successful Was Naturalism?* Georg Gasser, ed. (2007): 203–26.

For parts of Chapter 6:

- *Grazer Philosophische Studien* 84 (2012): 31–50, "From Consciousness to Self-Consciousness";
- *The Modern Schoolman*, 84 (2007): 155–70, "First-Person Externalism";
- *Phenomenology and Mind* 1 (2011): 48–57, "Beyond the Cartesian Self";
- With Kind Permission from Springer Science + Business Media B.V. "How to Have Self-Directed Attitudes" by Lynne Rudder Baker in *Self-Evaluation*, Anita Konzelmann Ziv, Keith Lehrer, and Hans Bernhard Schmid, eds. (2011): 33–43.

For a part of Chapter 7:

- Cambridge University Press. "Personal Identity: A Not-So-Simple View." In *Personal Identity: Complex or Simple?* (in press) Georg Gasser and Matthias Stefan, eds.

For parts of Chapter 9:

- Blackwell Publishing Company. "First-Personal Aspects of Agency," *Metaphilosophy*, 42(1–2): 1–16, 2011.

INTRODUCTION

WHAT IS THE PROBLEM?

The problem that concerns me here was effectively posed years ago by Thomas Nagel. (T. Nagel 1983) Although I demur from his resolution of the problem,[1] Nagel raised it in a particularly pointed way: If there is an impersonal conception of the world that includes all the individuals and all their properties, then we have the ingredients of all the facts about every individual. How, then, is there a place for the putative fact that some particular person is me?[2] Since all the individuals, including LB, would already be represented in such an objectively described world, how could there be room for an additional fact that one of the individuals is me? How could a centerless world accommodate me? How can we understand the apparent fact that I am LB?

1. One way that I demur is from Nagel's idea of an objective self; another way is that I use the term "properties" to include relations.
2. On one point I differ with the way that Nagel expresses the problem. He distinguishes between an ordinary use of "I am LB" when I introduce myself at a party from a philosophical use, which he takes to be perplexing. (T. Nagel 1983, 216) I treat ordinary and philosophical uses of "I am LB" the same way.

The answer of naturalism is that there is no such fact. On the heels of science, naturalism takes the world to be impersonal; what exists are all individuals and all their properties, but none of these requires appeal to anything expressible in the first person. So, the answer to the questions in the last paragraph, on naturalistic views, is that there are no irreducibly first-person facts.[3] I shall argue otherwise: If we take first-person facts to entail properties expressible only in the first person ("first-person properties"), then, as I shall argue, there are irreducible first-person facts. There is a long and, I believe, provocative story to be told about the first-person perspective, and it is not until Chapter Eight that I shall show how there can be an irreducible fact that I am LB.

Naturalists try to show that the problem of *my* being LB is a pseudo-problem. There are several tacks that they may take to show that there are no first-person properties. For example, they may take a semantic line. They may treat "I am LB" as a special kind of statement—one governed by truth-conditions expressible without the token-reflexive "I." All the facts, they may say, are expressible in the third person; "I am LB" expresses no "further fact." Sentences with the indexical "I" are treated just like sentences with other indexical terms ("here," "now," "this"); this kind of treatment is quite free of any appeal to any special facts or any special semantic content. (Kaplan 1989)

However, this semantic diagnosis seems inadequate to the problem posed by Nagel, who was concerned with *his* being TN, not with particular utterances. It is still the case that I am LB even when I am not thinking or saying anything at all. No semantic rule seems adequate fully to explain my being LB.

---

3. I often use "first-person," as opposed to "first-personal," as an adjective. I use "first-person facts" to apply to facts adequately describable only by means of a first-person pronoun. First-person pronouns include not only "I," "me," and "mine," but also "I*," "he*," and "she*." (See Chapter Two.) I sometimes use "third-person facts" or "third-person ontology" as stand-ins for "non-first-person facts" or "non-first-person ontology."

Another naturalistic response aimed to show that there are no irreducibly first-person facts or properties is epistemic. According to the epistemic line, "I am LB" does express something inexpressible in the third person; however, the reason for the inexpressibility is not that "I am LB" expresses a special fact. "I am LB" expresses belief or knowledge of an ordinary truth under a first-person description. My belief about myself under a first-person description has special behavioral consequences that a similar belief about myself under a third-person description lacks. (See Chapter 3 for a discussion and critique of John Perry's view. (Perry 2002a))

My response to Nagel's question is to argue that my assertion, "I am LB," entails that I have a first-person perspective, which is irreducible and ineliminable. Consequently, not all the facts are expressible without reference to the first person. Thus, insofar as naturalism provides a conception of the world that has no room for first-person properties, it cannot be true.[4] I rest my case not on simple thoughts or assertions like "I am LB," but on more complex ones like "I believe (know, said, and so on) that I am LB," which entails that I am not only the thinker of my thought but also I am the object of my thought: what I am thinking *about*, conceived of in the first person.[5] Anyone with the capacity to have such thoughts about herself conceived of in the first person exemplifies an irreducible and ineliminable first-personal dispositional property. Or so I shall argue.

In this book, I have three main goals: (1) to show that no wholly impersonal account of the world can be adequate; the apparently first-person aspects of reality are genuine—irreducible and

---

4. This is not Nagel's response. Nagel's solution is to say that I am an objective self, now seeing through the eyes of LB. According to Nagel, I, like everyone else, have an impersonal conception of the world containing LB and everyone else.

5. I take "conceived of in the first person" to mean "thought of using a first-person concept."

ineliminable; (2) to give a detailed non-Cartesian account of the first-person perspective and its contribution to reality; (3) to shape a "near-naturalism" that is more accommodating to the world that we encounter than is the dominant scientific naturalism.

The Claim of Naturalism

Naturalism is a philosophical view about the nature of reality and our knowledge of it. Like many other philosophical views, naturalism has both stronger and weaker construals. The weaker construal is just that there is no supernatural reality.[6] The stronger construal is that science is the arbiter of reality and of knowledge.

If we take ontology to be a complete inventory of all the individuals, kinds, and properties that must exist for reality to be as it is, then the claim of the stronger form of naturalism—scientific naturalism—is twofold: (1) At bottom, reality is what natural science says it is and nothing more, and (2) our beliefs are ultimately justifiable only by the methods of science. So, the stronger form of naturalism, as I am construing it, comprises both an ontological and an epistemological claim about science. My arguments will focus on the ontological claims—ontological naturalism—and my use of "naturalism" will refer to the stronger form of naturalism.

A corollary of the ontological claim is that reality is completely describable in "scientific language"—language that contains no

---

6. Some philosophers, like Alvin Plantinga, discuss naturalism on its weaker construal (that there is no supernatural reality). As he construes naturalism, science conflicts with naturalism. (Beilby 2002; Plantinga 2011) On the stronger construal (that science is the arbiter of reality and of knowledge), naturalism is in fact incompatible with supernaturalism. Although strong naturalism in fact precludes supernaturalism, Quine himself would countenance immaterial objects if there were an explanatory need for them. "If I saw indirect explanatory benefit in positing sensibilia, possibilia, spirits, a Creator," Quine said, "I would joyfully accord them scientific status too, on a par with such avowedly scientific posits as quarks and black holes." (Quine 1995, 252) I thank Michael Rea for the reference. (Rea 2002, 42)

tenses or indexicals. Scientific language is "generally stated as applicable to arbitrary speakers, places, times, and the like; if modality is involved, to arbitrary possible worlds as well." (Kripke 2011, 294)

If the ontological claim of scientific naturalism is correct, then all the elements of reality must fall within the purview of science. There are numerous kinds of things—mathematical entities, normativity, modality, responsibility, and freedom—that seem to exist, but are not obviously within the purview of science. So, according to scientific naturalism, these "controversial cases" either must be described by science or explained away by science. (De Caro and Voltolini 2010, 70) I want to add another such case: the first-person perspective.

Some philosophers simply take for granted that the first-person phenomena of the sort to which I shall draw attention are compatible with naturalism. For example, Frankfurt, Velleman, and Bratman (Frankfurt 1971; Velleman 1992; Bratman 2001) all speak of an agent's reflective participation in her action as if reflective participation (on a non-instrumentalist construal) is compatible with a third-person ontology. Many philosophers do not acknowledge that the first-person perspective presents a problem for scientific naturalism. Philosophers who explicitly discuss first-person phenomena at all—with the exception of hard-core Cartesians—aim to show that first-person phenomena are either reducible to third-person phenomena or eliminable altogether. Even John Perry, who argues for the essential indexical, takes first-person phenomena compatible with third-person naturalistic ontology. (Perry 1979, 2002b)

At least one philosopher takes the epistemological preeminence often assumed for the first-person perspective to stem from a kind of mystified view of reflection. "The first-step toward mystification... involves a perspectival shift in which first-order mental processes are viewed from the third-person point of view, but reflection—[e.g., 'I believe that I am honest']—is instead presented from a first-person perspective." (Kornblith 2012, 206–7) In positing a perspectival shift between first- and second-order mental processes, Kornblith is not aiming at my view; however, if I am right, a perspectival shift already presupposes that the subject has a first-person perspective. In a world without first-person properties, I shall argue, there could be no second-order (or reflective) mental processes at all; so, a scientist who wants to study second-order (or reflective) mental processes must presuppose that her subjects have first-person properties. Whatever the fate of the epistemological preeminence of the first-person perspective, its ontological significance—I shall argue—is secure.

Naturalists may want to treat the first-person perspective in the same way that they treat other naturalistically problematic notions: Give truth conditions for statements about some putative domain that do not require accepting the putative domain into ontology. For example, according to David Lewis's Humean supervenience, there is no possibility or necessity in the actual world: "all there is to the world is a vast mosaic of local matters of particular fact, just one little thing and then another." (Lewis 1986, ix) But no worry: We still have true and false statements about possibility and necessity, and Lewis has supplied a semantics for such statements. His semantics defines statements about possibility and necessity in terms of relations between possible worlds. With such a semantics on hand, no ontological question about possibility and necessity remains. All the facts about possibility and necessity are reconstrued in terms of facts about possible worlds, together with interest-dependent metrics of similarity.

Or consider a very different kind of naturalist. According to Philip Kitcher, the universe is devoid of value, but he provides a naturalistic account of the how hominids came to make value judgments. (Kitcher 2011, 41–42) A common strategy for naturalists who find some apparent phenomenon that seems resistant to being naturalized (e.g., modality or normativity) is to give a naturalistic account of a closely related phenomenon (a semantics for modal statements or the origin of moral judgments) that leaves the original (putative) phenomenon out in the cold as something that has no purchase on actual reality.

Can first-person perspectives be treated in the same way?[7] Perhaps people think of perspectives as analogous to kinds of graph paper. Just as an equation can be graphed in rectangular coordinates or in polar coordinates, perhaps the same bit of reality may be considered from the first- or the third-person perspective. But note: The case of the first-person perspective is not analogous to the case of rectangular or polar coordinates. There is no third-person perspective at all. The so-called third-person perspective is centerless; it is the "view from nowhere." (T. Nagel 1986) The world as conceived by naturalists is the world "as simply existing…as simply there." (T. Nagel 1986, 56) The naturalist view is that reality is without perspective.[8] It is not surprising that naturalists tend to be unfazed by any appeal to the first-person perspective. They may think that the first-person perspective is nothing in reality, or if they agree that there is such a thing, it is—to borrow from Fodor in another context—"really something else." (Fodor 1987, 97) I shall try to show that the first-person perspective cannot be downplayed in this way.

A Challenge to Naturalism

The robust form of the first-person perspective is the capacity to think of oneself, conceived in the first person, as the object of one's thought. (As I shall explain in Chapter 2, I use a "*" to signal this use

---

7. I am not implying that this strategy is successful in the non-first-person cases either.
8. If one took reality to be the nonperspectival world together with all the perspectives on it, one would still be treating the perspectives in a non-first-person way, treating all of them equally.

of first-person pronouns.)[9] It is manifested every time one thinks of what she* wishes or what she* believes, where "she*" is an attribution to the thinker or speaker of a first-person reference. Canonically, the thinker or speaker would express her thought by "I hope that I* survive the war," or "I whispered that I* was sorry," or some other sentence of like structure. Indeed, the robust first-person perspective is manifested with every thought, utterance, or action that exhibits self-consciousness. Many simple "I" sentences—for example, "I am LB"—also indirectly manifest the robust first-person perspective when they are assertible only by someone who has the capacity to think of herself as herself* in the first person.

As important as the robust first-person perspective is, many philosophers have not appreciated the force of the data from it and suppose that what I am calling "the robust first-person perspective" presents no particular problems for the naturalizing philosopher. For example, David Kaplan, who has done groundbreaking work on indexicals (e.g., the pronoun "I") has not—as far as I know—taken up the sentences of interest here, like "I believe that I* am a slow reader." The robust first-person perspective is required for self-consciousness, but philosophers often bypass self-consciousness: For example, Ned Block commented, "It is of course [phenomenal] consciousness rather than…self-consciousness that has seemed such a scientific mystery." (Block 1995, 230) And David Chalmers said that self-consciousness is one of those psychological states that "pose no deep metaphysical enigmas." (Chalmers 1996, 24)

---

9. I use "I*" to mark cases in which I (conceived of in the first person) am the object of my thought. Canonically, "I*" is embedded in a "that" clause of a complex first-person sentence with a psychological or linguistic main verb—for example, "I believe that I* am LB" or "I'm glad that I* study philosophy" with a "*" to signal that the thinker or speaker, conceived of in the first person, is also part of the object of the attitude. This use of "*" is an extension of Castañeda's use of "he*," which attributes to someone else a first-person reference. (Castañeda 1966, 1967)

I shall counter dismissals of the significance of the robust first-person perspective by showing that it can neither be explained by science nor explained away: it can neither be eliminated nor be reduced to anything nonperspectival or non-first-personal. It is, in fact, a dispositional property that must appear in basic ontology. If that is correct, then there are genuinely first-person properties. Since the scientific picture of the world is of a totally objective, totally impersonal reality, the scientific picture cannot accommodate the first-person perspective. If I am successful, the first-person perspective is a serious challenge to naturalism.

What Is at Stake

What is at stake is the fundamental character of natural reality. If naturalism is correct, then the world, at bottom, is wholly impersonal. If I am right about the first-person perspective, then the world has an ineliminably personal element.[10]

If there are first-person properties that cannot be eliminated or reduced to non-first-person properties, then reality is not wholly impersonal. This consequence has significant implications both for the nature of reality and for the possibility of knowledge. For example, what Bernard Williams has called "the absolute conception" is not feasible, even as an ideal. The absolute conception is a maximally inclusive representation of the world, which includes all the other representations and their relations to reality. (Williams 1978, 64–66) The absolute conception is a conception of the reality

---

10. To say that the world, at bottom, has a personal element is not to say that it always has had a personal element. As is apparent from the properties present immediately after the Big Bang, not all properties have existed from the beginning: some properties come into existence by natural selection (being a mammal), and perhaps by human invention (being an MRI machine). To put it another way, the properties that did exist at the beginning of the world are not sufficient to illuminate reality as it is today. For further detail, see Chapter 10 where I offer an account of emergent properties.

which is "there anyway," a conception required by the thought that "knowledge is of what is there anyway." The absolute conception is a picture of reality as wholly mind-independent.

If reality is, as I shall argue, not wholly impersonal, then the absolute conception cannot include all reality. In this case, we should rethink the conception of reality as being exhausted by objects that are mind-independent or "there anyway." The upshot is that the mind-independence/mind-dependence distinction is not metaphysically fundamental, as I have argued for decades (Baker 1995). The result of locating the first-person perspective in ontology, as I propose to do, is that we live in a stoutly minded world without appeal to imaginary skyhooks.

An Overview

This book has two parts. Part I (Chapter 1—Chapter 5) comprises the core argument that both reductive and nonreductive versions of naturalism, without first-person properties, are in error. Part II (Chapter 6—Chapter 10) adds my own metaphysical background picture to the Core Argument. It shows one way (my way) to situate the first-person perspective in a metaphysical view; since the Core Argument does not depend on my particular way of developing the background picture, a reader may accept the major conclusion of the book while taking issue with the background picture.

In Chapter 1, I discuss two ways of construing science and the resulting forms of reductive and nonreductive naturalism. In Chapter 2, I discuss what would be required to naturalize a property, and then I introduce the two stages of the first-person perspective: (1) the rudimentary stage, which human infants (and some other people with out language) share with certain nonhuman animals, and (2) the robust stage, which is available only to persons with complex conceptual and linguistic abilities.

Beings at the rudimentary stage of the first-person perspective have consciousness and intentionality; beings at the robust stage have, in addition, the capacity to conceive of themselves *as* themselves, in the first person. This second, robust stage brings with it a cascade of new capacities. In Chapter 3 and Chapter 4, I survey four attempts to naturalize the first-person perspective, either by reduction or by elimination (John Perry and David Lewis in Chapter 3; Daniel Dennett and Thomas Metzinger in Chapter 4) and conclude that each is inadequate. Each attempt either leaves a residue of the first-person perspective in the metaphysical account or suffers from internal incoherence.

In Chapter 5, I give two positive arguments against naturalization of the first-person perspective. First, I give a linguistic argument that starts from first-person concepts and argues for first-person properties that are neither reducible nor eliminable. Then, I give a metaphysical argument against ontological naturalism.

Then, I turn in Part II to a deeper look at the idea of the first-person perspective. Chapter 6 is an account of the road from the rudimentary to the robust stage of the first-person perspective, or more colloquially, from consciousness to self-consciousness. The focus is on a social conception of language and the acquisition of a self-concept. The chapter concludes with a summary of my non-Cartesian account of human persons. Chapter 7 is a presentation and defense of a first-personal approach to diachronic personal identity. I then explore Mark Johnston's recent account of self-identity as illusory and argue that my view does not fall to his arguments.

Then, in Chapter 8 and Chapter 9, I turn to the metaphysics of the first-person perspective. In Chapter 8, I discuss first-personal properties, dispositional properties and, briefly, haecceities. In Chapter 9, I describe some of the contributions to reality that the first-person perspective makes. Without first-person perspectives, there would be no persons, no agency, and no moral responsibility.

Finally, in Chapter 10, I discuss a conception of natural reality that I take to be adequate to the commonsense world that we interact with. The conception, which I call "near-naturalism," is a very weak version of nonreductivism that recognizes first-person perspectives in the inventory of properties that make an irreplaceable contribution to reality. Using a notion of property-constitution, I argue that everyday properties are casually efficacious without being reducible to micro- or micro-based properties. I argue for the reality of ontological emergentism and downward causation. Finally, I consider in what respect this conception of natural reality is naturalistic.

PART I

THE CORE ARGUMENT

Chapter One

Varieties of Naturalism

Success has catapulted science and technology into the intellectual spotlight all over the world. Naturalism, the philosophical companion of science, now dominates Anglophone philosophy. As befits a reigning worldview, naturalism comes in many varieties, with little in common save (1) a commitment to science as the discoverer of what really exists and how we know it and (2) a repudiation of anything that smacks of the supernatural.

Without trying to survey all the kinds of naturalism in philosophy, I shall emphasize the one that concerns me here: ontological naturalism. As I mentioned, I take ontology to be an inventory of the objects, kinds, and properties required for a complete description of reality, without redundancy.[1] For purposes here, I shall confine discussion of naturalistic ontology to concrete objects and the properties that they exemplify. (I'll omit consideration of numbers, for example.) According to ontological naturalism, science tells us what exists and cannot be omitted from a complete description of reality.

Obviously, it would be tautologous to define "ontology" as comprising only whatever our best science quantifies over, or what

---

1. The question of whether there are multiple admissible complete descriptions of reality is complicated, and I am not taking a stand on it here. Nor am I taking a stand on whether there are *qualia* or not.

appears in the austere "first-class" conceptual scheme of regimented science, used for "official scientific business." (Quine 1969a, 24) I use "ontology" to apply to the objects, kinds, and properties that suffice for all of reality, not to apply to some privileged part of reality from which the rest of reality cannot be deduced.[2]

A large burden of my project is to show that the first-person perspective is a dispositional property that should be included in ontology, along with properties like having a charge, being mammalian, and being ambidextrous.[3] If I am right, then no exclusively non-first-person ontology can be complete. In that case, science cannot be a complete account of everything there is, as long as it omits reference to first-personal properties. Although my main concern with naturalism is ontological, naturalism also makes claims that connect methodology to epistemology, and connect both to ontology.[4]

The origin of current naturalism lies in Quine's naturalized epistemology, according to which epistemology—study of knowledge and justification—"simply falls into place as a chapter of psychology and hence of natural science." (Quine 1969b, 82) Traditionally, knowledge and justification were analyzed a priori or by introspective reflection. Quine introduced a new project: Knowledge and justification should be investigated empirically, in terms of what science (e.g., cognitive psychology) discovers about our cognitive faculties.

2. Throughout, I am using "reality" to be natural reality. I remain neutral here about whether natural reality is all there is.
3. I use the term "properties" very loosely, to pick out "ways things are." A nominalist (who does not think that there are any properties) may then replace "ways things are" by "objects' being different ways." Then a complete description of reality would include mention of all the objects and the ways that they could be. (This note was prompted by a comment from Sam Cowling.)
4. There are other versions of naturalism that I cannot discuss here—for example, Rea (2002), Almeder (1998), and the essays in Shook and Kurtz (2009).

Some methodological versions of naturalism accept the Quinean view that philosophy is continuous with science and that both are empirical: "A metaphysics that goes beyond the commitments of science is simply unsupported by the best available evidence." (Kornblith 1994, 40; cf. Kitcher 1992) Other influential forms of naturalism have a place for a priori conceptual analysis alongside scientific method: We analyze our concepts and use science to see what, if anything, satisfies the concepts. (Lewis 1983; Jackson 1998) Even naturalists who do not confine philosophical method to scientific method would agree with Wilfrid Sellars's well-known epigram, "In the dimension of describing and explaining the world, science is the measure of all things, of what is that it is, and of what is not that it is not." (Sellars 1963, 173).

To sum up the terminology that I use: Ontological naturalism is the view that ontology (i.e., the complete inventory of reality) is exhausted by the entities and properties invoked by scientific theories. Epistemological naturalism is the view that epistemological questions (e.g., what can we know or what is the nature of knowledge or justification) are to be investigated empirically by, for example, scientific accounts of our cognitive faculties. Methological naturalism is the view that the methods of philosophy should be restricted to the methods of science. A corollary of methodological naturalism is explanatory naturalism, the view that all genuine explanations are scientific explanations. Any and all of these kinds of naturalism fall under the rubric "scientific naturalism."

The term "naturalistic" is sometimes used in a weaker way to mean only "without God or a designer" or "pertaining to the realm of nature," but even in this weaker usage, naturalism at least requires consistency with the laws of nature.

WHAT COUNTS AS "SCIENCE"?

A major feature that divides the many varieties of naturalism is what conditions to put on "science" or "natural science." Everyone agrees that sciences try to find laws of nature and to produce successful explanations and predictions; the disagreement concerns whether there are multiple autonomous sciences or whether physics alone—together with what strictly follows from physics—suffices to account for everything. Reductionists say "yes": Ontology is determined by physics and what logically follows from physics. Nonreductionists say "no": Ontology is determined by all the sciences—psychological, social, historical—whether they are reducible to physics or not. If reductionists are correct, then it is a condition for even *being* a science (e.g., biology, psychology, sociology) that a discipline be reducible to physics.

Nonreductionists may take biology, psychology, and sociology to have domains on ontologically distinct levels that are not reducible to physics. Reductionists hold that there is only one ontological level, the level of physics, and that biology, psychology, and sociology have scientific legitimacy only if they are reducible to physics. According to one reductionist, what we think of as biological evolution by means of natural selection is really only the outworking of the second law of thermodynamics on physical particles. (Rosenberg 2013).

REDUCTIVE NATURALISM

All forms of reduction have a direction toward physics; they all reduce a "higher-level" item (theory, property, law, or term) to a "lower-level" item (theory, property, law, or term), where the lower-level item is privileged by being "closer" to physics. For example, when heat is identified with the motion of molecules, the property of being heat is reduced to the property of being motion of molecules, where the property of being motion of molecules is a property found in physics.

The nature of reduction is a very complicated and contested issue in philosophy. Traditionally, reduction has been understood as derivability of higher-level theories from physics, together with bridge laws that connect properties mentioned in physics to properties mentioned in the reduced theory—for example, motion of molecules and heat. (E. Nagel 1961) Others take reduction to be an explanatory relation: A property is reduced if it is reductively explainable in terms of underlying properties. (Kim 1993a, 10) More recently, Jaegwon Kim has taken reduction of a property to depend on whether it can be construed in terms of its causal/nomic relations to other properties (its "functionalizability"). (Kim 2000, 24–27) Finally, David Chalmers takes reduction to entail that the lower-level facts determine the higher-level facts.[5]

Reductive naturalism requires that reduction go all the way to microphysics. If mental properties were reducible to neural properties, say, but neural properties were not further reducible, there would be only a partial reduction. All the layers between the neural and the microphysical would still be intact; but the aim of reductionism is to reduce all the levels to the bottom level, if there is one. Jonathan Schaffer has argued persuasively that whether there is a fundamental level is an open empirical question. (Schaffer 2003). However, even if there is no bottom level, there will be some level

---

5. (Chalmers 1996, 107) Although I think that he does not appreciate the problem of self-consciousness (Chalmers 1996, 24), Chalmers, who is an anti-reductionist about consciousness, does admit that "David Chalmers is me" may express "an indexical fact that may have to be taken as primitive." It is "a fact about the world as I find it, and it is the world as I find it that needs explanation." However, "admitting this primitive indexical fact would require far less revision of our materialist worldview than would admitting irreducible facts about conscious experience." (Chalmers 1996, 85)

at which objects have no "physically significant proper parts" that make a difference in physics. (Kim 2000a, 15) In that case, any level at which objects lack physically significant parts is tantamount to a bottom level. The point is that for a reductionist there are not multiple ontological levels.

For purposes here, I shall formulate a generic version of reductive naturalism: Say that a property P is reduced if and only if there are properties $Q_1, Q_2, \ldots, Q_n$ mentioned in a successful theory of microphysics, such that $Q_1, Q_2, \ldots, Q_n$ (1) are local and (2) P strongly supervenes on $Q_1, Q_2, \ldots, Q_n$. Then, reductive naturalism is true if and only if all properties P are reducible to some microproperties $Q_1, Q_2, \ldots, Q_n$.

Let me explain each clause, beginning with the second: (2) Technically, strong supervenience is a relation between sets of properties, A and B. A strongly supervenes on B if and only if: "necessarily, for any object x and property F in A, if x has F, then there exists a property G in B such that x has G, and necessarily if any y has G, it has F." (Kim 1993b)[6] This definition applies to reductive naturalism by taking A to be the set of macroproperties and B to be the set of microproperties mentioned in a successful theory of physics. Although some philosophers take strong supervenience still to be too weak for reduction, I shall argue that even reductive naturalism in the sense of (1) and (2) is false, and so would still be false if reduction were construed in a stronger sense.

(1) By "local," I mean to underscore the point that the lower-level microproperties are instantiated by the bearer of the reduced macroproperty P. Reductive naturalists typically confine

---

6. Strong supervenience on the microphysical is not just covariance, or the claim that there is "no difference without a microphysical difference." Strong supervenience on the microphysical is the claim that microphysical properties necessitate the macrophysical properties.

macroproperties to the intrinsic properties of their bearers—properties that an object has independent of its relations to other objects.[7] I am using "local" to enforce this restriction: Since the supervenient macroproperties are intrinsic properties of their (macro-object) bearers, the instantiation of the subvenient microproperties depends on nothing beyond the spatial boundaries of the bearer of the macro-property.[8]

Reductive naturalism, as I am construing it, is the view that all properties reduce to local microphysical properties. If a property P reduces to microphysical properties $Q_1, Q_2, \ldots, Q_n$, then only $Q_1, Q_2, \ldots, Q_n$ appear in the ontology. Reduced properties are not among those required for a complete description of reality. If, as reductive naturalists hold, all science is reducible to microphysics, then all reality reduces to the microphysical. What appears to be a single individual thing—a person, a chair—is really just an aggregate of microphysical particles, and what appear to be macroproperties of single individual things (e.g., being a person, being a chair) just reduce to microproperties. So, if reductive naturalism is true, then it seems that the whole perceived world ontologically collapses.

Many reductivists would protest, "Of course, I believe that what we perceive exists: there are people, computers, and so on. I do not deny that chairs exist. I'm just saying that what they are—really are—is just aggregates of microphysical particles." OK, but if reductivism

---

7. In Chapter 2, I'll allow for nonreductive naturalists who are externalists, but here we are discussing reductionists.

8. I am deliberately formulating the locality restriction without appeal to mereology, because I believe that the wholesale use of mereology as the key to understanding the physical world has pulled philosophy way off course. Moreover, by forgoing the standard uses of mereology in favor of my view of constitution, I have no worry about maximality considerations. On my view, a table with one atom removed is still a table (indeed, the same table) but is now constituted by a different sum of atoms. (Baker 2007, 181–98)

is true, the difference between a being chair and being an aggregate of particles amounts to a difference in the description: "chair" versus "aggregate of particles."[9] Whether one then claims that the chair does not exist (eliminativism) or that the chair is just an aggregate of particles (reductionism) is small beer. If reductionism is true, then, ontologically speaking, no single object is a chair (or a person-sized object). What seems to be a difference in reality between aggregates of particles and people is only a difference in description. All that really exist, all that deserve a place in a complete description of reality, are microphysical particles and their properties. Such particles and microproperties exhaust the ontology.

Alternatively, a reductive naturalist may hold that there is a property of being a chair, but that it is reducible to the property of being an aggregate (or plurality or sum) of particles organized in a certain (chairlike) way. So, necessarily, anything that has the property of being an aggregate of particles organized in a certain way has the property of being a chair. Reductivists hold that higher-level properties, like being a chair or even like being a mammal, are causally inert. So, if they hold Alexander's Dictum that to be real is to have causal powers, reductive naturalists hold that there are no higher-level properties that have any effects. (Kim 1993c, 348) So, reductivists who adhere to Alexander's Dictum become eliminativists about higher-level properties.

NONREDUCTIVE NATURALISM

Nonreductive naturalism is the view that there are genuine properties that do not strongly supervene on local microphysical

---

9. On my nonreductive view, a chair is constituted at t by a particular aggregate of particles, but is not identical to the aggregate of particles that constitutes it at t. I take aggregates to be "ontologically innocent" (Lewis's term).

properties. "Local" is important here. Nonreductivists may well hold that genuine properties globally supervene on microphysical properties, but global supervenience is obviously nonlocal; so, the restriction on nonreductive naturalism is only that there are genuine properties that do not strongly supervene on local microphysical properties. For example, a nonreductionist (an externalist) may hold that having the thought that there is water in lakes does not strongly supervene on *local* microproperties, but is nonetheless a genuine property.

In general, mentalistic terms are used in successful explanation and prediction, and they are ineliminable from successful psychological theories. The ineliminability of mentalistic terms from "a successful scientific theory gives us reason to believe that these terms genuinely refer. This is all the evidence one needs for holding that mental states and processes genuinely exist." (Kornblith 1994, 41) And if nonreductive naturalism is correct, mental states and the properties instantiated by people in those states are irreducible.

Moreover, nonreductivists also deny explanatory reductionism. There may be biological, psychological, sociological and other explanations that do not reduce to explanations in the vocabulary of physics. Nonetheless, nonreductivists remain materialists in the sense that they hold that every concrete object is ultimately constituted or composed by microphysical particles. Although nonreductivists are monists about the ultimate constituents of concrete objects, they are not monists about ontology *simpliciter*. The ultimate micro-constituents do not exhaust what exists in the material world. There are irreducible macro-objects that have causal powers. (For example, a lion may be an irreducible entity that has the power to bring down a gazelle.)

In short, nonreductive naturalists are open to pluralism about the sciences (and hence about ontology). Kornblith joins Kitcher (Kitcher 1992; Kornblith 1994), for instance, in including the biological, psychological, social, and historical sciences among the successful sciences whether or not they are reducible to physics. "Physics does not provide us with the only [successful scientific] theory, nor do physics and chemistry, or physics, chemistry, and biology. The suggestion that (some of) these sciences are the sole determinants of what exists is a suggestion which does not derive from science itself." (Kornblith 1994, 40) If the task of the naturalistic metaphysician is, as Kornblith says, "simply to draw out the metaphysical implications of contemporary science," the naturalist should not appeal to extrascientific restrictions like limiting ontology to the ontology of physics. (Kornblith 1994, 40) "For the naturalist," as Kornblith says, "there is simply no extrascientific route to metaphysical understanding." (Kornblith 1994, 40)

A few nonreductivists go still further. So-called liberal naturalists aim to carve out logical space between scientific naturalism and supernaturalism, where supernaturalism is "characterized by the acceptance of entities that could break the causal closure of the world studied by natural sciences (for instance, Cartesian mental properties)," or entities that require a "special mode of understanding that would be irreconcilable with rational forms of understanding." (De Caro and Voltolini 2010, 81)

However, liberal naturalism, so understood, faces a dilemma: If liberal naturalism grants that all entities are reducible to or ontologically dependent on entities mentioned in scientific theories, then it collapses into scientific naturalism; but if it denies that possibility for some entities, then it "loses its naturalistic credentials." So liberal naturalism seems either too liberal or not liberal enough. (De Caro and Voltolini 2010, 69)

Liberal naturalists try to thread the horns of the dilemma by showing that there can be philosophically legitimate entities that are irreducible and ineliminable, without being supernatural. (Throughout this discussion, "supernatural" applies not just to divine beings or to entities presumably known by revelation but to "any special modes of understanding that would be irreconcilable with rational forms of understanding." (De Caro and Voltolini 2010, 70))

De Caro and Voltolini formulate what they call "the constitutive claim of contemporary naturalism" like this: "No entity or explanation should be accepted whose existence or truth could contradict the laws of nature, insofar as we know them." (De Caro and Voltolini 2010, 71) To find room in naturalism for a nonscientific variety that does not court supernaturalism, liberal naturalists buttress the constitutive claim with two provisos: (1) They are prepared to countenance modes of inquiry that are neither scientific nor supernatural. Among these, they mention conceptual analysis, imaginative speculation, and introspection. (2) They are prepared to countenance entities (e.g., numbers) that "do not and cannot causally affect the world investigated by the sciences and that are both irreducible to and ontologically independent of entities explained by science," without being supernatural. (De Caro and Macarthur 2010, 75; cf. De Caro and Macarthur 2010, 12)

Neither of these provisos seems to help the liberal naturalist avoid the dilemma. (1) Of the nonnaturalistic modes of inquiry mentioned, two are used by scientific naturalists—David Lewis and Australian naturalists avail themselves of conceptual analysis, (Braddon-Mitchell and Nola 2009) and Galileo used imaginative speculation in thought-experiments. (Sorenson 1992, 8) Introspection, the other mode of inquiry mentioned, is arguably one of the "special modes of understanding that would be irreconcilable with scientific explanation" and hence in violation of the constitutive claim of naturalism. (De Caro and Macarthur 2010, 13) So, the first two modes of inquiry are used by scientists or by scientific naturalists, and the third courts "supernaturalism" as De Caro and Voltolini construe it.

(2) In the second proviso, the only example that De Caro and Voltolini give—numbers—is admitted by many naturalists. The arch-naturalist Quine countenanced numbers, on the ground that mathematics is committed to them and science requires mathematics.[10] Moreover, the entities of interest to liberal naturalists are not just numbers anyway but include more generally "entities that are implicit in other sound and successful ordinary transactions of ours." (De Caro and Macarthur 2010, 76) Legitimating entities like numbers does not ipso facto legitimate concrete entities that are not investigated by science but that are "implicit in other sound and successful ordinary transactions of ours." Since scientific naturalists are prepared to admit entities that "do not and cannot causally affect the world investigated by science," it is difficult to see how either of the provisos seems to provide logical space for a view distinct from both scientific naturalism and supernaturalism.

In their defense of liberal naturalism, De Caro and Voltolini seem to trade on an ambiguity on the two ways the word "natural" is used. In its first use, "natural" applies to anything that is not supernatural, or anything not in the realm of nature. In its second use, "natural" applies to items connected to science. Anything natural in the first way is (merely) consistent with the laws of nature; anything natural in the second way is derived from, or guided by, the laws of nature. Scientific naturalism takes these two senses to be extensionally equivalent, but liberal naturalism pries them apart and endorses only naturalism as pertaining to nature and not supernatural. Similarly, the term "naturalistic philosophy" may be read either as "philosophy with no supernaturalistic elements" or as "philosophy constrained by science." In contemporary philosophical literature, "naturalism" has come to refer to philosophy constrained by science.

---

10. De Caro is quite aware that Quine countenances numbers but holds that to be a consistent scientific naturalist, he should not. (De Caro, personal communication, October 13, 2011).

When De Caro and Voltolini say what makes their view of liberal naturalism *liberal*, they use "naturalism" in the first way, as pertaining to the realm of nature and as allowing "entities that are implicit in other sound and successful ordinary transactions of ours." (De Caro and Macarthur 2010, 76) Liberal naturalism allows acceptance of "entities that cannot be studied by the methods of natural sciences." (De Caro and Voltolini 2010, 78) Appeal to "ontological tolerance plus methodological discontinuity" shows how their view differs from scientific naturalism.

But when they say what makes their view of liberal naturalism *naturalism*, they seem to use "naturalism" in the second way, as guided by, or derived from, science. They limit the controversial entities that they admit—that is, entities that cannot be studied by natural science—to those that lack causal power. This limitation is, as they say, "perfectly compatible with the claims of the natural sciences," since the existence of entities that lack causal power "would not imply any violation of the causal closure of the natural world." So, "in a liberal naturalist perspective, the fact that a controversial kind of entity has no causal power, far from being a problem, is a necessary condition (albeit, of course, not a sufficient one) for accepting it as real."[11] (De Caro and Voltolini 2010, 78)

Taken together, these two defenses of liberal naturalism run into trouble. On the one hand, De Caro and Voltolini defend liberalism by admitting entities that are not investigated by science but are "implicit in other sound and successful ordinary transactions of ours." On the other hand, they defend naturalism by restricting such entities to those lacking causal power: To repeat, on their view,

---

11. However, De Caro has recently said that he recognizes concrete objects (like artifacts and artworks), and that they "obviously causally interact with us." (personal communication, October 16, 2011) De Caro subsequently told me that Voltolini agreed that controversial entities could have causal powers. (personal communication, October 18, 2011) Hence, De Caro and Voltolini seem no longer to take it to be a necessary condition for accepting a controversial kind of entity as real that it have no causal power.

it is a necessary condition (recently retracted) for a controversial kind of entity to be admissible that it have no causal power. (De Caro and Voltolini 2010, 78) But how can entities that lack causal power be "implicit in other sound and successful ordinary transactions of ours"? If De Caro and Voltolini open ontology to entities that are "implicit in other sound and successful ordinary transactions of ours," how can they close it to controversial entities that have causal power?

If all admissible entities that cannot be studied by the methods of the natural sciences lacked causal power, we would have no reason to think that such entities existed: Lacking causal power, they could have no influence on our successful ordinary transactions or on anything else (including our perceptual systems). So, entities that lack causal power are incompatible with the defense of liberalism. (However, see note 11.)

As sympathetic as I am with the aims of liberal naturalism, I think that it should admit concrete ordinary objects that have causal powers, as the published version of their view does not.

Liberal naturalists do not want to tie naturalism to science the way that Kornblith and other nonreductive naturalists do. Liberal naturalists want to show that there is logical space between scientific naturalism and supernaturalism; I agree, but I do not think that De Caro and Macarthur have exactly located the "extra" space. Liberal naturalism aims to widen "the realm of the natural" by allowing "entities that are implicit in other sound and successful ordinary transactions of ours" and by countenancing modes of inquiry that support such entities. (De Caro and Macarthur 2010, 76) Fine, but the controversial entities admitted will have causal powers. Otherwise, how would we know what to admit?

I think that if there is space for entities outside the purview of both scientific naturalism and supernaturalism, it will not be occupied by entities lacking causal powers. I think that it is mistaken to hold that consistency with the laws of nature (the constitutive claim of naturalism) requires that all entities that have causal power are reducible. (In Chapter 10, I shall suggest a modification of De Caro and Voltolini's liberal naturalism.) In any case, from the constitutive claim of naturalism, it does not follow that all naturalism is scientific naturalism. I suggest that liberal naturalists not locate their naturalism in entities lacking causal powers but rather espouse naturalism only in the sense of "pertaining to the natural realm."[12] In that way, they could be more liberal than nonreductivists like Kornblith and still be naturalistic.

TWO RESPONSES TO NATURALISM: DISENCHANTMENT AND OPTIMISM

There is another distinction among proponents of naturalism that I want to discuss: disenchanted naturalists versus what I'll call "optimistic naturalists."[13] The notion of disenchantment, adopted from Friedrich Schiller by Max Weber, concerns a pessimistic personal reaction to a fully rationalized world devoid of mystery or

---

12. De Caro and Voltolini make a distinction similar to the one that I am advocating here. They distinguish between (1) the claim that no entities can violate the laws of nature, and (2) the claim that "ontology should be shaped by natural science alone." (De Caro and Voltolini 2010, 76) However, where I disagree is in the assumption that to disallow entities that can violate the laws of nature is to disallow entities that have causal powers without being in the purview of science. (As I mentioned, in a personal communication from De Caro to me, October 18, 2011, after their publication of 2010, they withdraw the assumption.)

13. Rosenberg uses this same pair of terms, but a little differently from the way that I use them. (Rosenberg 2011b, 22–24) Roughly, I think, for Rosenberg, disenchanted naturalists are eliminativists about anything beyond the domain of physics and optimistic naturalists are reductionists who hope to save, say, purpose by supposing that science naturalizes it. To Rosenberg, optimistic naturalism just changes the subject

magic. Naturalism induces disenchantment in some, but not all, philosophers.

The disenchanted naturalist thinks that physics alone tells us what the world is like; disenchanted naturalists advise that we need to accept the unpleasant fact that what we care about is an illusion. The disenchanted naturalist thinks that once we understand the scope and import of basic physics, what we might call "life's questions" disintegrate. Questions about values, meaning, love, purpose actually have simple answers that we can read off science.[14] (Rosenberg 2009, sec. 1)

Darwin's discovery of blind variation and natural selection is just "the foresightless play of fermions and bosons producing, in us conspiracy theorists, the *illusion* of purpose." (Rosenberg 2011b, 4) The "thermodynamic noise among the molecules present on the Earth about three billion years ago every so often randomly produced molecules that combined stability with replication, the first sliver of an adaptation, produced from zero adaptation." The process of piling on adaptations upon adaptations is temporally asymmetrical, driven by the second law of thermodynamics—the law that entropy increases almost everywhere almost all the time. Repeat the process of thermodynamically random variations enough times "and the rest is history—natural history. That's how physics fakes design." (Rosenberg 2011b, 4)

Moreover, since the second law of thermodynamics is the only law that has a direction (from earlier to later), according to Rosenberg, physics shows that Darwin's mechanism is the only one

by redefining the target of inquiry (e.g., purpose). I think that Rosenberg has a point here, but it is not my point. I do not use these terms to distinguish different varieties of naturalism, but different attitudes toward it.

14. Rosenberg sometimes appeals not just to physics but to "the mature sciences—from physics across to biology and increasingly neuroscience" to rule out life's questions. But his argument relies exclusively on physics, to the second law of thermodynamics in particular. (Rosenberg 2011b, 1)

that could drive adaptational evolution in a universe like ours. "If the 2d law makes Darwinian natural selection inevitable, then the notion that Darwinian natural selection naturalizes purpose has to be surrendered"—not just in biology, but *tout court*, even "in the sciences of man." (Rosenberg 2011b, 22) So, Darwin did not just naturalize purpose; he annihilated it. (Rosenberg 2011b, 7)

Ontologically speaking, the disenchanted naturalist disavows everything but the laws and entities recognized by microphysics. So, there is a single answer to any of life's questions that assume that there is anything else in reality: the questions make no sense because they have false presuppositions. Values, meaning, love, and purpose are illusions. Physics has ruled them out.

The disenchanted naturalist leaves us with pervasive nihilism. There is no more to mind than what is discovered by neuroscience (which is reducible to physics). Rosenberg warns that introspection misleads us into supposing that we represent facts about the world in our brains, perhaps in a language of thought; but in fact neuroscience has disproved any such thing. (I doubt that any nonphilosopher ever thought that introspection tells us anything at all (true or false) about the brain, much less about a language of thought.) But for the disenchanted naturalist, disenchantment is far-reaching. Rosenberg argues that "science has to be nihilistic about ethics and morality." There are no moral facts, or right morality, just adaptations. (Rosenberg 2011b, 7) (For a full report from a disenchanted naturalist, see Rosenberg 2011a.)

I have a couple of questions for the disenchanted naturalist: If he is right that there are only bosons and fermions and the like, how could we ever be under the illusion that there is love, morality, and meaning? The disenchanted naturalist should give us a clue (in terms of bosons and fermions, the laws of physics, etc.) as to how such illusions are even possible; what is it about bosons and fermions and the like that can give rise to such an illusion?

An error theory should show us how, with only the resources of microphysics, we ever could have made such an error.

Rosenberg gives a partial answer. The illusion that we can think about things outside the mind, says Rosenberg, "gets built up in each brain anew during the developmental ontogeny of every language learning child and has been built up in hominem evolution from grunts, shrieks, eventually clicks and gestures coordinated with behavior, all the way to Chinese characters and Kanji calligraphy." These features have great adaptive value and perhaps were selected for. (Rosenberg 2011b, 14) What Rosenberg makes a case for here is that there is no "original intentionality," that our brains do not "operate on statements that are 'about' things, facts, events that are outside the mind." But this conclusion does not imply that there is no intentionality at all, only that the representational theory of mind is incorrect. It swings wide of any theory of mind that does not claim that there are representations in the brain.[15] Nevertheless, Rosenberg goes on to say that our "plans, projects, purposes, plots, stories, narratives and the other ways we organize our lives and explain ourselves to others and ourselves"—anything that requires intentionality—are all illusions.

Although I suspect that a "just-so" story as Rosenberg gives is probably the best that can be done at this stage of knowledge, notice that it is not given in the language of bosons and fermions; it is not a scientific argument at all.[16] Nor does Rosenberg's discussion show how it is possible that we could ever think that we were planning or making a narrative if plans and narratives are illusions. If there are no plans, how could things work out as if there were

15. Also, the error theory does not apply to animals whose behavior seems intentional. What error are they making?
16. Indeed, Rosenberg's "just-so" story is a piece of speculative natural history. In light of Rosenberg's view that "history is bunk," I wonder how he regards natural history? (Rosenberg 2011b, 16)

plans? "They" succeed or seem to; "they" are thwarted or seem to be; "they" are sold for lots of money, which seems to be in your bank account. (Rosenberg has a response to such worries: natural selection. Plans, and so on, "seem to succeed or to be thwarted, just like the apparent designs in nature." (personal communication, October 3, 2011) However, if all the things I have mentioned and much more are illusions, we seem to be back in Descartes's Evil-Demon territory.

So, I leave disenchanted naturalism with a final question: Given the resources that Rosenberg allows (natural selection), how is global deception even possible?

In contrast to the disenchanted naturalist, some naturalists are far from pessimism. They take very seriously what I called "life's questions" and look for answers consistent with naturalism. Thomas Nagel, for example, has identified a religious temperament as one characterized by a desire for completion, a desire for connection with the whole of reality, "a yearning for harmony with the whole cosmos." (T. Nagel 2005, 6; 2010) Nagel, who is a professed atheist, has explored several ways to respond to this desire in a naturalistic and atheistic framework.

More particularly, since the existence of living things is a necessary condition for the operation of natural selection, Nagel considers how to explain the beginning of all life, without dissolving any sense of purpose with which we may have started our inquiry. The hypothesis that he considers is that there are "natural principles of organization and development of complexity over time" that are compatible with the principles of basic physics, but not determined by them. His suggestion is a revival of a discredited natural teleology, as an alternative to both chance and creationism. The suggestion is naturalistic in the sense that the teleological principles would be an irreducible part of the natural order, but it is in conflict with scientific naturalism, at least of the reductive stripe. (His aim is only to show that being an atheist does not entail being a reductionist.) (T. Nagel 2005, 33)

However, Nagel does not end up opting for natural teleology, even tricked out with a Platonic picture in which the world's "intelligibility and the development of beings to whom it is intelligible are nonaccidental." The Platonic picture, without being religious and without being reductionist, makes intelligible the existence and authority of reason. (T. Nagel 2005, 35) But if both the Platonic picture and the religious one are rejected, Nagel will vote for the absurd. A vote for the absurd places Nagel outside the tent of the disenchanted; a disenchanted naturalist would find the absurd as illusory as purpose or love.

A fully optimistic naturalist is Philip Kitcher, who is in the secular humanist tradition of John Dewey. Unlike the disenchanted naturalist, the optimistic naturalist recognizes human beings' concerns as real and tries to improve their lot. The optimistic naturalist does not rule out talk of values and life-questions. Kitcher discusses religious challenges to the view that there are no supernatural entities (secularism) and gives naturalistic replies that are in a loose way connected to science. (Kitcher 2011a) I'll discuss two challenges and Kitcher's replies: (1) Ethical judgments and claims are meaningless in the absence of a deity. (2) Without a deity, human life is robbed of purpose.

(1) Does ethics need a religious foundation? As Kitcher rightly says, Plato answered this question in the *Euthyphro*: Is something good because the gods say that it is, or do they say that it is good because it *is* good? The voluntarist line, that something is good because the gods say so, falls apart; the rationalist line, that the gods say that something is good because it is, prevails.[17]

---

17. In "The Euthyphro Problem," Gareth B. Matthews provides a clear and persuasive argument (Matthews 2009).

Suppose that Kitcher and many others are right that attempts at providing a religious foundation for ethics fail. Can naturalists do any better? Kitcher offers a brief sketch to show how ethical judgments and practice can be "understood in a thoroughly naturalistic fashion." (Kitcher 2011a, 23) He sketches a genealogy from our ancestors' acquisition of the capacity for normative guidance, which consisted in rules of behavior to prevent social disruption. Next, according to the story, normative guidance became socially embedded in the social units that experimented in various ways that were in cultural competition. Today's ethical practices descended from the winners of that competition. (Kitcher 2011a, 27–28) So, secularism finds a place for ethical judgments and practice—and more generally for value—in the natural world.[18]

(2) With ethical practice thus grounded in basic human desires, the secular humanist can overcome the suspicion "that lives without God (or gods) are deprived of purpose and significance." (Kitcher 2011a, 29) There is still purpose, understood as of our own making, as part of the human practice of valuing. Indeed, the purposes that make life meaningful for the religious believer and for the secularist have the same origin. The religious believer's identification with divine purposes itself springs from an act of evaluation, a recognition "of the *value* of serving a broader purpose accepted as *good*." (Kitcher 2011a, 32) So, like the secularist, the believer bases her life on an act of evaluation, an initial decision to value one particular course. So, without cosmic or transcendent purposes, secularism has a reply to the charge that it robs human life of purpose.

Realizing that I have not done justice to Kitcher's well-worked-out argument, I want only to raise a question about its

---

18. For a full-dress account of Kitcher's naturalistic approach to ethics, see (Kitcher 2011b).

scientific-naturalist credentials. I agree that the argument is naturalistic in the (weak) sense that it appeals to nothing supernatural, but its connection to natural science is less clear to me. Kitcher's response to the second religious challenge—that godlessness robs human life of purpose—may well be grounded in psychology and sociology. Decisions to value one thing rather than another and to commit oneself to a particular way of life are just the sorts of phenomena that one expects psychology and sociology to explain. So, Kitcher's second response is an example of a nonreductive version of scientific naturalism. The Euthyphro argument, though not an example of scientific naturalism, is only a negative argument that religious foundations for ethics are inadequate. In any case, the Euthyphro argument certainly is compatible with the natural sciences.

However, Kitcher has a more important, positive response to the religious charge that without God, ethical judgment and practice are meaningless. The relation of Kitcher's response to natural science seems tenuous to me (rather like Rosenberg's "just-so" story). Kitcher's naturalistic account of ethical judgment and practice is a genealogical speculation about origins. Even if some genealogies may count as scientific, not all can. And Kitcher's account seems more like Nietzsche's genealogy of morals (not a scientific theory) than like Darwin's genealogy of species (a scientific theory). The latter but not the former is bolstered by a good deal of empirical evidence. Both Darwin and Nietzsche are naturalistic, but only Darwin is a scientific naturalistic. If, as Kornblith put it, the task of the naturalistic metaphysician is "simply to draw out the metaphysical implications of contemporary science," then I do not think that Kitcher's account meets that standard. (Kornblith 1994, 40) Whether Kitcher *should* meet Kornblith's standard I leave open here. In any case, Kitcher is an optimistic nonreductive naturalist.

The difference between Rosenberg and Kitcher points to an obvious difference between the disenchanted and optimistic reactions to naturalism: The disenchanted naturalist is a reductionist, and the optimistic naturalist is a nonreductionist. However, even if all disenchanted naturalists are reductionists, not all reductionists are disenchanted. A reductionist who is not disenchanted may well think that the language in which we talk about meaning, purpose, morality, and so on is legitimate; it just lacks ontological import.[19] (Rosenberg is—rightly, in my opinion—dismissive of this line.) Daniel Dennett is a prime example of a philosopher who takes this position. Dennett, whose ontology is wholly at the level of physics, is an eliminativist about the intentional stance; but he cheerfully admits that we cannot do without it. So, I would include Dennett as a nondisenchanted naturalist (even if not quite an optimist), along with noneliminativists like David Lewis and Jaegwon Kim.

Nondisenchanted reductionists may be what Kim has called "conservative reductionists" rather than eliminativists. After all, genes were reduced, not eliminated; witches were eliminated, not reduced. (Kim 2005, 160) Nevertheless, neither conservatively reduced items nor eliminated items are in the ontology. As mentioned earlier, the difference between reduction and elimination is conceptual, not ontological. The difference between disenchanted naturalists (like Rosenberg) and nondisenchanted naturalists (like Dennett) is just a matter of attitude.

The concern in this book, however, is ontological (not attitudinal), and reductive (and eliminative) naturalists, disenchanted or not, agree on what is fundamentally real. So, the ontological line should be drawn between reductive and nonreductive

---

19. From the premise that, say, moral language has its uses, these nondisenchanted reductionists insist that we cannot draw any conclusions about ontology. Agreed! Further premises are needed.

naturalism, not between disenchanted and nondisenchanted naturalists.[20] Reality, according to the reductive naturalist— disenchanted or not—is thoroughly dehumanized. The disenchanted naturalist does not want to gloss over that fact: The disenchanted naturalist's mission is to exhort us to face up to the (putative) fact of dehumanization. The disenchanted naturalist, for whom morality is an illusion, cannot even raise the questions that occupy the optimistic naturalist.

The optimistic naturalist stands in stark contrast to the disenchanted naturalist. Kitcher, for example, is a humanist who believes we can find naturalistic ways to think about, and to account for, all or most of the things that we care about. All optimistic naturalists are nonreductionists, and nonreductionists accept the full panoply of the sciences that includes not only psychology, but also sociology, history, and political science. They use scientific theory, which has "proven its value in prediction, explanation, and technological application," in a project of epistemic improvement. (De Caro and Voltolini 2010, 78; cf. Kitcher 1992) The optimistic naturalist is confident that further research on our perceptual faculties and the standard environments in which we perceive and reason will lead to increasing our knowledge and improving our cognitive skills.

The moral of this chapter is that there is a wide range of philosophical views under the heading of "scientific naturalism" or just "naturalism." Scientific naturalism is guided by or derived from science; naturalism *simpliciter* is consistent with science, whether or not it is guided by science. Despite the wide range of nonscientific naturalists—think of McDowell, Stroud, Putnam, Hornsby, Brandom, De Caro, and Voltolini, to name a few—my focus will

20. Even so, a difference in attitude toward worldviews by their adherents can be revealing of the adherents' values, and thus be worthy of philosophical consideration.

be on ontological varieties of scientific naturalism, both reductive and nonreductive. In some sciences (for example, psychology and cognitive science), first-person reports are regarded as evidence for various hypotheses, but none of the sciences take first-person properties to be ontologically significant. Consequently, none of these versions of naturalism—reductive or nonreductive—recognize first-person properties in their ontology.

Chapter Two

On Naturalizing the
First-Person Perspective

As we saw in Chapter 1, the core of scientific naturalism is ontological: Science is the exclusive arbiter of what is. As long as science has no room for anything first personal, ontological naturalism must rid reality of the appearance of first-personal properties. The way to rid reality of unwelcome phenomena is to "naturalize" them.

WHAT IS NATURALIZATION?

"Naturalization" is not an altogether pellucid term. Roughly, the project of naturalization is the project of bringing all phenomena into line with scientific naturalism. The point of naturalizing projects is to show that phenomena that appear to be incompatible with a complete scientific ontology (e.g., consciousness, intentionality, normativity) can really be accommodated by a complete scientific ontology. Otherwise, according to naturalism, they are not real. If apparent phenomena conflict with a complete scientific ontology, then they are *only* apparent—and do not really exist. Although ontology includes objects, kinds, and properties, I shall focus on properties; objects and kinds may be treated similarly. Properties may be naturalized in either of two ways: by reduction or by elimination, as follows:

(R) Property P is naturalized by reduction if and only if property P strongly supervenes on "appropriate" microphysical properties.

(E) Putative property P is naturalized by elimination if and only if a complete ontology does not entail that there is such a property P.

I use the term "appropriate" to allow externalists who are nonreductionists about explanation and laws to be naturalists. As I said in Chapter 1, I take reductionist accounts of naturalism to hold that macroproperties strongly supervene on local microproperties, properties whose instantiations are within the spatiotemporal boundaries of the bearers of the macroproperties. So, I specified that a condition for reductionism is that macroproperties strongly supervene on *local* microproperties, where local microproperties are intrinsic properties of the bearer of the macroproperties.

Although this is fine for reductive naturalists who take all sciences to reduce to physics, the condition that supervenient properties supervene on local microproperties is too strong. Nonreductive naturalists like Hilary Putnam (Putnam 1975) and Richard Boyd (Boyd 1980)—along with more recent nonreductivists like Kornblith (Kornblith 2012) and Pereboom (Pereboom 2011; Kornblith 2012)—are externalists who may hold that some macroproperties strongly supervene on microproperties whose instantiations exceed the boundaries of the bearer of the macroproperties. For example, Sam's thinking about water may strongly supervene not only on intrinsic neural properties of Sam but also on their relation to quantities of H_2O. So, "local" would be too restrictive a condition for these externalists. On the other hand, "global" would be too permissive.

I use "appropriate" as a stand-in for whatever way such naturalists want to restrict the supervenience base for a given property.

Now we can cover both reductive and nonreductive naturalists by holding the following: Scientific naturalism is true if and only if every apparent property is naturalized either by reduction or by elimination. The main goal of this book is to show that the first-person perspective is not naturalized—either by reduction or by elimination.

Although I am going to give a detailed account of human persons and the two-stage first-person perspective, I expect these to be controversial. You do not have to accept these constructive accounts in order to recognize the adequacy of my arguments for the ontological significance of the first-person perspective. My main goal—to show that no form of naturalism as a "view from nowhere" is a sufficient account of reality—will be accomplished if my arguments against naturalization of the first-person perspective are sound.

THE ROBUST FIRST-PERSON PERSPECTIVE

Having specified what counts as naturalization, I need to gather appropriate first-person data to see whether they can be naturalized. First-person data are phenomena that entail a first-person perspective. That is, the occurrence of such phenomena entails that something has a first-person perspective.

On my view, the first-person perspective has two stages—a rudimentary stage, manifested by many mammals and human infants, and a robust stage, manifested by language-users who have mastered first-personal language.[1] Very roughly, the distinction

---

1. For convenience, I sometimes drop the qualification "stage" and speak of the robust first-person perspective or the rudimentary first-person perspective *simpliciter*. But my view is that there is a single dispositional property that has a greater variety of manifestations at its robust stage than at its rudimentary stage.

between the rudimentary and robust stages of the first-person perspective corresponds to the distinction between consciousness and self-consciousness.[2] I shall explain in detail in Chapter 6. A person has a first-person perspective (rudimentary or robust) essentially; an animal at best has a rudimentary first-person perspective, and that only contingently.

The first-personal data that I shall select are from the robust stage of language-users. A robust first-person perspective is a conceptual ability that is uniquely human,[3] an ability to conceive of oneself as oneself, from the first person, without recourse to a name, description, or other third-person referring device. I employ the phrase "conceive of oneself as oneself* in the first person" despite its redundancy in order to emphasize both the conceptual and first-personal aspects of the robust first-person perspective.

From a robust first-person perspective, one conceives of oneself as oneself in the first person. A robust first-person perspective guarantees that one knows which one she is without any need to pick herself out from items in the environment. (A nonhuman animal, with only a rudimentary first-person perspective, simply acts from a certain first-person point of view without needing to pick itself out from items in the environment either; but the nonhuman animal has certain first-person abilities—it nurses its own wounds—but does not *conceive* of itself as itself.) It is the robust first-person perspective (as I call the second stage of the first-person perspective) that distinguishes persons from every other kind of thing that exists.

2. There are some intriguing similarities (as well as differences) between my view of the first-person perspective and Dan Zahavi's phenomenological view. (Zahavi 2005)

3. Or at least unique among animals. I allow that a human person could come to be constituted by so many bionic parts that she would no longer qualify as human; yet she would still be a person.

Here's a true story that illustrates a toddler's robust first-person perspective: When one of my nieces was two years old, she had a birthday party to which her many cousins were invited. One of her cousins (his name was Donald) went into her bedroom and began systematically taking toys out of my niece's toybox. When my niece saw what was happening, she was outraged. She cried out, "Dammit, Donald, mine!" Her parents were appalled: Where, they wondered with embarrassment, had she learned the profanity "dammit"? What interested me, however, was not her saying "dammit," but her competent use of the word "mine." She had a robust first-person perspective of herself: She knew that she—she herself—was the rightful owner of the toys, and that her permission was required for anyone else to play with her toys. This little story illustrates, I think, what is unique about human persons. Of all the beings in the world, we alone have robust first-personal perspectives. We alone can conceive of ourselves from "within," so to speak; we can think of ourselves *as* ourselves. My niece's shouting, "Dammit, Donald, mine!" indicates that she can conceive of herself from her own point of view. That shout is a clear (even if indirect) manifestation of a robust first-person perspective.

To have a robust first-person perspective is to have the ability to conceive of oneself as oneself, in the first person. A robust first-person perspective is often manifested by a reflexive use of pronouns: "I (myself)" or "he (himself)" embedded in sentences whose main verbs are linguistic or psychological verbs—for example, "I protested that I was overcharged," or "I wonder how I will die." If I protest that I was overcharged or I wonder how I will die, then I am thinking of myself as myself; I am not thinking of myself in any third-person way (e.g., not as Lynne Baker, nor as the person who is thinking a certain thought, nor as a woman in the front of a computer) at all. I am not only the thinker of the thought, but also I (thought of in the first person) am part of the object of my thought.

Call a concept by means of which one conceives of oneself as oneself from the first person a "self-concept"—a concept of oneself from one's own point of view. The thought that you would express by saying, "I'm glad that I am a philosopher" contains the concepts *glad, philosopher,* and your self-concept. Unlike the concepts *glad* and *philosopher,* your self-concept is nonqualitative; your self-concept simply manifests your robust first-person perspective. Following Matthews, I'll use an asterisk, or star, beside the pronoun "I" to signal that its user has a robust first-person perspective.[4] Let me explain.

Canonically, "I*" (pronounced "eye-star") is embedded in a "that"-clause of a complex first-person sentence with a psychological or linguistic main verb—for example, "I doubt that I* will live to be ninety," or "I whispered that I* am sorry." As Matthews characterized "I*," "I*" pronouns, indeed first-person pronouns generally, when they are used reflexively, seem to pick out subjects from the individual subject's own point of view, and not under any particular name or definite description, either.[5]

Let I*-sentences be sentences that contain "I*," and let I*-thoughts be thoughts expressible by I*-sentences. (I take thinking to be interior speech.) Corresponding to I*-sentences and

---

4. Hector-Neri Castañeda introduced "he*" to attribute a first-person reference to someone else, for example, "The editor believes that he* is wise," which is not true unless the editor would express his belief in the first person, by "I am wise." Gareth B. Matthews extended the "he*" from sentences with a third-person subject to "I*" for sentences with a first-person subject. Castañeda studied phenomena expressed by sentences like "The editor believes that he* is F." (Castañeda 1966; 1967) Gareth B. Matthews extended the discussion to phenomena expressed by "I think that I* am F." (Matthews 1991)

5. Matthews 1992, 4. Matthews's interest is in "I* sentences" that are used to express philosophical questions: "Can I doubt that I* exist?" or "How do I know that I* am not dreaming?" My interest is somewhat broader. All I* sentences, no matter how mundane, entail that the speaker has a robust first-person perspective.

I*-thoughts are reflexive uses of third-person pronouns, for example, "Jane doubts that she* will live to be ninety" or "Jane whispered that she* was sorry." In these particular cases, her first-person sentences would be I*-sentences: "I doubt that I* will live to be ninety," and "I whispered that I* was sorry." Other "she*" sentences might be expressed in the first-person with simple I-sentences. For example, Jane may express someone's saying, "Jane believes that she* is wise," by saying "I am wise." Whether "I am wise" (indirectly) manifests a robust perspective depends on whether Jane has the conceptual resources to say or think, "I said [thought, denied, etc.] that I* am wise."

Whereas I*-sentences and I*-thoughts are *self-attributions* of first-person reference, he*- (or she*-) sentences and he*-thoughts are *attributions to others* of first-person reference. Although both I*-thoughts and he*-thoughts are attributions of first-person reference, the difference between self-attribution and attribution to others of first-person reference is important: I*-thoughts contain self-concepts; he*-thoughts do not contain self-concepts. At most, he*-sentences only attribute self-concepts but are no less first-personal for all that.[6]

Having a robust first-person perspective is not just having the capacity to emit what sounds like, for example, "I think that I* need more sleep." Rather, beings with robust first-person perspectives integrate I*-thoughts and I*-sentences with action in myriad ways. We make sense of actions by asking for reasons and getting answers that start with "I thought that I*..." or "I did not realize that I* was doing that." (Anscombe 1957) Although I am not sanguine

6. I say "at most" because he* sentences attribute self-concepts only to those with robust first-person perspectives. We attribute first-person thoughts to dogs and others with only rudimentary first-person perspectives. For example, "The dog believed that he was about to be fed." We could say that if the dog could speak, he would say, "I am about to be fed," but lacking language, he would lack a self-concept. I'll use the "*" device only with respect to people with robust first-person perspectives.

that anyone could build a machine that had a robust first-person perspective, I do not rule out the possibility a priori. If someone claimed to have built a machine that had a robust first-person person, evidence of having a first-person perspective would be the same as for human persons: coherent use of I*-language integrated with action in indefinitely many ways.

To sum up: The robust first-person perspective is the capacity to conceive of oneself as oneself* in the first person. This capacity is directly manifested in I*-thoughts and I*-sentences; it is indirectly manifested in other thoughts and sentences that presuppose that the thinker/speaker has the capacity to conceive of herself as herself* in the first person.

It is important to see the range of first-person phenomena. They are not just subjective phenomena that are available to creatures with only rudimentary first-person perspectives—like smelling an acrid odor or hearing a high-pitched whistle. First-person phenomena also include nonsubjective phenomena like my swearing that I* saw the defendant running away, or the newspaper report, "She swore that she* saw the defendant running."

First-person phenomena are not limited to "Cartesian" thoughts about what one is thinking; they include mundane thoughts like "I wish that I* were a movie star," or "I am glad that I* live in Amherst." First-person phenomena are rather phenomena that occur only if there are first-person perspectives; and many such phenomena— like a wish that one* were a movie star—are inextricably tied to what Descartes would call the "external world." One could not wish that one* were a movie star unless one had the concept of being a movie star in addition to a self-concept, and there would be no concept of being a movie star in a world in which there were no practices of making movies. First-person phenomena are not logically private, nor are they phenomena about which a single person is allegedly infallible. So, first-person phenomena should not be thought of in a Cartesian way.

When one entertains an I*-thought or asserts an I*-sentence, one manifests a robust first-person perspective. This does not imply that there is any special subpersonal entity, "the self." As we shall see later, I*-thoughts need no recourse to any peculiar object like a self, or a soul, or an ego. What one thinks of from a first-person perspective is oneself, an embodied person. All I*-thoughts are manifestations of robust first-person perspectives.

Someone may object that we do not need "I*" because the simple pronoun "I" following a psychological or linguistic verb in a first-person sentence has the same effect as "I*." After all, "I" and "I*" are both first-person pronouns that do not differ in reference: Both pronouns refer to the person who is the subject of the sentence in question.

Such points notwithstanding, it is useful to mark occurrences of "I" in "that"-clauses of first-person psychological or linguistic sentences with a "*," because whoever asserts I*-sentences (as opposed to simple I-sentences) ipso facto has a robust first-person perspective. The reason it is useful to mark that a sentence or thought entails a robust first-person perspective is this: It is the robust first-person perspective that resists naturalization. Moreover, the distinction between "I" and "I*" (or at least the importance of "I*") can be brought to the fore in other ways:

(1) "I" is a pronoun of direct reference. "I" is used to refer directly to oneself, regardless of how one characterizes oneself. "I*" is referentially opaque. "I*" is used to refer to oneself characterized in the first person, by means of a self-concept.[7] The significance of this difference comes out in truth-conditions. Someone's—say, Mary's—simple first-person sentence, "I am underweight," is true

---

7. I want to retain direct reference for ordinary pronouns (without "*"s) and for proper names. It would pull me off course to be a full-fledged Fregean. So, I treat self-concepts as surds that do not fit into standard categories.

if and only if Mary is underweight, independent of how Mary conceives of herself. However, Mary's saying, "I believe that I* am underweight," is true only if Mary has a self-concept. The difference between "I" and "I*" captures the difference between making a first-person reference (by direct reference) and self-attributing a first-person reference (by means of a self-concept).

(2) Use of "I*" draws attention to the fact that the speaker has two roles: one as the producer of the sentence ("I") and the other as the one who is spoken of in the first person ("I*"). That the speaker is speaking about herself in the first person is guaranteed by the self-concept. Since "I*" is used to attribute a first-person reference to oneself (and not just to make a first-person reference), the speaker—by means of her self-concept—is part of the object of her attitude in an I*-sentence. For example, if you said, "I believe that I* am short," the first occurrence of "I" would identify you as the believer, and the second occurrence of "I" would place your self-concept in the proposition believed.

(3) Someone may suppose that we would not need any "I*" if we eliminated "I." There is a fairly long-standing line of thought that the use of "I" is eliminable, at least in soliloquy.[8] For example, Peter Geach said that the use of "I" in "soliloquies...is redundant and has no special reference; "I am very puzzled at this problem" really says no more than "This problem *is* puzzling." (Geach 1957, 120) And Moritz Schlick attributed to Lichtenberg, "the wonderful eighteenth century physicist and philosopher," the view that "Descartes had no right to start his philosophy with the proposition 'I think', instead of saying, 'it thinks.'" (Schlick 1949, 166) Similarly, Russell said that Descartes's "I think" could be paraphrased as "there is thinking."

---

8. John Perry argued that "I" cannot be eliminated from any context, but my point here is that even if "I" were eliminable, "I*" would not be. (Perry 1979) "I*" occurs in the content clause of a complex sentence. A sentence that attributes to the speaker a first-person reference would not be true unless there were a first-person reference.

(Russell 1945, 567) There is some reason to think that the simple "I" could be paraphrased away. (But see Williams 1978, 95)

However, to suppose that eliminating "I" would eliminate "I*" is a pipe dream. Whether or not "I" is eliminable in simple first-person sentences, "I*" is not eliminable from sentences where the "that"-clause contains a self-concept. Such sentences—for example, "I regret that I* find this problem puzzling"—do not succumb to strategies adopted to challenge Descartes. This suggests, as I shall argue in Chapter 5, that even if "I" could be eliminated, "I*" could not be. So, we would still need "I*."

As I have emphasized, use of an I*-sentence is a direct manifestation of a robust first-person perspective; however, use of a simple I-sentence is an indirect manifestation of a robust first-person perspectives if an I*-sentence can be inferred from the from the I-sentence. For example, Ernst Mach famously told the story of getting in at one end of a bus and seeing a shabby-looking man at the other end. Mach thought to himself something like, "That is an unkempt person." Unbeknownst to Mach, he was looking at himself in the bus mirror; so he did not realize that he* was the unkempt person referred to: He was referring to himself without realizing that it was himself* he was referring to.[9] Soon, Mach realized that it was himself whom he was looking at. It was only then that he was able to say, "I am that unkempt person."[10] (Mach 1949, 4n) And because Mach had a robust first-person perspective, with that realization came a raft of others: "I know [think, believe] that I* am that unkempt person," or perhaps "I wish that I* didn't look so unkempt."

9. "He*" is an analogue of "I*": "Al said that he* was wise" is not true unless Al said, "I am wise."
10. There are numerous examples of this kind. See Lewis (1979); Baker (1981); Kaplan (1989); Perry (2002, 202); Castañeda (1967); Perry (2002); Matthews (1992).

As we see in the case of Mach, one can refer to oneself without realizing that it is oneself* whom one refers to, but one cannot attribute a first-person reference to oneself without realizing that it is oneself* to whom she attributes the first-person reference. In general, once a person has a robust first-person perspective, then his simple assertions using "I" are connected to "I*" sentences. For example, if Joe says, "I am tall," and you ask him what he said, he may well reply, "I said that I* am tall."

In short: A robust first-person perspective is the capacity to think of oneself as oneself* in the first person. Constitutive of this capacity is the possession of a special self-concept, and constitutive of the possession of a special self-concept is the ability to use language of a certain complexity. The assertion of I*-sentences is the canonical manifestation of the capacity to think of oneself as oneself* in the first person, but it is not the only manifestation. Once one has a robust first-person perspective, many different kinds of one's sentences indirectly manifest it. (Think of my niece's shouting, "Mine!" or Mach's thinking, "I am that shabby fellow.")

The capacity to use I*-language (i.e., a robust first-person perspective) is constitutive of self-consciousness.[11] A being with the capacity to conceive of herself as herself* in the first person has the most basic kind of self-consciousness, on which all other forms of self-consciousness depend. For example, phenomena such as constructing a "narrative self," trying to get oneself* invited to the White House, keeping a diary, and so on all presuppose that one has a robust first-person perspective.

---

11. Nonlinguistic animals (e.g., chimpanzees) have been shown to display self-recognition in tests with mirrors. (Gallup 1977) Since such self-recognition does not blossom out into the myriad manifestations of what I call "the robust first-person perspective," I am not supposing that passing mirror tests is a sufficient condition for having a robust first-person perspective.

THE RUDIMENTARY FIRST-PERSON PERSPECTIVE

Lacking a self-concept, a human infant lacks a robust first-person perspective. Nevertheless, a human infant has a rudimentary first-person perspective, and has it essentially; any being that has a first-person perspective (rudimentary or robust) essentially is a person.[12] Human persons acquire robust first-person perspectives around the age of two, when they learn enough of a natural language to be able to conceive of themselves as themselves*, in the first person. But persons come into existence before they are exposed to natural language. So although what is distinctive about human persons is their robust first-person perspectives, the property in virtue of which they are persons—a property that they have essentially—is a first-person perspective, rudimentary or robust.

A person comes into existence when a human organism—perhaps around birth—develops to the point of supporting a rudimentary first-person perspective. At that point, on my view, a new entity—a person—comes into existence, constituted by a human organism. Like everything else that we know of (from solar systems to trees to mobile phones to paintings), a person comes into existence gradually. There is no precise moment after which a person exists and before which a person does not exist. (See Chapter 7.)

When a person comes into existence, on my view, what comes into existence is an entity with a rudimentary first-person perspective. Here are three important features of a rudimentary first-person perspective: (1) It is a perspective. A perspective is not an object; it

---

12. A terminological point: I use "human person" and "human being" interchangeably. I distinguish between human persons (that have first-person perspectives essentially) and human organisms (that lack first-person perspectives at early stages in their existence). See Baker (2007, 72–82).

is not something that one occupies. To have a perspective is to be disposed to perceive the world from a particular spatiotemporal location. (2) It is first personal, but it does not explicitly refer to a subject (first personally or otherwise); it is simply the default location of the conscious subject, the origin of her perceptual field, the location from which the subject perceives the environment that she interacts with.[13] (3) It is independent of linguistic or conceptual abilities, as I shall argue. So, entities that lack concepts (e.g., human infants and nonhuman animals) may enjoy rudimentary first-person perspectives.

Let us consider rudimentary first-person perspectives in greater detail. There are two conditions for an entity to have a rudimentary first-person perspective: (1) the entity be sentient; (2) the entity have intentionality.[14] Sentience is a primitive form of consciousness; one has consciousness only if one is capable of being conscious *of* something. The term "perspective" is appropriate, because all consciousnesss is perspectival. What intentionality adds to sentience is minimal agency, goal-directed behavior. (See Chapter 9.) A being that meets these conditions (a newborn human being, a dog) is conscious and can display intentional, goal-directed behavior.[15]

---

13. This feature of a rudimentary first-person perspective brings to mind Wittgenstein's remark (on another topic) that "nothing in the visual field allows to you infer that it is seen by an eye." (Wittgenstein 1921, 5.633)
14. Intentionality is not mere sentience. What intentionality adds to sentience is minimal agency, goal-directed behavior (Baker 2011), which is more flexible than just sensing and responding.
15. I should call attention to the fact that I hereby revise my earlier conditions for a rudimentary first-person perspective. In (Baker 2000; 2007), I added a third condition: the ability to imitate. I added imitativeness as a condition because I do not think that the rudimentary first-person perspective extends too far down the phylogenetic scale. I do not believe that spiders have any sort of first-person perspective: their sentience and intentionality (if they have them at all) seem *too* rudimentary. However, I have removed the condition of imitativeness as superfluous; imitativeness is a combination of perception and intentionality. So, now I take sentience and intentionality to be sufficient for a rudimentary first-person perspective, with the stipulation that the intentionality be enough to make any entity with a first-person perspective a minimal agent capable of goal-directed behavior. (See Chapter 7.)

There is ample psychological evidence that human infants have rudimentary first-person perspectives. (1) They are clearly sentient: they feel pain. (2) They have intentionality: They display goal-directed behavior—for example, escape behavior (head retraction and interposing hands between face and object) in the presence of a looming person. (Bower 1974, 84)[16]

These conditions for a rudimentary first-person perspective imply that beings with rudimentary first-person perspectives are, in Tyler Burge's terms, not just sensors but perceivers—beings with states that take the world to be one way rather than another. (Burge 2010, 74) Perceivers have "capacities systematically to represent a given particular or attribute as the same—despite significant variations in proximal stimulation."[17] These constancies are "explanatorily associated with systematic filtering mechanisms that yield sensitivity to a single environmental particular or attribute." (Burge 2010, 274) So, beings with rudimentary first-person perspectives can perceive (and misperceive) their environments and can intentionally interact with things in it; their capacity for goal-directed behavior makes them, at least minimally, agents.

A being with only a rudimentary first-person perspective has no self-concept or self-understanding; it simply stands at the origin of that part of reality which it can perceive and with which it can interact. All its perceptual mental states are first personal by default, but the bearer of those mental states does not think of them

16. With goal-directed behavior come veridicality conditions. "Representation" is a generic term that does not indicate the specific ways in which representation is effected. Perception, belief, desire, and intention are "representational in the sense that they are about something, indicate a subject matter as being a certain way, and (constitutively and nontrivially) have veridicality conditions." (Burge 2010, 27) We need not suppose that nonhuman animals represent themselves in order to explain their behavior. For another argument that we need not ascribe first-person reference to explain the actions of "simple creatures," see O'Brien (2007, 59–65).

17. I am taking the vexed term "represent" in a nontheoretical way, simply to mean that the perceiver takes the world to be one way rather than another.

as first personal. Nonhuman primates and other higher animals have rudimentary first-person perspectives: They are conscious, and they have psychological states like believing, fearing, and desiring. They have points of view (e.g., "danger in that direction"), but there is no evidence that they can conceive of themselves as the subjects of such thoughts. Much the same can be said for young human beings who can assert simple I-sentences without having a self-concept. For example, a toddler, just learning to speak, may say, "I want..." without yet having a concept of herself. Indeed, her assertion of "I want" may be equivalent to her assertions of or "Baby want" or just "Want."

From a rudimentary first-person perspective, there is no chance of misidentification—just as there is no chance of misidentification from a robust first-person perspective—but for different reasons: from a robust first-person perspective, one conceives of oneself from the first person and hence always succeeds in referring to the intended person, but from a rudimentary first-person perspective, one does not identify oneself at all, and hence there is no room for misidentification.[18] All the objects of the attitudes of an entity with only a rudimentary first-person perspective—whether a human being or a nonhuman animal—are in the entity's perceptual field. Since she is the origin of her perceptual field (and hence not to be found in it), all her perceptions are, by default, first personal.

Now a difficulty looms: Not only do human infants have rudimentary first-person perspectives, but so also do many higher animals (e.g., dogs, chimpanzees). Nonhuman animals that can interact consciously and intentionally with their environments likewise have the rudimentary stage of a first-person perspective. When

18. I think that distinguishing between a rudimentary and a robust first-person perspective may show where Anscombe went wrong in denying that "I" is a referring word. (Anscombe 1981) She was wrong with respect to "I" (or rather, "I*") from a robust first-person perspective, but she was right with respect to "I" from a rudimentary first-person perspective.

a dog fetches a stick on command, she is manifesting a rudimentary first-person perspective—as is a human baby who shrinks from a looming figure. If human infants with only rudimentary first-person perspectives are persons, why aren't primates and other higher animals, who also have rudimentary first-person perspectives, persons as well? What is the difference between dogs and persons? (cf. Povinelli and Vonk 2004) Why aren't dogs canine persons?

The quick answer is that animals have first-person perspectives only contingently, and persons have first-person perspectives essentially.[19] The better answer is that a human infant, a person, is of a *kind* that develops robust first-person perspectives; an animal with a rudimentary first-person perspective is of a kind that does not. For animals, there is only the first stage of a first-person perspective; an animal may have only a rudimentary first-person perspective, and that's it. The difference between human infants who go on to develop robust first-person perspectives and nonhuman animals (e.g., chimpanzees) who do not is this: Creatures with only rudimentary first-person perspectives, along with creatures with no first-person perspectives at all, have only biologically given goals and drives that they cannot evaluate or modify, whereas beings with robust first-person perspectives can evaluate and modify their goals. Unlike chimpanzees, persons have many goals that are unrelated to survival and reproduction.[20]

---

19. An animal develops a first-person perspective at or near birth. Since the organism existed before developing a first-person perspective, it has a first-person perspective only contingently. An human fetus also develops a first-person perspective at or near birth; but when that happens, a person comes into existence constituted by the human organism. The relation between an animal (human or not) and its body is identity; the relation between a person and her body is constitution. Constitution is time-bound; identity is not. (Baker 2007) The person, not the constituting organism, has the first-person perspective essentially. The constituting organism then has the first-person perspective derivatively, in virtue of constituting a person who has it nonderivatively.

20. Persons may even have goals that conflict with their biologically given goals. As Steven Pinker, a well-known evolutionary psychologist, writes, "A Darwinian would say that

Rudimentary first-person perspectives bind human persons to the seamless animal kingdom. Chimpanzees—with which human beings share 98.6 percent of their genetic material (Povinelli 2004)—and other higher animals also have rudimentary first-person perspectives (consciousness). They are sentient: Descartes notwithstanding, they feel pain if struck hard. Their behavior exhibits intentionality: Chimpanzees share food with conspecifics. In contrast to more broadly shared properties like having a heart, the properties in virtue of which an organism has a rudimentary first-person perspective are what we might call "person-making" properties, or perhaps better, "proto-person-making" properties. But in the case of a nonhuman animal, the development of a rudimentary first-person perspective is *not* the coming-into-being of a person. The reason is that nonhuman animals never move to the robust stage of a first-person perspective.

However, as I mentioned, a person comes into being when a human organism can support a rudimentary first-person perspective. So, it is unsurprising that a rudimentary first-person perspective has different roles in nonhuman and human animals. In nonhuman animals, it has a biological role in survival and reproduction. In human animals a rudimentary first-person perspective has the further role of bringing into existence a person who typically will come to have a robust first-person perspective.[21]

ultimately organisms have only two [goals]: to survive and to reproduce." (Pinker 1997, 541) But he also points out that he himself is "voluntarily childless," and comments, "I am happy to be that way, and if my genes don't like it, they can go jump in the lake." (Pinker 1997, 52)

21. Various thought experiments have been deployed to urge me to change "typically" to something more normative that invokes health or proper functioning. I resist because I think that it is built into the kind *person* that persons tend to develop robust first-person perspectives. If the dire thought experiments were to be realized, and statistically most human infants did not develop robust first-person perspectives, then I think that that would be the end of persons on earth (although there may still be human organisms with rudimentary first-person perspectives).

The development of a rudimentary first-person perspective in a human animal *is* the coming into existence of a person—a new entity—whom the animal then constitutes. Each human person has one exemplification of a first-person perspective, at first at the rudimentary stage and then later, with the development of a self-concept, the robust stage.

Almost twenty-five years ago, Gordon Gallup started a cottage industry of mirror experiments with primates and young humans. (Gallup 1977) He found that chimpanzees could be taught to recognize themselves in mirrors. The acquisition of this recognitional ability by the chimps required intervention beyond the species, human intervention; the chimps so trained did not pass on the newfound recognitional ability to their offspring, nor did the recognitional ability spread throughout the species. Nor does recognition require a self-concept or any kind of conceptual awareness. Perhaps this recognitional ability is a step toward self-consciousness, but it is far from a robust first-person perspective—which requires a self-concept. As I mentioned, passing the mirror test is not enough to guarantee a robust first-person perspective. Chimpanzees, even those "mirror-trained," have only rudimentary first-person perspectives. (cf. Baker 2000, 60–62) Human persons with robust first-person perspectives, by contrast to mirror-trained chimpanzees, can evaluate their desires, change their habits, and generally be moral beings.

To sum up: Human infants and higher nonhuman animals are conscious without being self-conscious. Lacking self-concepts, they have rudimentary, but not robust, first-person perspectives. Even lacking any pronouns like "I," all the mental states of beings with only rudimentary first-person perspectives are, by default, first personal. Typically, human infants (very young persons) develop into mature persons with robust first-person perspectives; nonhuman animals do not develop robust first-person perspectives.

I have now explained rudimentary and robust stages of the first-person perspective, the former as nonconceptual and the latter as requiring language and a self-concept. It is on the robust stage that I shall focus, both in my critiques in Chapters 3 and 4 and in my positive arguments against naturalization of the first-person perspective in Chapter 5. Now let us turn to John Perry and David Lewis, and then to a comment on John Searle, to see whether their reductive views can naturalize the first-person perspective.

Chapter Three

Reductive Approaches to the First-Person Perspective

Many philosophers agree on the importance of a first-person perspective expressed by I* thoughts. Any kind of self-evaluation (e.g., "I regret that I* was being mean-spirited" or "I hope that I* am up to the task") requires a robust first-personal perspective. (Baker 2011b) Achievements like self-understanding and emotions like regret and gratitude presuppose a robust first-personal perspective. No entity lacking a robust first-person perspective is morally responsible for anything. (Without a robust first-person perspective, one could not know that she herself (she*) had done anything.) Our manifestations of agency are suffused with robust first-personal perspectives—the perspective from which we deliberate and engage in practical reasoning. The question here is whether these first-person phenomena can fit into a non-first-person ontology.[1]

A successful reduction of the first-person perspective would be stated in entirely third-person terms and show that the first-person perspective strongly supervenes on local microphysical properties. (See Chapter 1.) In this chapter, after considering specific philosophers, I consider whether cognitive science can save the day for naturalism.

---

1. For purposes here, I use "non-first-person" and "third-person" interchangeably.

JOHN PERRY AND AN EPISTEMIC ACCOUNT OF THE SELF

Almost all philosophers use what I'm calling "I*-sentences" and "he*-sentences"—without using the "*"—to express their views on agency and the philosophy of mind. See, for example, Frankfurt (1971), Velleman (1992), and Bratman (2001), who assume that a special neural state or process of one sort or another can play "I*" roles—without showing how the trick can be pulled off.

John Perry, by contrast, takes on the task of trying to show how first-personal phenomena can fit into a non-first-person ontology. Agreeing on the importance of first-personal phenomena in our actions and self-knowledge, Perry argues that first-personal phenomena are just epistemic or pragmatic. In that case, first-person concepts have no first-personal ontological import and hence do not imply the exemplification of first-person properties. So, ontological naturalism seems secure. But the devil is in the details, as we shall see.

John Perry, famous for his work on the "essential indexical," uses a non-first-person ontology to explain first-person phenomena. I want to turn to first-person phenomena that are not described in terms of consciousness of our own minds. The first example that I want to consider is John Perry's famous case of the messy shopper. (Perry 1979)

Suppose that JP is shopping in a supermarket, and he notices that somebody has a torn bag of sugar that's leaking. He follows the trail of sugar to inform the messy shopper that he or she is making a mess. He forms various beliefs—for example, that the messy shopper isn't paying attention to his cart. JP catches a glimpse of the messy shopper in the security mirror and forms the belief that the person he sees in the security mirror is the messy shopper. As he keeps going around and the trail gets thicker, it finally it dawns on him that he (himself) is the messy shopper. Until then, he had beliefs about the messy shopper (that is, about himself), but he didn't realize that he himself was the one that they were about. When he came to believe that he (himself) was the messy shopper, his behavior changed: He stopped and checked his cart and, sure enough, there was the leaking bag of sugar. When he had the beliefs about himself, without *realizing* that they were about himself, he kept pushing the cart. When he realized that he* was the messy shopper, he stopped—his change in behavior was explained by his change of belief.

The locution "one knowingly refers to oneself" seems to entail "one refers to oneself in the first-person and realizes that it is oneself* that one is referring to." When Perry referred to himself by means of the description "the messy shopper," he didn't realize that it was himself that he was referring to. He did not refer to himself knowingly. It is only when he could say from a first-person point of view, "I am the messy shopper" that he knowingly referred to himself. And the change in Perry's behavior was explained by the change in his belief from unknowingly referring to himself (in the third person) to knowingly referring to himself (in the first person).

No acquisition of any belief in which Perry didn't knowingly refer to himself would have led to a change in his behavior. It was his realization, "Oh! It's me! I'm the one making the mess!" that led him to look in his cart. Perry's first-personal belief that included his knowingly referring to himself led to his stopping and looking in his cart; acquisition of any third-personal belief about himself would not have led to his change of behavior. It follows that the first-personal belief that included knowingly referring to himself (1) is explanatory (of the change in his behavior), and (2) cannot be replaced by any third-personal belief about himself. Hence, Perry's belief that he (himself) was the messy shopper is irreducibly first personal.

A belief that JP would express or someone else would attribute to him as an instance of "x came to believe that x was the messy shopper" is not the belief that explains his change of behavior. The first-person way of thinking of himself is essential to the belief that explains his change of behavior—the belief that he would express by "I came to believe that I* was the messy shopper." If science is, as we are assuming, devoid of first-person pronouns, then the change of belief that explains his change of behavior is invisible to science.

Someone may object, "So what? You are just making the mistake of treating an epistemic case as an ontological one." Indeed, Perry might make this objection inasmuch as for him "the self" is a pragmatic/epistemic category. Perry may aver that his ontology is wholly third personal and is in no conflict with ontological naturalism.

Let me respond. Perry explains "knowingly referring to oneself" in terms of a self-notion. A self-notion is similar to what I refer to as my self-concept, with the crucial difference that Perry's self-notions are nothing but "the normal repository of normally self-informative ways of perceiving and the normal motivator of normally self-dependent ways of acting." (Perry 2002b, 202) That is, for Perry, self-notions play a pragmatic/epistemic role in how one obtains information; the information so obtained has no first-person ontological significance.

Perry distinguishes a notion (the idea of a thing) and a file (a number of beliefs with a common notion). (Perry 2002a, 193–94) On Perry's view, each of us has a self-notion, one that each would express by "being me." Perry's theory diagnoses the case of the messy shopper as follows:

> The problem of the messy shopper was that the shopper had two "unlinked" notions of himself—the notion of the messy shopper and his self-notion. The shopper had two beliefs with

the same content (expressed by, say, "someone made a mess in this aisle" but associated with different files. Files are unified, not by the fact that they are about same person but that "they contain the same notion or linked notions." (Perry 2002a).

The messy shopper came to realize that he* was making a mess when his two notions of himself—his self-notion and his messy-shopper-notion—became linked.

I want to make two points here. (1) Perry does not give a non-first-person account of how the two notions of himself—the notion he expresses by "being me" and the (third-person) notion of the messy shopper—became linked, and (2) Perry attempts to construe first-person phenomena in terms of ways of knowing associated with identity; but ways of knowing associated with identity are insufficient for first-person phenomena without a capacity to conceive of oneself as oneself* in the first person. So, there is no real reduction of the first person.

(1) What does it mean to say that the two notions of the messy shopper become linked? Perry does not say, but he does give another example which suggests, I think, that he has not given a third-person account of the linkage that is supposed to explain the acquisition of the first-person beliefs: Perry has a friend, Al. He sees Al limping toward him, but doesn't yet recognize him. Perry says:

> I form a notion of this person. At that moment I have two unlinked notions of Al. ... I accumulate information about him as he gets nearer; *finally, I recognize him as Al. At that point the notions become linked;* the newly acquired perceptual information combines with the old information, and I say, "Why are you limping, Al?" If the identification is tentative, the notions may retain their identity; if not, they may merge and become one. (Perry 2002a, 196; my emphasis)

But notice: The linkage of the two notions of Al seems to depend on Perry's recognizing the limping man, and not the other way around. This does not serve the purpose of reduction: Recognition seems to effect the linking of the notions. (To object that the linking just *is* the recognition (token-identity), without any suggestion of what triggered the linking, would be no explanation of how the two notions became linked.)

Elsewhere Perry seems to take the person, conceived in the first person, to be the agent of linkage. Before I can use objective information as being about myself (e.g., "I have grey hair"), "I need to recognize myself, to associate the information with my self-notion." (Perry 2002b, 229) In other words, it seems that Perry is saying, "The information is linked to my self-notion, because I linked it."

Perhaps Perry chose this first-person way of putting his view for felicity of expression. My point is that he has offered no third-person alternative to the first-person phenomena. Furthermore, if Perry holds that linkage constitutes the recognition or explains it, he needs to explain linkage without running into problems analogous to Davidson's deviant causal chains. That is, he would have to say what are the "right" ways of linkage—ways that yield recognition—without reintroducing what he is trying to explain. At this point, the only evidence there is for linkage is the recognition. Perry has offered no third-person reduction. So, I think that Perry's account falls short of a reduction.

Similarly, in the case of the messy shopper, it was when the messy shopper realized that he* was the messy shopper that the linkage between his self-notion and his messy-shopper notion occurred. But again, this gives us no clue about how the realization—"I am the messy shopper"—can be understood in terms of a subpersonal linkage between two third-person items.

Perry may respond that his account concerns only representations and knowledge and that self-notions accomplish what he needs without any first-personal ontological commitment. On the contrary, I do not think that his self-notions do the trick: Although Perry can distinguish his self-notion from a John-Perry-notion, he does not show how to distinguish his (JP's) self-notion from my (LB's) self-notion. He says, "my self-notion is a notion *of* me because it is *my* self-notion; that is, (i) it is a self-notion…and (ii) it is mine." (Perry 2002a, 234) This explanation of one's self-notion is not adequate: it implies that my self-notion is mine in virtue of being mine, and Perry's is his in virtue of being his.[2] So, I do not believe that Perry gives an account of a self-notion adequate to his reductive needs.

(2) Perry says that "'self' expresses an agent-relative role, that of identity"; and "there are special ways of knowing and acting that are associated with identity." (Perry 2002, 212) As already mentioned, I agree that we do not need special entities like selves in ontology. As Perry puts it, "we do not need to postulate anything but the person himself or herself for the knowledge to be about." (Perry 2002a, 213) Of course, I agree with this too.

But the person must have a first-person perspective. Otherwise, we have no way to distinguish between referring to oneself knowingly and referring to oneself unknowingly. Without a robust first-person perspective, how would you know the difference between genuine self-knowledge and knowledge about someone who merely happened to be yourself? (cf. Mach) Having a self-notion would not even suffice to make the distinction, unless you knew which notion was your self-notion. You would not know which notion was your self-notion unless you knew which kinds of information were normally picked

2. I admit that I make a move similar to Perry's in Chapter 7. I cannot give a noncircular answer to the question: What makes my first-person perspective at time t the same first-person perspective as my first-person perspective at time t'? But I am not trying to give a naturalistic or noncircular account of a self-notion, or of a first-person perspective. I explain my noninformative answer by contending that being a person is not reducible to any subpersonal properties or parts, whereas Perry is aiming to give a reductive explanation of a self-notion.

up in self-informative ways. And if you didn't know which kinds of information were normally picked up in self-informative ways, you would not know which "channel" any particular piece of information came from. By holding that "*self* is an agent-relative role, being identical with the agent, that is associated with special epistemic and practical methods" (Perry 2002b, 229), Perry has not shown how to avoid an irreducibly first-person perspective.

Perry may respond that he has no truck with irreducible first-person perspectives or with any irreducible any first-person facts. He says, for example, "The facts that make it the case that Tom Nagel realizes he is TN are all objective facts." (Perry 2002a, 239) One of the objective facts that makes Nagel's belief that he is TN true is what Perry calls the "reflexive content" of the belief. On Perry's view, there are two kinds of content or truth-conditions of a belief or utterance: subject-matter truth-conditions and reflexive truth-conditions. Reflexive truth-conditions (or content) are "conditions on the things we take for granted in getting to the subject matter, namely, the words themselves." (Perry 2002a, 232) Reflexive content is not part of the subject-matter content but is part of the total content. For a belief involving a self-notion, the reflexive content is a way of believing but not what is believed or what is asserted. Different reflexive content provides different ways of having the same belief. The beliefs—with the same total content—that Thomas Nagel, say, would express by, "I am TN" and "TN is TN" differ in reflexive content. The first is that, TN is the owner of TN's self-notion.[3] The second is that TN is the owner of TN's TN-notion. It is this reflexive content that distinguishes Nagel's belief that he* is TN from his belief that TN is TN.

However, I do not believe that Perry's idea of reflexive content can accomplish what is needed for a wholly non-first-personal

---

3. "The reflexive content of his belief needs to be true, but he need not believe it." (Perry 2002a, 239)

ontology. Indeed, it cannot distinguish the informative belief that Nagel expresses by

(a) "I am TN"

from the uninformative belief that Nagel expresses by

(b) "I am I."

Perry treats (a) and (b) in exactly the same way: Both express the same trivial and necessary proposition also expressed by "TN is TN"; and both have the same true reflexive content, entailing the same self-notion: TN is the owner of TN's self-notion. (Perry 2002a, 232) So adding reflexive content to subject-matter or propositional content does not make the distinction Perry needs. The beliefs expressed by (a) and (b) have the same total truth-conditions: the same subject-matter content *and* the same reflexive content. So, I do not believe that Perry's use of the idea of reflexive content can result in "no need for any kind of facts other than objective facts, no need for true propositions that are 'subjective' or agent-relative." (Perry 2002b, 239)

In addition to the problems with Perry's idea of a self-notion just canvassed, Perry—to be an ontological naturalist—must construe the capacity to think of oneself as oneself* in third-person terms. I doubt that Perry (or anyone else) can achieve that. (See Chapter 5.)

DAVID LEWIS ON DE SE BELIEF

Although David Lewis had too much confidence in the a priori to be a mainstream naturalist, his fundamental ontology contains only natural microphysical properties—like spin and charge— and is a wholly third-person ontology. Moreover, Lewis's analysis of de se knowledge and belief may seem to provide a third-person account of the objects of knowledge and belief. Lewis proposed a novel view of objects of attitudes that is to accommodate I*-beliefs and I*-knowledge. On his view, the objects of the attitudes are not propositions, but properties: To have an attitude is to self-ascribe a property. All knowledge and belief, on Lewis's view, is self-ascription of properties—and hence is broadly de se. (Lewis 1979, 139)

Lewis, who calls himself "a robust realist about beliefs and desires,"[4] very neatly distinguishes self-belief expressed by I*-sentences from de re belief and de dicto belief. De dicto belief that p is self-ascription of the property of being in a world in which p. De re belief is ascription of a property X to an individual Y under a suitable description Z, where a suitable description either denotes an essence of Y or a relation of acquaintance with Y.[5] Finally, I*-belief is a special case of de re belief, where the relation of acquaintance is identity. "Self-ascription of properties is ascription of properties to oneself under the relation of identity." (Lewis 1979, 156) Lewis says that de se belief "concerns not the world but oneself." It is belief whereby I "self-ascribe the properties I think myself to possess." (Lewis 1999, 317)

So, if I say, "I believe that I* live in Amherst," I self-ascribe the property of living in Amherst. ("The de se content of my belief that I have F is just the property F itself." (Lewis 1999, 318)) If I say, "I believe that you live in Amherst," there is a relation of acquaintance (or a description that captures essence) that I uniquely bear to you, and I self-ascribe bearing that relation uniquely to someone who lives in Amherst. If I say, "I believe that many people live in

4. Lewis 1999, 322. I take this to imply that Lewis would not consider use of "I*" a user-illusion.
5. Relations of acquaintance include relations to my acquaintances, present or absent; people prominent in the news; famous dead people; authors whose works I have read; strangers I am face to face with; strangers I am tracing (such as the driver in the car in front of me); myself. (Lewis 1979, 155)

Amherst," I self-ascribe the property of inhabiting a world in which many people live in Amherst. The first belief—the I*-belief is (narrowly) de se; the second, de re; and the third, de dicto.

My question is this: Does this account capture first-personal phenomena in non-first-person terms? Not obviously so: All belief is self-ascription of properties, and self-ascription as Lewis is using the term is not just ascription to someone who happens to be oneself. To self-ascribe a property is to ascribe it to oneself as oneself*, in the first person. Self-ascription (of any property) requires that the self-ascriber realize that it is she* to whom she is ascribing the property. Oedipus may have self-ascribed the property of being in a world in which someone killed Laius at a crossroads. But Oedipus would not have self-ascribed the property of being the killer of Laius at a crossroads, if he did not realize that he* himself killed Laius at a crossroads. But self-ascription of *either* property—of being in a world in which someone killed Laius at a crossroads, and of being the killer of Laius—requires that the self-ascriber have a robust first-person perspective. Lewis's whole account in terms of self-ascription presupposes that every believer has a robust first-person perspective.

This observation, though true, understates the role of the first-person perspective in Lewis's account. The robust first-person perspective shows up, not only in all self-ascribing of properties, but also in some of the properties that are the *objects* of belief and knowledge. Suppose that Smith is trying to recall how she felt when she* won the booby prize. She says, "I believe that I* was embarrassed (and not amused) that I* won the booby prize." How would Lewis construe Smith's remark? Considering how he treats other cases, I think that he should say this:

> Smith self-ascribed the property of being embarrassed that she* won the booby prize.

So, in addition to the first-person perspective embedded in any self-ascription of any property, the particular property that Smith self-ascribed—the property of being embarrassed that she* won the booby prize—is a first-person property that is the *object* of Smith's belief, a property that itself involves attribution of a first-person reference. If the attribution is correct, then Smith made a first-person reference that we have no idea how to paraphrase in third-personal terms.

So, Lewis's analysis has not eliminated the first-person perspective from the objects of belief, and objects of true belief belong in a full account of reality. In order to reduce the self-concept to make it naturalistically suitable, we would have to give a third-person account of the distinction between Smith's self-ascribing the property of being embarrassed that she* was F (with its first-person implication) and Smith's self-ascribing the property of being embarrassed that Smith was F in wholly third-personal terms.[6] I'll make two stabs at doing this.

(1) Perhaps Lewis could eliminate the "I*" by embedding the self-ascribing—for example, "Smith self-ascribed the property of self-ascribing the property of winning the booby prize." This sentence goes too far; it eliminates all reference to being embarrassed, and hence does not capture Smith's belief: she did not self-ascribe the property of winning the booby prize, but rather the property of being embarrassed that she* won the booby prize. It is the expression of the self-ascribed property that contains the "she*"

(2) Perhaps Lewis would give a functional paraphrase of what Smith said by "I believe that I* was embarrassed that I* won the

6. For the same reason that worlds were not fine-grained enough to handle self-locating beliefs, worlds plus individuals (centered worlds) seem not fine-grained enough to handle beliefs whose objects include I*-properties. This suggests that I*-properties cannot simply be construed as self-locating properties.

booby prize." However, we do not even have a toy example of a third-person functional analysis of any sentence self-ascribing a concept expressible by "I*." If Smith was sincere, then what she said was true; but if it was true, then the world cannot be completely described without first-person reference. That is, the truth of a sentence with "I*" embedded in her belief about the object of her embarrassment requires that the world contain a referent of "I*"—not just a person *simpliciter*, but a person picked out *by her own first-person reference as herself.* (See Chapter 5.) I do not see how the phenomenon of picking out someone as herself by her own first-person reference can occur in a world without (robust) first-person perspectives. In any case, as it stands, Lewis's analysis of de se belief gives scant comfort to the naturalist.

Moreover, there are many I*-states that fall outside the purview of belief and desire. The state of being embarrassed is only one of them. As mentioned, Lewis must distinguish between "I'm embarrassed that I* won the booby prize" (said by LB) and "I'm embarrassed that LB won the booby prize." It seems unlikely that there is a functional state with which to identify being embarrassed, and even less likely that there is a first-order physical state that plays the being-embarrassed-role, as Lewis's account would require. (Lewis 1999) (Why suppose that there is such a role? Do we have any idea of what it would be?) The state of being embarrassed is just the beginning. Being glad, being apprehensive, swearing, promising, regretting, apologizing, hoping, and on and on are subject to the same distinction between "I*" and "LB."

Lewis may suppose that I*-properties can all be functionalized at once through one massive definition. Even if belief ascriptions are holistic, the plausibility of this move is diminished by the range of I*-properties that extend far beyond belief. (For example, "I was embarrassed that I* won the booby prize.") There is no glimmer of the required massive definition on the horizon, and I see no reason to believe that there could be one, or that we could grasp such a definition. So, the need for I*-properties stubbornly persists, and the functionalization route to reduction seems blocked.

It seems unlikely that functionalism has the resources to account for the relevant distinction with respect to all, or even any, of them. At least, we have no clue how they might be construed functionally.

A COMMENT ON JOHN SEARLE

Perry and Lewis represent attempts to place robust first-person perspectives in a naturalistic ontology. Ordinary consciousness, a major component of a rudimentary first-person perspective, has also received a great deal of attention. I want to look at John Searle's views as another kind of example of scientific naturalism, this time applied to ordinary consciousness.

John Searle takes consciousness—"inner, qualitative, subjective states and processes of sentience or awareness" that distinguish waking life from dreamless sleep—to be a neurobiological problem. (Searle 2000, 559) Conscious states are "essentially subjective." But to think that the essential subjectivity of conscious states puts them out of the reach of science, says Searle, is to conflate two senses of the objective/subjective distinction. One sense is epistemic: Science is objective in that its claims can be settled in a way that is "independent of the feelings and attitudes of the investigators." Subjective matters are not so settleable in this sense. The subjective sense is ontological: Conscious items such as tickles and itches have a "subjective mode of existence," in the sense that "they exist only as experienced by a conscious subject." Entities in the environment, such as mountains and molecules, have an "objective mode of existence, in the sense that their existence does not depend on any consciousness." (Searle 2000, 561, 563, 564) Searle notes that "the scientific requirement of epistemic objectivity does not preclude ontological subjectivity as a domain of investigation." (Searle 2000, 564)

Since the realm of consciousness, on Searle's view, is the only subjective domain, it seems a little awkward to hold that consciousness "is a biological phenomenon like any other" and hence can be investigated neurobiologically. To Searle, the so-called "hard problem of consciousness" (cf. Chalmers 1995) is no problem at all. Skeptics doubt that anyone can ever explain why red things look red or why warm things feel warm. Searle's response is, "We know it happens. We know that brain processes cause all of our inner qualitative, subjective thoughts and feelings." What's left is the neurobiological question, *How* do brain processes cause subjective states of thought and feeling, and "how, exactly, is consciousness realized in the brain?" (Searle 2000, 366) How, indeed? If conscious states are essentially subjective, they seem unique. In that case, the neurobiological questions about consciousness hardly seem on a par with other biological questions, like how do microorganisms cause disease symptoms?

Searle argues that because, as he thinks, natural science can explain consciousness, his naturalism is intact. Perhaps his methodological naturalism is intact, but ontologically, he is no naturalist. Indeed, he explicitly appeals to "ontological subjectivity." (Searle 1992) If ontological naturalism were true, then "ontological subjectivity" would be an oxymoron: Subjectivity would have to be eliminated or cashed out in third-personal terms.

Moreover, an *epistemically* objective science of consciousness, even if successful, provides no reason to include consciousness in *ontology*. An epistemically objective science of consciousness or of anything else may be an "error theory." An eliminativist about consciousness may well hold that the verdict of an epistemically objective science of consciousness is that it does not exist. (For example, Patricia Churchland observed that "just as it turned out that there was no such thing as impetus, there may be no such thing as awareness." (Churchland 1988, 309)) Although ontological naturalism is at the core of scientific naturalism, Searle's view cannot accommodate both. There is a seemingly unresolvable tension between Searle's scientific naturalism and his ontological nonnaturalism.

So, I stand by my claim that an ontology exhausted by (impersonal) natural science cannot include consciousness. Since, as I agree with Searle, consciousness is both irreducible and ineliminable, it belongs in the ontology. Since ontological naturalism denies that there are any first-person entities, properties, or kinds in the ontology, the conclusion to draw is that ontological naturalism is false.

DOES COGNITIVE SCIENCE SAVE THE DAY FOR NATURALISM?

Naturalists are likely to object that metaphysics should follow science, and science has no problem with any robust first-person perspective or I*-thoughts. They may try to turn the tables on me with "one philosopher's modus ponens is another's modus tollens." Consider: If there is a robust first-person perspective, then there is a distinction between thinking of oneself as oneself* in the first person and thinking of someone who happens to be oneself. I go the "modus ponens" route: we have robust first-person perspectives and hence can make the distinction. Cognitive scientists may go the "modus tollens" route: Science does not make the distinction and hence does not have robust first-person perspectives (as I have characterized them).

Naturalists may advance an objection like this: "Cognitive science is a natural science in the broad sense, and there is a myriad of experiments on what is called 'the first-person perspective.' The thrust of the experiments is to call into question the reliability of the first-person perspective and thus to diminish its significance.[7] So, rather than saying that the first-person perspective impugns naturalism, the cognitive-science objector concludes, we should say that naturalism (by means of empirical studies) impugns the first-person perspective."

Such an objection may be backed up with a good deal of psychological literature to show that we often confabulate. (For an example of confabulation, see Goldman 1997, 532.) However, the objection quite misses my ontological concern. My concern is upstream from such psychological and epistemological matters. I would ask, not about mistaken beliefs about the sources of our first-order beliefs, but rather under what conditions can we have beliefs about our beliefs at all? The answer in part is that we must have a robust first-person perspective, whether we confabulate often or rarely. Similarly with self-evaluation: It is not the accuracy of our self-evaluations that concerns me; a robust first-person perspective is required to make a self-evaluation—whether accurate or not. (Baker 2011)

I shall respond to the above objection by trying to convince you that if science does not recognize a distinction between thinking of oneself as oneself* in the first person and thinking of someone who happens to be oneself, then science leaves something important about reality. I'll organize my response around a crucial distinction, which I call "The Datum":

(D) There is a distinction between conceiving of oneself as oneself in the first-person and conceiving of someone who is in fact oneself (perhaps unbeknownst to the thinker).

---

7. For example, "reflection on the manner in which our beliefs are formed may...lead to entirely erroneous beliefs about the source of our first-order states." (Kornblith 2012, ms 189)

Distinction (D) issues in two kinds of belief about oneself, one tied to a robust first-person conception and the other not.

Turn back to the cognitive scientist's objection in light of distinction (D). In the first place, this objection from cognitive science, I believe, misses the thrust of my argument. The cognitive-science objector unsurprisingly is concerned with cognition, but cognition is only a tiny sliver of my concern. I'm concerned with the fact that we (many of us) have inner lives; I am not concerned here with the contents of our inner lives, or with how reliable we our in reporting our reasons for thinking as we do. Rather, my concern is this: What is required for us to have inner lives at all? And my answer is that we have robust first-person perspectives—our capacity to conceive of ourselves as ourselves*. It is this capacity that makes the crucial distinction between conceiving of oneself as just another object and conceiving of oneself from the "inside," as it were. Regardless of how reliable or unreliable first-person perspectives are for acquiring beliefs about ourselves, we in fact make distinction (D)—as we saw in the case of Mach—and thus have first-person perspectives. If we were to fail to make distinction (D), we would never have any beliefs about what we* were doing or thinking.

In the second place, as I shall argue in several cases, cognitive-science theories lack the resources to recognize distinction (D) at all. I'll argue that failure to recognize distinction (D) is a serious conceptual shortcoming for any theory of cognition.

(1) Many cognitive scientists distinguish two systems of cognitive processing—System 1 and System 2. System 1 operates "automatically and quickly, with little or no effort and no sense of voluntary control." System 2 "allocates attention to the effortful mental activities that demand it, including complex computations. The operations of System 2 are often associated with the subjective experience of agency, choice and concentration." (Kahneman 2011,

20–21) System 1 seems to coincide with what I call "the rudimentary first-person perspective": "The capabilities of System 1 include innate skills that we share with other animals. We are born prepared to perceive the world around us, recognize objects, orient attention, avoid losses and fear spiders." (Kahneman 2011, 21–22) By contrast with System 1, Kahneman says, "When we think of ourselves, we identify with System 2, the conscious, reasoning self that has beliefs, makes choices, and decides what to think about and what to do." (Kahneman 2011, 21)

System 2 is certainly closer to the robust first-person perspective than is System 1. However, System 2 does not have conceptual space for the distinction between thinking of oneself as oneself* and thinking of someone who happens to be oneself. Consider some of the diverse examples that Kahneman gives of the operations of System 2: Some seem to require or presuppose a robust first-person perspective ("Tell someone your phone number"); others do not ("Look for a woman with white hair"), and still others are ambiguous with respect to the robust first-person perspective ("Monitor the appropriateness of your behavior in a social situation" is ambiguous between monitoring the behavior of yourself as yourself* from the first person or the behavior of someone who is in fact yourself, via a surveillance camera). The examples have in common only that they "require attention and are disrupted when attention is drawn away." (Kahneman 2011, 22) Requiring attention is not going to distinguish between cases in which you are manifesting a robust first-person perspective and cases in which you are not.[8] There seems to be no way in the dual-process view to distinguish between thinking of oneself as oneself and thinking of someone who is in fact oneself.

---

8. Nonlinguistic entities that lack a robust first-person perspective are able to pay attention when, say, they are tracking their prey.

So, although the dual process conception of System 1 and System 2 may make an important distinction about mechanisms, it does not underwrite the crucial distinction between conceiving of oneself as oneself* in the first person and conceiving of someone who happens to be oneself; hence, the dual process view does not have room for the robust first-person perspective.

(2) Cognitive scientists are concerned with introspection and its epistemic warrant or lack of it. For example, Carruthers (2010) argues that we do not have introspective access to our decisions and (nonperceptual) judgments; our attributions of decisions and judgments to ourselves depend on self-interpretation, just as our attributions of decisions and judgments to others depend on interpretation of their behavior. The only difference is that we have a much greater evidential base in our own case. However, whether we know our decisions and judgments by introspection or by self-interpretation is irrelevant to my argument about the first-person perspective. Self-interpretation raises the same basic issue about the first person as introspection.

What is self-interpretation? Cognitive science seems not to distinguish between an interpretation of somebody who happens to be yourself, and interpretation of yourself from the first person. But this, again, is the crucial distinction (D). Suppose that a cognitive scientist is studying the results of an Implicit Association Test of an anonymous subject and judges that the subject is biased. Unbeknownst to the cognitive scientist, he (himself) is that subject. His judgment is indeed about himself, but not about himself in the relevant (first-personal) sense. (The scientist may recommend therapy for the subject, but balk at the idea of therapy for himself.) This plausible example shows the need to recognize distinction (D). If self-interpretation is to have to do with what we want from self-knowledge, it had better be interpretation of oneself conceived of *as* oneself, from the first person, and not just interpretation of someone who happens to be oneself. So, the robust first-person perspective is presupposed as much by self-interpretation as by introspection (Cartesian or not).[9]

As I said, the cognitive scientist's interest in the first-person perspective is not per se in eliminating or reducing it but in ascertaining its reliability as a cognitive faculty. No matter how unreliable cognitive scientists deem the first-person perspective, they have not begun to show how an impersonal science can accommodate it.[10]

(3) Let's consider an explicitly representationalist view. On this kind of view, Jack thinks of Jill by tokening a mental representation that refers to Jill. Now consider a real-life case. New York *Times* columnist Maureen Dowd nicknamed presidential candidate Mitt Romney "Mittens." Not realizing that he* was Mittens, suppose that Romney formed many beliefs about Mittens—for example, "I think that the man in the photo with his back to us is Mittens," but he denied that the man in the photo was himself. Perhaps a representationalist would say that when Romney is thinking of himself as Mittens, he tokens one mental representation, but when he is thinking of himself as himself* in the first person, he tokens a different mental representation.

But this does not seem right: There is a big difference between believing that you are talking about yourself and believing that you are talking about someone else, and this difference is not reflected in a difference about which mental representation is tokened. If conceiving of oneself as oneself* were simply the tokening of a special

---

9. I'll later consider the possibility that Carruthers would reject distinction (D) altogether and deny that here is a robust first-person perspective.

10. It is noteworthy that in many of the empirical studies that impugn introspection, the subjects are not typical believers like you and me. They are commissurotomy patients (Carruthers 2009, 2010), subjects who confabulate following hypnosis (Carruthers 2010), subjects given a forced choice or are duped—as in studies of position effect (Nisbett and Ross 1980, 207)—or are primed (Frankish and Evans 2009, 14). They are in obviously nonoptimal (even nonnormal) epistemic situations. Moreover, the studies are statistical, and hence inapplicable to a particular individual.

mental representation, then our mental lives would be flat. The only difference between Mach's thinking, on seeing himself in the mirror, "That guy looks unkempt," and his coming to think, "I look unkempt" would be which mental representation he tokened. This would put his disgust that he* looked unkempt on a par with his disgust that the man whom he took to be someone else looked unkempt.[11]

To hold that the difference between conceiving of oneself as oneself* and merely conceiving of someone who happens to be oneself is just a matter of which mental representation is tokened does no justice to the importance in our lives of I*-thoughts, nor to their moral significance. So, appeal to mental representations seems inadequate to reduce distinction (D). (cf. 117–122.)

(4) No notion of the first-person perspective in terms of self-monitoring can make the crucial distinction (D): A self-monitor cannot make a distinction between monitoring the thing that is itself and monitoring itself as itself*. An object x can monitor x without realizing that it is himself* that it is monitoring.

(5) Metacognition fares no better. Metacognition is a trivial shift of mind reading—that is, a trivial shift to ourselves of third-personal attribution of mental states to others on the basis of their behavior: Metacognition is "merely the result of turning our mindreading capacities on ourselves." (Carruthers 2009, 123) This is ambiguous between my turning my mind reading capacities on someone who is in fact myself and turning them on my myself conceived of as myself* in the first person.

So, there seems to be a dilemma: Either metacognition requires an I*-concept or not. If metacognition does not require an I* concept (if it is the trivial shift from mind reading that it is billed as being), then it cannot make distinction D and leaves out the robust first-person perspective altogether. On the other hand, if metacognition does

11. Moreover, this example (like others) raises the imponderable question of how many boxes—belief box, hope box, disgust box and so on—we will need.

require an I*-concept, it is no trivial shift, but covert introduction of a robust first-person perspective, without reducing it to non-first-personal terms. In neither case can metacognition, understood as mind reading turned on ourselves, make the distinction D without presupposing an irreducible robust first-person perspective. Metacognition either fails to make distinction D or it does not reduce or eliminate the first-person perspective.

(6) In an important new book, *The Opacity of Mind* (Carruthers 2011), Peter Carruthers argues that "there is a single mental faculty underlying our attributions of propositional attitudes, whether to ourselves or to others." (Carruthers 2011, 1) In that case, given the inference from an underlying mechanism to the phenomenon that it supports, "self-knowledge" and "other-knowledge" are on a par.[12] This view clearly has no ability even to recognize distinction (D), which implies a distinction between two kinds of knowledge and belief about ourselves. Suppose then that we follow Carruthers and reject The Datum.[13]

Which half of distinction (D) do we reject? (Since "self-knowledge" implies truth, I'll switch the locution to "self-belief.") On Carruthers's theory, there is nothing distinctive about self-belief except that it happens to be about ourselves—that our access to our own current discursive mental states is "no different in principle from our access to the mental states of other people, at least insofar as both are equally grounded in sensory input [as he thinks they are]." (Carruthers 2011, 1)

This passage strongly suggests that Carruthers's theory would retain the notion of self-belief as belief about someone who is in fact ourselves, and reject the notion of self-belief as

12. Although I do not have space to support it here, I think that such inferences are fallacious. In Chapter 10, I sketch an alternative account that avoids such inferences.

13. Alternatively, Carruthers may accept distinction (D), but on pain of admitting an ineliminable and irreducible first-person element into his view. The general tenor of his view suggests that he would reject The Datum.

belief about ourselves as ourselves*. If this is right, then to follow Carruthers, we should reject the robust first-person perspective and with it our ability to conceive of ourselves as ourselves* in the first person, without aid of a name, description, or other third-person referring device.

But there are good reasons to recognize distinction (D). Here are two empirical reasons: (i) The fact that we need distinction (D) to make sense of what people do and say is good empirical evidence that there is such a distinction. (Remember Mittens and of course, Mach.) (ii) Distinction (D) makes a difference in what happens. Contrast: "I believe that I* destroyed Jack's property" versus "I believe that Suspect 2 destroyed Jack's property," where the speaker is in fact Suspect 2. If the former is true, then the speaker may take steps to make restitution to Jack; but if the latter is true (and the former is false), then the speaker will not take steps to make restitution to Jack. (This is a variation of Perry's argument for the "essential indexical" (Perry 1979)). Since the beliefs lead to a difference in ensuing action, and the only difference between them is that the former directly manifests a robust first-person perspective, distinction (D) makes a difference in what happens.

Finally, there is a theoretical reason not to reject distinction (D): Distinction (D) and the robust first-person perspective unify all our self-directed attitudes—being glad that I*..., anticipating that I*..., being embarrassed that I*..., regretting that I*... and all the rest. Carruthers's theory, which concerns only epistemic states like knowing and believing, leaves us with a disunified motley of self-directed attitudes. In the interest of theoretical unity, we should prefer the robust first-person perspective to a view that provides no natural way to unify all of our self-directed attitudes or even to acknowledge such attitudes.

So, rather than denying a robust first-person perspective, I suggest taking Carruthers's theory to cast doubt on the notion—I believe it is his own—that "differences at the personal level are only possible if realized in subpersonal differences." (Carruthers 2011, 23–24) The problem with a subpersonal level—with any level of mechanisms and processes—is that it leaves out actual phenomena at the personal level, the level of distinction (D) and the robust first-person perspective.

To sum up: On the one hand, cognitive science cannot reject distinction (D) and the robust first-person perspective without serious impairment. On the other hand, cognitive science cannot recognize distinction (D) without acknowledging the robust first-person perspective. The arguments in the sections on Perry and Lewis suggest that the robust first-person perspective is unlikely to be reduced or eliminated by the natural sciences. Hence, no wholly impersonal theory—including cognitive-science theories—can accommodate The Datum, distinction (D).

CONCLUSION

We have now considered three philosophers' attempts to treat first-person perspectives in a third-person, naturalistic way, and we have considered more generally the empirical approach from cognitive science. None of these actually vindicates ontological naturalism by reducing the robust first-person perspective to non-personal terms.

The robust first-person perspective plays a central role in many garden-variety things we do. Consider making a vow. Vows are typically made by I*-sentences: "I promise that I* will care for you in sickness and in health." Your life may depend on my keeping my vow, which could not have been made without a robust first-person perspective . Or consider regret, which is also expressed by I*-sentences: "I regret that I* caused you such pain." Again, this is a mundane example. But these everyday phenomena could not occur at all in the absence of robust first-person perspectives. Whether we appeal to science or not, we should not embrace a metaphysics that makes mundane but significant phenomena unintelligible.

Chapter Four

Eliminative Approaches to the First-Person Perspective

Even if the first-person perspective cannot be reduced, perhaps it can be eliminated. Several important philosophers have attempted to eliminate the first-person perspective from ontology altogether, and in this chapter, I shall consider two of the most interesting of them: Daniel Dennett and Thomas Metzinger.

DANIEL DENNETT ON CONSCIOUSNESS

Daniel Dennett is sanguine about a science of consciousness: "The defeatist idea that consciousness is a mystery beyond human ken has nothing going for it." However, "the gulf between the view from the inside and the view from science is unlike any other explanatory gulf in nature—even greater that the gulf between living things and inanimate matter." (Dennett 2009a, 28, 27)

Dennett wants to close the gulf by eliminating the first-person perspective altogether, by showing that it has no place in reality—even as something to be reduced. Dennett explicitly aims to construct a model of consciousness "from the third-personal point of view since all science is constructed from that perspective." (Dennett 1991, 71) His strategy is to show how a theorist can describe a subject's mind from the subject's own point of view—without assuming any first-person elements.

Dennett's account has two phases. Both phases rely on Dennett's intentional-systems theory. Intentional-systems theory "is in the first place an analysis of the meanings of such everyday 'mentalistic' terms as 'believe,' 'desire,' 'expect,' 'decide' and 'intend': the terms of folk psychology." (Dennett 2009b, 339) An intentional system is one whose behavior is predictable from the intentional stance, and the intentional stance "is the strategy of interpreting the behavior of an entity (person, animal, artifact, whatever) by treating it as if it were a rational agent." (Dennett 2009b, 339)

Although the physical stance and the design stance are the "more basic stances of strategies of prediction," the intentional stance is extremely far-reaching. It can be used not only to predict the behavior of persons, animals, and artifacts, but also to predict the behavior of subsystems, subpersonal agents that are composed of teams of still "simpler," "stupider" agents, until we reach a level where the agents are "so stupid that they can be replaced by a machine." (Dennett 2009b, 344) So, the intentional stance is part of an "as-if" strategy that can be used for predicting the behavior of any entity whose behavior is predictable by attributing mental "states," without any commitment to whatever internal mechanisms are running the show.

The first phase of Dennett's theory of consciousness is what he calls "heterophenomenological"—a theorist's (putatively) third-personal view of the way a subject sees herself. The second phase is a neuroscientist's account of what is really going on in the subject's brain. The result, interpreted intentionally, is Dennett's "Multiple Drafts model" of consciousness. The first phase is to purge the account of anything first personal, and the second phase is—again with the help of the intentional stance—to identify the neural states that explain the third-person data.

The theorist of the first phase, the heterophenomenologist, prepares data given by a subject who reports her subjective experiences. The raw data are the uninterpreted output of a sound tape, perhaps accompanied by a videotape and an electroencephalogram. These devices record observable features of the subject: the sounds the subject emits, her bodily motions, her brain states. I shall focus only on the sounds the subject emits, as Dennett does. The heterophenomenologist puts the data through several processes of interpretation—first by interpreting the noises from the tape as sentences,[1] then by interpreting the sentences as speech acts. The result is a text of the world from the subject's own point of view, like the world according to Garp, or Sherlock Holmes's London—all without giving up science.[2]

These processes of interpretation do not remove the theorist from the realm of science because, understood in terms of Dennett's intentional-systems theory of content, the processes of interpretation are just a means to reach the level explained by physical science; they make no ontological claims. Again, the value of intentional-systems theory is that it provides a way to use intentional language like "Jill believes that she heard a siren" without commitment to any particular state of affairs in reality; the intentional language is only a tool for prediction. Intentional-systems theory legitimates heterophenomenological interpretations in which "we *treat* the noise-emitter as an agent, indeed, a rational agent, who harbors beliefs and desires and other mental states that exhibit intentionality or "aboutness," and whose actions can be

1. For example, if the subject says what sounds like "the spot moved from reft to light," the theorist interprets the subject's utterance as "the spot moved from left to right." (Dennett 1991, 75)
2. Dennett 1991, 76. Recent brain research has shown that certain parts of the brain are more active when a person is lying or trying to deceive. So, brain imaging techniques can be used to show that subjects are sincere in their reports, and hence that they really had the beliefs in question.

explained (or predicted) on the basis of the content of these states." (Dennett 1991, 76) But the theory is indifferent to "the internal structures that accomplish the rational competences." (Dennett 2009b, 346)

The data to be explained, then, are a theorist's interpretations of the subject's verbal expressions of belief. The subject's expressions and reports of conscious events are never taken to *refer* to conscious events (like hearing a siren), but are taken only as data concerning what the subject thinks. ("Pain-talk," for example, "is non-referential" (Dennett 1993, 96)) As Dennett puts it, "what has to be explained by theory is not the conscious experience, but your belief in it (or your sincere verbal judgment, etc.)." (Dennett 2001, 4)

Heterophenomenology, Dennett says, "maintains a nice neutrality: it characterizes [subjects'] beliefs, their heterophenomenological worlds, without passing judgment, and then investigates to see what could explain *the existence of those beliefs*."[3] The point of heterophenomenology is to purge the data of any reference to conscious events, and hence to purge the data of any commitments to any first-person phenomena. This process is to render the data suitable for explanation by physical theory.

The Multiple Drafts model of consciousness then tells us what is really going on in the brain that explains the subject's beliefs about private subjective experiences. What is really going on in the brain can also be interpreted from the intentional stance.[4] From the intentional stance, we can say of the continual stream of processing

3. Dennett 2001, 4. And: Heterophenomenology is "a neutral path leading from objective physical science and its insistence on the third-personal point of view to a method of phenomenology that can (in principle) do justice to the most private and ineffable subjective experiences, while never abandoning the methodological scruples of science." (Dennett 1991, 72; 2001, 2)
4. Indeed, Dennett says that intentional-systems theory is ubiquitous in computer science, animal psychology, and evolutionary biology. (Dennett 2009b, 349)

that the brain is constantly editing and creating content. Hence, the title "Multiple Drafts model."[5]

As I mentioned, the theory of consciousness must not assume that the subject's beliefs are true, but only that she has them. But this leads to a problem in Dennett's account: There remains a residual first-person reference, even from the theorist's point of view. Suppose that a subject says, "I'm seeing a continuously moving dot." The datum would have to be "She believes that she* is seeing a continuously moving dot."[6] Then, it is the task of neuroscience to explain what is going on in her brain when she says, "I'm seeing a continuously moving dot." Although the neural evidence may render it doubtful or false that the subject actually sees a continuously moving dot, from the point of view of Dennett's theory, it remains the case that she *believes* that she* sees a continuously moving dot. That's the datum to be explained by the theory.

However, it may not be obvious, but that datum retains the commitment to a first-person perspective. If the datum were only "The subject reports that she* sees a continuously moving dot," the datum could be confirmed by the audiotape interpreted in terms of the intentional stance. But the datum would still entail that a first-person

5. Any line drawn between what is conscious and what is preconscious is arbitrary. Indeed, "the fundamental implication of the Multiple Drafts model" is this: If "one wants to settle on some moment of processing in the brain as the moment of consciousness, this has to be arbitrary.... [T]here are no functional differences that could motivate declaring all prior stages and revisions to be unconscious or preconscious adjustments, and all subsequent emendations to the content...to be postexperiential memory contamination. The distinction lapses in close quarters." (Dennett 1991, 126) And: "There is no reality of conscious experience independent of the effects of various vehicles of content on subsequent action (and hence, of course, on memory)." Dennett is willing to classify the Multiple Drafts model as "first-person operationalism, for it brusquely denies the possibility in principle of consciousness of a stimulus in the absence of the subject's belief in that consciousness." Indeed, "the Multiple Drafts model makes 'writing it down' in memory criterial for consciousness: that is *what it is* for the 'given' to be 'taken'—to be taken one way rather than another." (Dennett 1991, 132)

6. The datum could also be "She reports seeing a continuously moving dot," which is equivalent to "She reports that she* sees a continuously moving dot."

reference was made. The "she*" is the theorist's expression of the subject's attribution to herself of a first-person reference. That is, it is not just the subject of the experiment who makes a first-person reference, but also Dennett's *theorist* must attribute to the subject a first-person reference. The theorist's attribution is false unless the subject actually makes a first-person reference. So, the theorist as well as the subject is committed to there being a first-person reference. And without a first-person reference there is no datum.

Perhaps there was a datum that was misdescribed as containing a first-person reference. Well then, what *was* the datum? Perhaps it was some cognitive processing in a particular brain. That cannot be right. The data are supposed to be bits of the world from the subject's point of view, according to Dennett's characterization of heterophenomenology. The subject does not think of the world from her point of view in terms of cognitive processing. So it is difficult to see how there could be a heterophenomenological datum without the theorist's attribution to the subject of a first-person reference.

Consider a slightly different heterophenomenological datum, "The subject believes that she* saw a witch." The theorist who takes this to be a datum is not committed to the existence of witches, but the theorist *is* committed to the subject's having made a first-person reference. If the subject did not really see a witch, then the subject was mistaken; but if she didn't make a first-person reference, then there is no datum.[7] But if *the theorist* must suppose that the subject actually made a first-person reference, then first-personal phenomena are not eliminated from the world. The first-personal phenomenon may be concealed, but it is still there. Heterophenomenology does not succeed in purging the data of first-personal elements.

---

7. Someone may object that the datum does not require that the subject make a first-person reference. She may simply report seeing a continuously moving dot or seeing a witch. Then, we could consider a more complex case of the subject's reporting being embarrassed that she* won the booby prize. The attribution of a first-person reference there is ineliminable.

But this is not really Dennett's last word. Although Dennett mentions that the intentional stance has been put to vigorous use by various sciences,[8] he takes his Multiple Drafts model to be a mere propaedeutic to a serious scientific study of the mind, for which he suggests "translat[ing] all the talk of personal access into subpersonal terms." (Huebner and Dennett 2009, 148–49) Indeed, Dennett advises banishing the word "I" from science that properly "treats the mind as a distributed computational system with no central controller." (Huebner and Dennett 2009, 149) But unless the subpersonal theory can capture a subject's first-person reports, it cannot yield complete knowledge of reality. Although the heterophenomenological data do not entail the existence of moving dots or witches, they do entail the existence of first-personal reference. Hence, Dennett's account of consciousness does not show how first-person phenomena can be replaced by wholly third-person phenomena.

We can express the point as a dilemma: The heterophenomenological theorist's attribution of a first-person reference to the subject is either true or not. If the attribution is true, then the theorist is committed to there being a first-person reference. If the attribution is not true, then the subject did not make a first-person reference and there is no datum. So, heterophenomenology does not purge the data of commitment to first-person reference.

THOMAS METZINGER ON A SELF-MODEL THEORY

Thomas Metzinger is a naturalistic philosopher who recognizes the complexity of self-consciousness and treats it in detail. Indeed, there are a number of points of broad agreement between Metzinger and

8. "I think the fact that the concept of the intentional stance has been put to such vigorous use (and some abuse) by the relevant sciences has … shown philosophers something about the role that we philosophers can play in the interdisciplinary quest to understand the mind." (Dennett 2009a, 26)

me. Here are some examples: (1) self-consciousness is importantly different from mere sentience, or the kind of consciousness that non-human animals have. (Metzinger 2003a, 396) (2) Self-conscious beings possess the distinction between the first and third person "on a *conceptual* level, and actually use it." (Metzinger 2003a, 396) (3) Philosophers cannot "decide on the truth or falsity of empirical statements by logical argument alone." (Metzinger 2003a, 3) (4) The phenomenology of conscious experience should be taken seriously. (Metzinger 2003a, 301, n.2) (5) A human being can "conceive of itself *as a whole.*" (Metzinger 2003a, 1) Nevertheless, despite the similarities between us, we fundamentally are at odds with each other.

Some years ago, I wrote an article, "The First-Person Perspective: A Test for Naturalism" (Baker 1998), in which I presented the first-person perspective as a challenge to naturalism—at least to the robust form of scientific naturalism that aims to provide accounts of all phenomena in terms accepted by the natural sciences. Metzinger has taken up this challenge, both in his article "Phenomenal Transparency and Cognitive Self-Reference" (Metzinger 2003b) and in his book, *Being No One: The Self-Model Theory of Subjectivity* (Metzinger 2003a). These works offer by far the most comprehensive naturalistic theory of the first-person perspective that I know of.

In particular, Metzinger sees clearly the distinction that I draw between rudimentary and robust (stages of) the first-person perspective. All conscious beings—dogs, as well as human beings—have a perspective. They have points of view from which they perceive and act in the world. They solve problems by employing perspectival attitudes. Although a dog has a certain perspective on its surroundings with itself as "origin," the dog does not conceive of itself as a subject of experience. Metzinger puts it well:

> As Baker points out, it is not only necessary to have thoughts that can be expressed using "I". What is necessary is the possession

of a concept of oneself as the *thinker* of these thoughts, as the *owner* of a subjective point of view. In short, what is needed is not only reference from the first-person point of view, but the capacity to mentally "ascribe" this act of reference *to* oneself while it is taking place. (Metzinger 2003a, 396; emphasis his)

Metzinger writes sympathetically about my account of the first-person perspective. He writes that the conceptual distinction between merely having a perspective and conceiving of oneself as having a perspective—a distinction at the heart of my account of the first-person perspective—"is important for cognitive science in general, and also for the philosophical notion of a true cognitive subject." (Metzinger 2003a, 396) However, when I say, "Attribution of first-person reference to one's self seems to be ineliminable" (Baker 1998, 331), Metzinger disagrees. He offers an alternative view that eliminates reference to any self or genuine subject of experience. On his view, "all that exists are conscious systems operating under transparent self-models." (Metzinger 2003a, 397) On my view, I (me, the person, a first-personal being, a genuine subject of experience, a "self") am an entity in the world. So, the issue between Metzinger and me is joined in a profound and intriguing way: When I affirm that there are persons with irreducible first-person perspectives in the world, I am affirming that there are genuine subjects of experience (essentially first-personal beings) in the world. When Metzinger denies that there are "selves," he is denying that there are genuine subjects of experience in the world.[9]

Let me make two terminological points: (1) I follow Metzinger's use of the word "phenomenal" to apply to the qualitative contents

9. If all Metzinger means by a self or a subject of experience is "an internal and nonphysical object" (Metzinger, 2003b, 271), then almost everyone agrees with him that there are none; and there is no argument. I do not suppose him to be taking on a "straw man."

of conscious experience; phenomenal experience is character-ized by how it feels or "what it's like" to have it. This leaves it open whether or not a phenomenal content represents anything real, or as Metzinger puts it, whether it is "epistemically justified." (Metzinger 2003a, 401) Phenomenal content may or may not depict anything in reality.

(2) Metzinger denies that there are any entities in the world that are "selves" or genuine subjects of experience. By the term "genuine subject of experience," I mean an entity that must be included as such in ontology—a first-personal entity that exists in the world and not just as an artifact of an information-processing system. Although I do not believe that there exist "selves" as dis-tinct from persons, I do believe that there are persons, who are essentially first personal, and are genuine subjects of experience (call them "selves" if you'd like). I prefer the word "persons" or "genuine subjects of experience" to the word "self," because "self" suggests some inner entity; but I'll use all of these locutions to mean the same thing.

Although Metzinger emphasizes the importance of the first-person perspective in the very terms in which I describe it, he argues that we can account for the first-person perspective without supposing that there are "selves" or genuine subjects of experience. The question, then, comes down to this: Can there be an adequate ontology—an inventory of what really exists—that includes no first-personal subjects of experience, but only information-processing systems and self-models that are under-standable in wholly third-personal terms?

The portion of Metzinger's argument that concerns me here has three parts: (1) a subpersonal, naturalistic account of subjec-tive experience, (2) an account of how it can *seem* to us that we are genuine subjects of experience, and (3) an account of the (puta-tive) fact that there really are no genuine subjects of experience in the world. Metzinger offers a theory both that denies that I am a genuine subject of experience and that (putatively) shows what is really going on when it *seems* to me that I am a genuine subject of experience.

The first part of Metzinger's argument aims to give an account of subjective experience. Metzinger holds that our brains activate mental models that contain mental representations. Mental representations have both phenomenal content (smells, colors, etc.) that supervene on brain states, and intentional content (wishing you were here, believing that global warming is a serious threat) that depend in part on relations to an environment. Our representations are parts of mental models, some of which represent the world (world-models) and some of which represent the system generating the models (self-models).

A "self-model is a model *of* the very representational system that is currently activating it within itself." (Metzinger 2003a, 302) The content of a phenomenal self-model (PSM) "is the conscious self: your bodily sensations, your present emotional situation, plus all the contents of your phenomenally experienced cognitive processes." (Metzinger 2003a, 299)

Some properties of a self-model are transparent—that is, we don't see them, we look through them; they are not introspectively accessible. Transparency here is a phenomenological, not an epistemological, notion. Other properties are opaque—that is, we are aware of them; they are introspectively accessible. For example, as G. E. Moore pointed out, when we try to introspect the sensation of blue, the *sensation* (what the sensation of blue has in common with the sensation of green) is transparent: "we look through it and see nothing but the blue." (Moore 1903, 446) But the blue is opaque; it is what we see. Metzinger says: "A transparent representation is characterized by the fact that the only properties accessible to introspective attention are their content properties." (Metzinger 2003a, 387) Our subjective experience, in the first instance, is activation of representations in transparent models— that is, only the representational contents are experienced, not the models themselves.

In other words, subjective experience is phenomenal experience. It consists of activation of models of representations. We cannot experience the models. We experience only the content properties of representations, whether the contents depict anything outside the model or not.

The second part of Metzinger's argument is to show how it can seem to us that we are subjects of experience. Metzinger distinguishes between a phenomenal first-person perspective and a cognitive first-person perspective. (Metzinger 2003a, 405) A phenomenal first-person perspective allows an information-processing system to have phenomenal (i.e., subjective) experience; a cognitive first-person perspective allows an information-processing system to have I* thoughts that make it seem that it is a genuine subject of experience in the world.[10] So, Metzinger's phenomenal first-person perspective corresponds to my rudimentary first-person perspective, and his cognitive first-person perspective corresponds to my robust first-person perspective.

---

10. To show how it can seem to us that we are subjects of experience, Metzinger begins with a transparent phenomenal self-model that can be generated by an animal or pre-linguistic being; then, a conscious cognitive subject emerges when the system generates opaque representations and integrates them into the transparent phenomenal self-model. In Metzinger's words,

> My claim is that, all other constraints for perspectival phenomenality satisfied, a conscious cognitive subject is generated as soon as a globally available representation of the system as currently generating and operating with the help of quasi-linguistic, opaque mental representations is integrated into the already existing transparent self-model. (Metzinger 2003a, 367–68; 2003b, 395)

I*-thoughts require integrating part of an opaque self-model into a preexisting transparent self-model.[11] (Metzinger 2003a, 402) The opaque self-model is a phenomenal model of the intentionality relation (PMIR) that "represents itself in an ongoing, episodic *subject-object relation.*" (Metzinger 2003a, 411) What we think about when we consciously think about ourselves is really just the content of a self-model. In having I* thoughts, we are unable to consciously experience that "we are referring to the content of a *representation* that is 'in ourselves' (in terms of locally supervening on brain properties)." (Metzinger 2003a, 402) Metzinger continues:

> Cognitive self-reference always is reference to the phenomenal content of a transparent self-model. More precisely, it is a *second-order* variant of phenomenal self-modeling, which, however, is mediated by *one and the same* integrated vehicle of representation. The capacity to conceive of oneself as oneself* consists in being able to activate a dynamic, 'hybrid' self-model: Phenomenally opaque, quasi-symbolic, and second-order representations of a preexisting phenomenally transparent self-model are being activated and continuously reembedded in it. This process is the process of [conscious cognitive self-reference]....Reflexive self-consciousness consists in establishing a subject-object relation within the [phenomenal self-model].[12] (Metzinger 2003a, 403)

Let me try to put this in my own words. If someone thinks, "I am hungry," she is activating a transparent phenomenal self-model.

---

11. Metzinger defines a minimal notion of self-consciousness as having three properties: "the content of the self-model has to be embedded into a currently active world-model; it has to be activated within a virtual window of presence; and it has to be transparent." (Metzinger 2003a, 373)

12. Metzinger 2003b, 403. I inserted "consciously experienced cognitive self-reference" for "introspection$_4$." Metzinger characterizes introspection$_4$ as "a conceptual (or quasi-conceptual) kind of metarepresentation, operating on a pre-existing, coherent self-model." (Metzinger 2000a, 367)

She sees through the "I" (so to speak) to the feeling of hunger. The "I" is invisible to her. But if she thinks, "I believe that I* am hungry," the first occurrence of "I" is part of an opaque self-model that is integrated into the preexisting transparent self-model. The second occurrence of "I" in "I believe that I* am hungry" (the "I*") is phenomenologically transparent. The first occurrence of "I" is opaque since she is thinking of herself as the subject of her thought. What remains invisible to her is precisely what she is referring to. A conscious information-processing system seems to be a subject of experience when it generates subjective experiences that include the experience of being a subject of experience. Thus, we seem to be subjects of experience in the world. But the experience of being a subject of experience remains phenomenal.

The third part of Metzinger's argument is to show that the experience of being a substantial subject is *merely* phenomenal. The conscious cognitive subject is not part of reality, but only part of a self-model. Metzinger holds that a cognitive first-person perspective (that is, the ability to have I* thoughts) is a special case of a phenomenal first-person perspective: "Cognitive self-reference is a process of phenomenally modeling certain aspects of the content of a preexisting transparent self-model, which in turn can be interpreted as the capacity of conceiving of oneself as oneself*." (Metzinger 2003a, 405). In cognitive self-reference, what is referred to is the phenomenal content of a transparent self-model. So, the reference will be to an element of the self-model, not to a self existing in the world. In short, the conscious cognitive subject is just an element of the self-model.

Metzinger says: "Any conscious system operating under a phenomenally transparent self-model will by necessity instantiate the phenomenal property of selfhood in a way that is untranscendable for this system itself." (Metzinger 2003b, 363) I believe that the word "untranscendable" in this passage means that the system lacks resources to uncover the fact that the phenomenal property of selfhood is *merely* the content of a self-model. But according to Metzinger, what we refer to in cognitive self-reference is a mental representation: "[I*]," he says, "is the content of the transparent self-model." (Metzinger 2003a, 400).[13]

Metzinger's claim that the *cognitive* first-person perspective can be reduced to a complex *phenomenal* first-person perspective has a strong consequence about subjects of experience: No belief about the worldly existence of *what* is being mentally represented is "epistemically justified." That is, we cannot conclude that what is represented exists in reality. Metzinger says that the belief that a self carries out the act of cognitive self-reference is not epistemically justified, and hence is apt for rejection (Metzinger 2003a, 403). Thus, we can see how the Cartesian claim of epistemic transparency (my certainty that I am a genuine subject of experience that exists in reality) is intelligible, even if it is false. (Metzinger 2003b, 363)

In sum, Metzinger denies that conscious experience really has a subject in the world (a self or person who does the experiencing). Our experience of being subjects of experience is only phenomenal. We are mistaken if we think that, because we experience being a subject of experience, there actually *is* (in reality) a subject of experience who we are. We lack epistemic justification for "all corresponding belief states about what is actually being represented." (Metzinger 2003a, 404; 2003b, 375) The subjective experience of being someone in the world is an illusion. Just as dreams and hallucinations tell us nothing veridical about what's really going on in the environment, so too does subjective experience tell us nothing veridical about what we are. There are no selves, just self-models. "For ontological purposes," he says, "'self' can therefore be substituted by 'PSM' [phenomenal self-model]." (Metzinger 2003a, 626)

---

13. "[I*]" denotes "I*" in thought as opposed to language. See note 13.

Metzinger says that the main thesis of his book, *Being No One*, "is that no such things as selves exist in the world: Nobody ever was or had a self. All that ever existed were conscious self-models that could not be recognized as models." (Metzinger 2003a, 1) The experience of oneself is only a phenomenological consequence of a system operating under a phenomenal self-model (Metzinger 2003a, 387). This is compatible with saying either that I (a subject of experience) do not exist, or that I exist but that what I am is only a part of the content of a self-model.

However, I believe that the most charitable way to read Metzinger is not as an eliminativist about subjects of experience, but as a reductionist. Despite the misleading title of his book, *Being No One*, and despite what I just quoted him as saying, perhaps he is not saying that I do not exist, or that I am no one. Perhaps he is saying that *what I am* is an information-processing system that has generated a phenomenal self-model (PSM), and that *what I think about* when I think about myself is only the content of a mental representation in my self-model.

In any case, whether Metzinger is an eliminativist about selves (as his quotations suggest) or a reductionist (as I think is the more charitable interpretation), he denies that there exist what I have called "genuine subjects of experience"—first-personal entities that must be included as such in ontology. If Metzinger is correct, then the fact that you and I seem to be subjects of experience has no ontological significance. The difference between reduction and elimination is only a conceptual or descriptive difference; it makes no difference in ontology. On Metzinger's view, a complete inventory of reality will not include persons (selves, subjects of I* thoughts).

I would like to critically discuss two issues internal to Metzinger's view, and then turn to the main difference between my view and Metzinger's: The main difference between us is the ontological difference, stemming from his commitment to reductive scientific naturalism. Whereas I think that a complete ontology must include persons ("selves" or genuine subjects of experience), Metzinger does not. That is, although I think that there are selves in reality (again, I really prefer the word "person"), Metzinger thinks that selves are only matters of appearance, not reality. On his view, as we have seen, reality includes no selves, only self-models.

The two issues internal to Metzinger's view that I want to discuss are, first, Metzinger's "analysis" of cognitive first-person reference from a third-person point of view, and second, his notion of phenomenal content and the use that he makes of it.

First, consider Metzinger's argument against my claim that attribution of first-person reference to oneself is ineliminable. In the article of mine that Metzinger discusses, I used the example of Descartes's I*-thought, [I am certain that I* exist],[14] and I pointed out that the certainty that Descartes claimed was from a first-person perspective: Descartes claimed that he was certain that he* (he himself) existed, not that he was certain that Descartes existed. Although Metzinger agrees that Descartes was not making a third-person reference to Descartes (Metzinger 2003a, 398), he also holds that the mental content of Descartes's thought [I am certain that I* exist] and the linguistic content of the sentence <I am certain that I* exist> can be understood in third-person terms.

All the mental content of the thought [I am certain that I* exist] is merely phenomenal and, as Metzinger says, "not epistemically justified." (Metzinger 2003b, 373)[15] In short, my certainty that I* exist is understood as a complex relation of parts of the

14. Metzinger uses square brackets ([....]) to denote thoughts, and pointed brackets (<....>) to denote linguistic expressions.
15. Such phenomenal certainty has two defining characteristics. The first is that "the object-component of the phenomenal first-person perspective is transparent and the respective person is therefore, on the level of phenomenal experience, forced into an (epistemically unjustified) existence assumption with respect to

content of a self-model. In general, I*-thoughts are to be understood without supposing that a subject of experience exists in reality.

Metzinger also treats *linguistic* self-reference by the sentence <I am certain that I* exist>. The linguistic content of <I am certain that I* exist> may be "analyzed," he says, from a third person perspective as follows:

(A)   <The speaker of this sentence currently activates a PSM (a phenomenal self-model) in which second-order, opaque self-representations have been embedded. These representations are characterized by three properties:

First, they possess a quasi-conceptual format (e.g., through a connectionist emulation of constituent-structure, etc.);

second, their content is exclusively formed by operations on the transparent partitions of the currently active PSM;

third, the resulting relation between the system as a whole and content is phenomenally modeled as a relation of certainty.> (Metzinger 2003a, 402)

Let us label this account (A). Can (A) be a correct analysis of a first-person assertion <I am certain that I* exist>? My assertion <I am certain that I* exist> is necessarily about me, Lynne Baker. But the analysis is not. The analysis is about anybody who asserts that she* is certain that she* exists. Neither my assertion <I am certain that I* exist> nor (A) entails the other. So, the proposed analysis (A) is not an analysis in a traditional sense. Nor can (A) replace

the object-component." The second defining characteristic is "transparency of the self-model yielding a phenomenal self depicted as being certain." (Metzinger 2003a, 374) anyone's assertion of "I am certain that I* exist." The target sentence and (A) simply do not convey the same information.[16]

What is at issue is not the specific Cartesian example <I am certain that I* exist>, however, but rather my broader claim that the attribution of first-person reference to oneself seems to be ineliminable (Baker 1998, 331). It is this broader claim—one that applies to all I*-thoughts and I*-sentences that is at stake.

So perhaps (A)—even if it is not an analysis—should be regarded as an application of part of an empirical theory. Metzinger predicts that the phenomenal self-model (PSM) is a real entity that will be empirically discovered—"for instance, as a specific stage of the global neural dynamics in the human brain, characterized by a discrete and unitary functional role." (Metzinger 2003a, 411) The only thing to say here is that we will have to wait and see whether neural correlates of phenomenal self-models are actually discovered in the brain.

Even if they are discovered, however, the most that a neurological theory of I*-sentences or I* thoughts can hope to do is to provide necessary and sufficient conditions for the production of I* sentences or I* thoughts. But this would be a far cry from eliminating or replacing I* sentences or I* thoughts by third-person sentences or thoughts. Even if (A) is part of an empirical theory that is eventually confirmed, it still cannot *replace* the I*-sentence, which remains ineliminable.

The second question that I want to raise that is internal to Metzinger's theory is whether the notion of phenomenal content can bear the load that Metzinger puts upon it. Phenomenal

---

16. Maybe (A) is what makes an assertion of <I am certain that I* exist> true. Maybe (A) is the truth-maker for such assertions. But the notion of truth-makers is part of a controversial metaphysical theory outside the purview of any empirical science known to me. So, as a naturalist, Metzinger should be reluctant to appeal to truth-makers. (And, as far as I know, he does not appeal to truth-makers.)

content is qualitative content and (supposedly) supervenes on the brain; representational content is intentional content. (Metzinger 2003a, 71)

Metzinger says: "The central characteristic feature in individuating mental states is their phenomenal content: the way in which they *feel* from a first-person perspective." (Metzinger 2003a, 71) In my opinion, this is not the way that mental states should (or even could) be individuated—at least those mental states that have truth-conditions, as all I*-thoughts do. We have no criterion for sameness of feeling: I wake up at night and on some occasion my subjective experience is hope that I'll get a certain paper finished on time; on another occasion, my subjective experience is hope that it won't rain tomorrow. My subjective experience is certainly not the same on both occasions of hope, but not because of any difference in feeling. The difference—even the difference in what it's like to be in the states—depends on the *intentional content* of the hopes, not on any feeling associated with them. So, I do not think that purely phenomenal content can individuate mental states.

According to Metzinger, "conceptual forms of self-knowledge" (I*-thoughts) are generated "by directing cognitive processes towards certain aspects of internal system states, the intentional content of which is being constituted by a part of the world depicted as *internal*." (Metzinger 2003b, 367; his emphasis.) He says that the phenomenology associated with this type of representational activity "includes all situations in which we consciously think about ourselves *as* ourselves (i.e., when we think what some philosophers call I*-thoughts; for an example see Baker 1998)." (Metzinger 2003b, 367)

It seems to me to be phenomenologically mistaken to suppose that the intentional contents of I*-thoughts depict part of the world as internal. When I think: "I believe that I* can get money from this ATM," the intentional content of my I*-thought is not constituted by a part of the world depicted as *internal*. Still less is internality "phenomenally experienced." When I consciously think, "I believe that I* can get money from this ATM," the intentional content of my thought depicts a relation between a cash machine and myself—a relation that is not internal to me.

Metzinger endorses a principle of local supervenience for phenomenal content: "phenomenal content supervenes on spatially and temporally internal system properties." (Metzinger 2003a, 112) He goes on: "If all properties of my central nervous system are fixed, the contents of my subjective experience are fixed as well. What in many cases, of course, is not fixed is the *intentional* content of those subjective states." (Metzinger 2003a, 112) But almost all subjective experience (mine, anyway) has intentional content. Any mental state that can be true or false, or that can be fulfilled or unfulfilled, has intentional content, no matter what it feels like.[17]

For example, it suddenly occurs to me that I locked my keys in my office, and I experience a feeling of panic. The subjective experience has intentional, not just phenomenal, content; it includes a thought that has a truth-value. And I'm greatly relieved if I discover that the truth-value of my thought is false: Here are the keys in my pocket. The subjective experiences were not just the panic and the relief; they included the sudden thought with its specific intentional content and the happy discovery that the thought was false. Not only are we embodied, but also we are embedded—embedded in a real world, not just in representations of a world. And the contents of our subjective experience are typically infected by relations with the environment.[18]

---

17. Although I cannot argue for it here, I believe that none (or almost none?) of our intentional mental states supervene on our brain states. (Baker 2007a)

18. Metzinger notes that one "of the most important theoretical problems today consists in putting the concepts of 'phenomenal content' and 'intentional content' into the right kind of logical relation." (Metzinger 2003b, 112) That seems to me a problem

Since, according to Metzinger, phenomenal content supervenes on brains, and most of our subjective experience has intentional content, which does not supervene on the brain, phenomenal content cannot account for our subjective experience. Our brains, and what supervene on them, are only one determinant of subjective experience. I may wake up in the night, thinking that a search committee meeting the next day may be unpleasant. That particular subjective experience would be metaphysically impossible (and not just causally impossible) in a world without search committees and all the intentional apparatus surrounding hiring new people. So my subjective experience of thinking that tomorrow's meeting may be unpleasant does not supervene on my brain. Hence, phenomenal content, which does supervene on my brain, does not suffice for ordinary subjective experience.

Metzinger asserts, "Phenomenal content can be dissociated from intentional content: a brain in a vat could possess states subjectively representing object colors as immediately and directly given." (Metzinger 2003b, 359) This claim brings to the fore the dilemma that phenomenal content faces: If phenomenal content is dissociated from intentional content, then phenomenal content does not account for much of our subjective experience, as the examples given here show. But if phenomenal content is not dissociated from intentional content, then phenomenal content does not supervene locally on brain states and it loses the neuroscientific legitimacy that Metzinger claims for it. Either way, phenomenal content cannot play the role that Metzinger assigns it.

To recapitulate, my two objections internal to Metzinger's view concern his attempt to eliminate I*-thoughts and I*-sentences (or to reduce them to the third person), and his use of phenomenal

---

easily solved: Do not insist that phenomenal content (content that is experienced) supervenes on brain states. With the exception of qualia (if there are any), all content depends on interaction with the environment.

content to carry the weight of subjective experience. Now let us turn to some consequences of Metzinger's theory.

I want to consider three kinds of consequences of Metzinger's view that I find untenable—semantic, epistemic, and moral consequences. First, I believe that Metzinger's view requires an ineliminable equivocation on the word "I." Sometimes "I" refers to the whole information-processing system, and sometimes "I" refers to the content of a part of a self-model. This becomes apparent if we consider I*-sentences. Consider an ordinary I*-thought—for example, "I believe that I* am in Austria." Metzinger says: "I experience myself as the thinker of the I*-thoughts." (Metzinger 2003b, 373) The reality that the first occurrence of "I" in this thought refers to is the whole information-processing system. "The content of [I] is the thinker, currently representing herself as operating with mental representations." (Metzinger 2003a, 401) It is the whole system that thinks of itself as the thinker of thoughts.

On the other hand, the second occurrence of "I" (the "I*" in "I believe that I* am in Austria") "is the content of the transparent self-model." As Metzinger explains: "Any conscious system operating under a transparent self-model will by necessity instantiate a phenomenal self to which, linguistically, it *must* refer using <I*>." (Metzinger 2003a, 400, emphasis his.) So, the referent of "I" is sometimes the whole information-processing system and sometimes the content of a self-model. It is utterly implausible that "I" could be equivocal in a single thought of a single thinker. This would make us all hopelessly schizophrenic: Which am I—the whole information-processing system or part of the transparent content of its currently active self-model?

We can see this tension in another way when we consider Metzinger's metaphor that "you constantly confuse yourself with the content of the self-model currently activated by your brain." (Metzinger 2003a, 1) Who is doing the confusing? On the last page of his book, Metzinger says that we should not take this metaphor, "being no one," too literally: "There is no one *whose* illusion the conscious self could be, no one *who* is confusing herself with anything." (Metzinger 2003a, 634). What, exactly, then is the confusion that has no bearer?

It is difficult to see how there is a confusion to be made (with or without someone to make it). When I think, "I believe that I* am in Austria," my belief is that I (all of me) am in Austria. Perhaps, Metzinger is saying that, unbeknownst to me, the information-processing system that I am has a transparent self-model representing being in Austria, and the system integrates part of an opaque self-model representing itself into the transparent self-model, and thus generates a representation of a representation of being in Austria within the self-model.

This would completely misrepresent the content of my thought "I believe that I* am in Austria." If you and I agree that I believe that I* am in Austria, then we are agreeing about me, about where I believe I* am (even if I am an information-processing system operating with a self-model); we are not agreeing about my self-model. So, I think that it is not coherent to construe the subjects of I* thoughts to be parts of self-models.

Second, consider an epistemic consequence of Metzinger's view. The theory cannot make sense of what is going on when people reflect on what they are doing while they are doing it. Suppose that a scientist using an electron microscope for the first time thinks to herself, "I can hardly believe that I'm looking at electrons." If the scientist is not a subject of experience that exists in the world, how is she to make sense of her own thought, on Metzinger's view? Well, maybe this: The scientist has the experience of being the subject of the thought expressed by "I can hardly believe that I'm looking at electrons," but she is not "epistemically justified" in supposing that she really is a genuine subject of experience in the world. From Metzinger's point of view, the scientist is an information-processing system that is integrating "its own operations with opaque mental representations, i.e., with mental simulations of propositional structures that could be true or false, into its already existing transparent self-model while simultaneously attributing the causal role of generating these representational states to itself." (Metzinger 2003b, 369)

But, on Metzinger's view, *the scientist herself* cannot see her own thoughts and activity in this light; indeed, she is deceived about what is going on. Of course, Metzinger has an account of why she cannot see her own thoughts and activity in this light; but that's beside the point. The point is that the scientist cannot comprehend what she is doing and thinking while she is engaging in scientific activity. Metzinger's theory would seem to make it impossible for anyone to think clearly about what she is doing while she is doing it. A view of subjectivity that makes it impossible for scientists (and everyone else) to think clearly about what they are doing as they are doing it is dubious.

Third, Metzinger's view has consequences that are morally questionable. Consider a soldier long ago who experienced excruciating pain while undergoing a battlefield amputation. Metzinger says that we should minimize "the overall amount of suffering in all beings capable of conscious suffering." (Metzinger 2003a, 570) I do not see what epistemic grounds we can have for this "simple principle of solidarity," as he calls it. If Metzinger's view is correct, then we are epistemically unjustified in supposing that there is any substantial entity in the world that actually undergoes excruciating pain; rather, there is an information-processing system with a self-model that makes it appear that there is such a subject of pain. There was a subjective experience of pain, but the bearer of the pain was just a phenomenal self, who was "epistemically unjustified." If we are unjustified in supposing that there was a substantial entity (the soldier) who was a subject of pain, then we would be under no obligation to alleviate the pain. I think that this consequence would make our moral experience unintelligible.[19]

I am prepared to accept theories with counterintuitive consequences (e.g., I find it counterintuitive that there's no absolute ongoing now; but I accept this as a result of well-confirmed theories of physics). But Metzinger's view of the first-person perspective and its I* thoughts is not just counterintuitive. It has consequences that seem to me to be semantically, epistemically, and morally untenable. So, what should we do?

Metzinger's theory is a naturalistic one. Naturalism is often characterized by two themes—an ontological one that is committed to an exclusively scientific conception of nature, and a methodological one that conceives of philosophical inquiry as continuous with science. (De Caro and Macarthur 2010, 3) Scientific naturalism recognizes as real only non-first-person entities and properties.[20]

Metzinger's third-person subpersonal account of the first-person perspective fits this characterization of scientific naturalism nicely. So, I shall continue to use Metzinger as a case study. On being presented with a theory, each of us decides: Do I accept this theory? I invite you to join me in thinking of Metzinger's theory from the point of view of a prospective adherent of it. Would it be *rational* for me to accept it? Would it even be *possible* for me to accept it? Let's consider each of these questions in turn.

(1) If Metzinger's view is correct, then there are no selves and no genuine subjects of experience in the world. I just argued that

---

19. In an email to me, Metzinger said that he was very interested in ethical consequences of his view. He said that he believes that there can be selfless suffering subjects, and that phenomenal suffering is real and should be minimized. I hope that he pursues these issues at length. It is not obvious to me how to work out a morally acceptable position within the confines of his view.

20. Whether nonreductive naturalism can allow irreducibly first-person phenomena remains to be seen.

without subjects of experience in reality, I cannot make sense of my own experience while I'm having it. A view with this consequence renders my experience unintelligible to me. Is it rational for me to endorse a theory that renders my experience unintelligible to me? My experience of being a conscious subject is evidence that I am a subject, and this evidence overwhelms any possible evidence that I may have for any scientific theory to the contrary. Hence, rationally, I should reject the view that would have me repudiate myself as a genuine subject of experience.

(2) It seems that Metzinger's theory cannot coherently be endorsed or accepted. I may report having the subjective experience that I* am accepting Metzinger's theory. I report thinking to myself, "I am having the experience that I* am accepting Metzinger's theory." But the "I*" having the experience is not an entity in the world; it is just part of the content of a transparent self-model. (Metzinger 2003b, 372; 2003a, 400) When I refer to myself by means of "I*," I am referring to the content of a mental representation. It is incoherent to suppose that a mental representation can actually accept a theory. On Metzinger's view, all there can be is a subjectless subjective experience of accepting his theory; but for me to accept a theory is not just for there to be a subjectless subjective experience of accepting. So, it seems doubtful that Metzinger's theory can be endorsed or accepted. If a theory cannot coherently be endorsed or accepted, it is self-defeating. It is paradoxical, if not self-contradictory, to suppose that I should accept a theory that I cannot coherently accept.

MY RECOMMENDATION

Here is my recommendation: Give up scientific naturalism. Do not confine ontological conclusions to those that can be gleaned by scientific methods. As we have seen in the best attempts to naturalize the first-person perspective, science (at least as it stands today) cannot intelligibly be the final word on what there is. We should distinguish between phenomena that interest philosophers and the underlying mechanisms that subserve those phenomena. For example, we may hope for a naturalistic theory of the mechanisms that underwrite a first-person perspective. (Metzinger 2003a, 395) But on my view, the "I" who is the genuine subject of experience is a person: an object in the world whose first-person perspective is irreducible and ineliminable.

Scientific naturalism often seems like a change of subject that lacks respect for the peculiar projects and puzzles that tradition-ally preoccupy philosophers. In particular, nonnaturalists resist the tendency to assimilate the phenomena that piqued our philo-sophical interest to the mechanisms that support those phenom-ena. No one doubts that there are underlying mechanisms and that they are worthy of understanding. The nonnaturalist resistance is to *supplanting* philosophical questions by empirical questions about the underlying mechanisms that make the philosophically interesting phenomena possible—as if questions about the 1985 world-championship chess match between Kasparov and Karpov could be replaced by questions about the physics involved in the motions of little bits of wood.

Taking Metzinger's view as the best case for eliminating the first-person perspective, I now suspect that the challenge that the first-person perspective poses for naturalism cannot be met.[21]

---

21. Parts of this chapter descended from a paper presented at the workshop, How Successful Is Naturalism? at the meeting of the Austrian Ludwig Wittgenstein Society, Kirchberg, Austria, August 6–12, 2006. I am grateful to Hilary Kornblith, Gareth B. Matthews, and Thomas Metzinger for commenting on a draft of this chapter.

Chapter Five

Arguments against
First-Person Naturalization

In the last two chapters, I argued that a number of attempts to reduce or eliminate the first-person perspective are unsuccessful. In this chapter, I want to mount a positive argument against scientific naturalization of the first-person perspective. I shall argue that there are irreducible properties that are ineliminably first personal and that a person has a first-person concept only if an irreducible first-person property is exemplified.

I shall assume, as seems generally agreed, that the sciences are wholly impersonal or objective. (Chalmers 1991) Finally, I take it to be a general methodological maxim that any putative objects, kinds, or properties that are neither eliminable nor reducible belong in the ontology.

If I am correct in these three claims—that there are ineliminable and irreducible first-person properties, that natural science is wholly impersonal, and that any ineliminable, irreducible objects, kinds, or properties belong in the ontology—then some first-personal properties belong in the ontology. My arguments in this chapter will conclude that as long as science (contrued reductively or nonreductively) does not recognize first-person properties and include them in the ontology, it cannot provide a complete inventory of reality. In that case, ontological naturalism is false.

The case of a first-person property that I shall press is what I call an "I*-property"[1]—the property of having a robust first-person perspective, the property of the capacity to conceive of oneself as oneself*. Recall from Chapter Two,

(R) Property P is naturalized by reduction if and only if property P strongly supervenes on "appropriate" microphysical properties.

(E) Putative property P is naturalized by elimination if and only if a complete ontology does not entail that there is such a property P.

My first argument is linguistic: It proceeds from I*-concepts to I*-properties, and then to the irreducibility and ineliminability of I*-sentences; the argument then moves to the irreducibility and ineliminability of I*-properties. The conclusion is that I*-properties are not entailed[2] by impersonal properties; and hence that an impersonal account of reality is incomplete. My second argument is ontological: it proceeds from conditions for ontological naturalism to the conclusion that properties exemplified by bearers of robust first-person perspectives are not naturalized (by reduction or elimination).

First, some preliminaries: Propositions are the primary bearers of truth-value. Propositions have concepts as constituents and are individuated by the concepts they contain. Call a concept of oneself as oneself* in the first person an "I*-concept" (or a "self-concept").[3]

---

1. There is really only one I*-property: the property of having a robust first-person perspective, but this property has many exemplifications. For simplicity, I'll use "I*-property" to refer both to the single property and to any of its many exemplifications.
2. Say that property P entails property Q if and only if necessarily, if P is exemplified, then Q is exemplified.
3. When I say, "concept of oneself as oneself* in the first person," or "concept of myself as myself* in the first person," I speak of an I*-concept. On this usage, there are as many I*-concepts as there are people with robust first-person perspectives, but it will turn out that they all express the first-person property. For more on this point, see Chapter 8.

A proposition expressed by an I*-sentence contains an I*-concept, a concept of oneself-as-oneself* in the first person. Having an I*-concept allows one to have all manner of I*-thoughts and I*-sentences, and thus to have an I*-concept is to have a capacity.[4]

To many concepts—but not to all—there correspond properties. I shall use the term "express" broadly to cover the relations (whatever they are) that hold between sentences and propositions, and between concepts and properties. Declarative sentences express propositions, and (some) concepts express properties. A sentence is true if and only if it expresses a true proposition.

One final preliminary point: The first argument relies on the irreducibility and ineliminability of I*-sentences, characterized as follows:

An I*-sentence S is *reducible* if and only if S is replaceable *salva veritate* by non-first-person sentences, where non-first-person sentences are sentences expressing propositions that neither entail nor presuppose a first-person reference.

An I*-sentence S is *eliminable* if and only if whatever purposes S serves could be served equally well by a sentence or sentences lacking any first-person constituent (e.g., "I," "me," "my," "mine," "he*," "she*").

Now let's turn to the linguistic argument from I*-sentences, and I*-concepts to I*-properties.

---

4. I have no theory of the individuation of capacities. However, a single capacity—say, the capacity to be a faithful friend—may be manifested in indefinitely many ways, and its manifestations may be unconnected by anything other than being manifestations of that capacity. When I say "I*-property," I mean the capacity expressed by an I*-concept, or anything that entails that capacity.

FROM FIRST-PERSON CONCEPTS TO
FIRST-PERSON PROPERTIES

Assuming that natural science is wholly expressible in the third-person, naturalists deny that there are any irreducible first-person properties. A first-person property is a property that can be exemplified by beings with first-person perspectives and *only* by those with first-person perspectives.[5] Even as they deny that there are any irreducible first-person properties, naturalists need not deny that we have first-person concepts (e.g., John Perry's self-notions (Perry 2002)). And we do have empty concepts that do not express properties. We have a concept *phlogiston*, for example, even though there is no property *being phlogiston*. Similarly, naturalists may argue, we can have first-person concepts even though there are no first-person properties.

Consider the concept *phlogiston*. The concept *phlogiston* is a constituent in the true propositions expressed by "Phlogiston does not exist," "Newton did not believe in phlogiston," and "Phlogiston was a theoretical posit." Yet the concept *phlogiston* does not express a property. So, the truth-conditions for the phlogiston-sentences cannot advert to any property of phlogiston: There is none. There are several ways to find appropriate truth-conditions for "phlogiston" sentences. For example, the proposition expressed by "Phlogiston does not exist" may also be expressed by, and have the same truth-conditions as, "There is no property expressed by the concept *phlogiston*." The proposition expressed by "Newton did not believe in phlogiston" may also be expressed by, and have the same truth-conditions as, "Newton did not believe that the concept *phlogiston* expressed a property," or perhaps by, "Newton did not have

---

5. This is not to suggest that a being must *antecedently* have a first-person perspective in order to exemplify the property. The manifestation of a first-person perspective is the exemplification of a first-person dispositional property. (See Chapter 8.)

the concept *phlogiston*." The proposition expressed by "Phlogiston was a theoretical posit" may also be expressed by, and have the same truth-conditions as, "The concept *phlogiston* appeared in theories as a theoretical posit."

We can account for the truth of sentences expressing propositions containing the concept *phlogiston* without supposing that the concept *phlogiston* expresses a property. A naturalist may say that, likewise, we do not need any first-person properties to account for the truth of I*-sentences. He may aver that I*-concepts will do.

Would such a naturalist be correct? Let's see whether or not the analogy between the *phlogiston*-concept and the I*-concept holds. I have no quarrel with the *phlogiston* example. Indeed, I want to contrast the case of *phlogiston* with the case of the I*-concept in three ways:

(1) In the *phlogiston* case, the concept *phlogiston* is empty. There is nothing in reality that satisfies that concept. If the I*-concept were likewise empty, there would be nothing in reality that satisfies it. What would it take to satisfy an I*-concept? It would take there being a capacity of someone's conceiving of oneself as oneself* in the first person. Just a quick look around shows regular exercise of the capacity to conceive of oneself as oneself* in the first person. For example, "I did not realize that I* was being rude." Therefore, we have good reason to suppose that there is such capacity. So, we have good reason to think that the I*-concept is not empty.

(2) Another contrast between the concept *phlogiston* and the I*-concept: In order to account for the truth of true "phlogiston"-sentences, we had to paraphrase true "phlogiston"-sentences so that they did not refer to phlogiston. However, the truth of true I*-sentences does not require that they be

paraphrased in a way that avoids reference to a person who can conceive of herself as herself* in the first person. Indeed, as we shall see shortly, they cannot be so paraphrased.

(3) A final contrast between "phlogiston"-sentences and I*-sentences: In order for an I*-sentence to be asserted, the speaker or thinker must be able to conceive of herself as herself* in the first person. There is no parallel with "phlogiston"-sentences. Although I*-sentences could not be asserted if there were no robust first-person perspectives, any of the *phlogiston*-sentences could be asserted even though there is no phlogiston. So, there are a number of disanalogies between the I*-concept and concepts like *phlogiston* that do not express properties.

On the positive side, we can see that the I*-concept is not empty by noting what an assertion of an I*-sentence entails. The assertion of an I*-sentence is an assertion that guarantees both that the subject of the I*-sentence exists and that the subject can conceive of herself as herself* in the first person—that is, she can conceive of herself without any name, description, or other third-person referring device. So assertion of an I*-sentence entails that someone has the capacity to conceive of herself without any name, description, or other third-person referring device. Since there are assertions of I*-sentences, there is such a capacity, and use of an I*-concept is the exercise of that capacity. Hence, an I*-concept, unlike *phlogiston*, is not an empty concept.

To put it somewhat differently: Since an I*-concept is a concept of oneself as oneself* from the first person, the only way that an I*-concept could fail to express a property would be for the capacity to conceive of oneself as oneself* in the first person to fail to exist. However, such a capacity is manifested in all aspects of life— from marriage vows to volunteering for a suicide mission. And the capacity is presupposed in yet other areas from suing a landlord to retrieve one*'s property to changing one*'s mind. Indeed, knowing what one* is thinking or doing in general presupposes the capacity in question. Any I*-sentence or I*-thought is a direct manifestation of that capacity.

Since the capacity to conceive of oneself as oneself* in the first person undoubtedly exists, the concept that makes that capacity possible expresses a property—a dispositional property. (For further details about dispositional properties, see Chapter Eight.) So, an I*-concept expresses a property.[6] The property that an I*-concept expresses—the I*-property—is the capacity to conceive of oneself as oneself* in the first person.

The argument just given is simple. There are I*-concepts. If I* concepts are empty, then there is no one who conceives of herself as herself* in the first person. But we have seen many examples of people who conceive of themselves as themselves* in the first person. So, I*-concepts are not empty. If I*-concepts are not empty, then I*-concepts express properties. If I* concepts express properties, they express first-person I*-properties. So, I*-concepts express I*-properties, and there are first-person properties. (See Chapter 8.)

Unlike "phlogiston," where the appearance of referring to phlogiston in true sentences can be paraphrased away, "I*" in true sentences cannot be paraphrased away. The very use of I*-concepts to express true propositions entails that there are first-person perspectives— properties of conceiving of oneself as oneself* in the first person. In the next two sections, we shall see that I*-properties are neither reducible nor eliminable.[7]

---

6. I*-sentences express I*-propositions that contain I*-concepts, and I*-concepts express I*-properties.
7. An I*-property is the capacity to conceive of oneself as oneself* in the first person.

A LINGUISTIC ARGUMENT: A COMPLETE ONTOLOGY MUST INCLUDE FIRST-PERSON PROPERTIES

First, I want to show that the robust first-person perspective, manifested in I*-sentences, is irreducible and ineliminable. Since "I*" occurs only in subordinate clauses, "I*" cannot be given a non-first-personal definition by itself. Second, as we shall see, even *in situ*, a sentence containing "I*" cannot be replaced by a sentence that is free of attribution of first-person reference, and hence the I*-concept cannot be reduced. My argument will show that the I*-sentences that entail the exemplification of I*-properties can neither be reduced nor eliminated.

In this section, I shall speak of reducibility with respect both to sentences and to properties. As I mentioned, a first-person property is reducible if and only if it is entailed by non-first-person properties. Again, I*-sentence S is reducible if and only if S is replaceable by non-first-person sentences without change of truth-value, and an I*-sentence is eliminable if and only if whatever purposes S serves could be served equally well by a sentence or sentences lacking any first-person constituent (e.g., "I," "me," "my," "mine," "he*," "she*").

I'll mount a linguistic argument, from I*-sentences, to the intermediate conclusion that I*-properties are neither reducible nor eliminable, and with the final conclusion that I*-properties belong in a complete ontology. (In the next section, I mount a metaphysical argument for the conclusion that ontological naturalism is false.) For perspicuity, I shall first set out the linguistic argument, which is fairly simple, without any justifications for the premises; then I shall present the argument with justification for each line. Here is a streamlined formulation of the argument:

1. I*-sentences are not reducible.
2. If I*-sentences are not reducible, then I*-properties are not reducible.

3. I*-sentences are not eliminable.

4. If I*-sentences are not eliminable, then I*-properties are not eliminable.

5. If I*-properties are neither reducible nor eliminable, then a complete ontology includes I*-properties.

∴6. A complete ontology includes I*-properties.

Here is the argument again, this time with indented justification for each preceding line.

1. I*-sentences are not reducible.

Consider an I*-sentence and what I call its "corresponding non-I* sentence":

   (i) I believe that I* am wealthy (assertively uttered by Jones).

   (ii) I believe that Jones is wealthy (assertively uttered by Jones).

There are circumstances in which (i) is true and (ii) is false, and circumstances in which (i) is false and (ii) is true.[8] Consider this fantasy (adapted from Baker (1981, 159)):

> Jones is a multimillionaire hedge fund manager, who has a belief that he expresses by saying at t, "I believe that I* am wealthy." One unhappy day, Jones is abducted, bopped on the head, and left on the side of the road in Vermont. When he recovers, he cannot remember his prior life. Eking out a living as a farmhand in Vermont, he regularly reads in the newspaper and on the Internet of Jones, the missing millionaire. He thus comes to believe at t′ that the missing Jones is wealthy and he expresses his belief at t′ by "I believe

8. I take it that attempts to confine the difference between (i) and (ii) to pragmatic matters that do not affect truth-value simply cannot be sustained. See examples in Chapter 3.

that Jones is wealthy"; not realizing that he* is Jones, he dissents at t′ from "I believe that I* am wealthy." In these circumstances at t′, (ii) is true and (i) is false.[9] Now suppose that farmhand Jones wins the state lottery; so Jones comes to believe at t″ that he* is wealthy; at about the same time (at t″), he reads that, due to mismanagement, the missing Jones's hedge fund has collapsed, and that Jones is a pauper. So he comes to disbelieve at t″ that Jones is wealthy. In these later circumstances, (i) is true and (ii) is false: At t″, (i) expresses a true proposition and (ii) does not. So, (i) cannot be replaced without changing truth-value by (ii).

Therefore, (i) is not reducible to (ii). So, I*-sentences like (i) are irreducible to their non-I* counterparts, like (ii)—counterparts that express propositions lacking first-person constituents. (This bears out the earlier claim that I*-sentences are not instances of "x believes that x is F.") Since (ii) is the most plausible non-first-person candidate for the reduction of (i), we can conclude that (i) is not reducible *simpliciter*.

2. If I*-sentences are not reducible, then I*-properties are not reducible.

I*-sentences express I*-propositions that contain I*-concepts, and—as I argued in the preceding section— I*-concepts express I*-properties. So, if I*-sentences are not reducible, then they express I*-properties. (I am using

9. For possible-worlds advocates (like Stalnaker 2008): A possible world in which Jones loses his I*-belief is a different possible world—different things happen—from a possible world in which Jones retains his I*-belief. One set of worlds is compatible with Jones's beliefs at t, and a different set of worlds is compatible with Jones's beliefs at t′. At t′, Jones had the non-I*-counterpart of his I*-belief that he* was wealthy without his first-person belief; as a result, he did what he never would have done before he was abducted: he found work as a farmhand.

"express I*-properties" here as short for "express propositions that contain I*-concepts that express I*-properties.")
So, I*-properties expressed by irreducible I*-sentences
must also be irreducible. If I*-properties were reducible, then they would be entailed by non-first-person
properties. In that case, the I*-sentences that express
the I*-properties would be replaceable without change
of truth value by non-first-person sentences. But we
have just seen that the I*-sentences are not replaceable
salva veritate by non-first-person sentences. Therefore, if
I*-sentences are not reducible, then I*-properties are not
reducible.

3. I*-sentences are not eliminable.
   The story about Jones also shows that I*-sentences are not
   eliminable. One of the main purposes that I*-sentences
   and thoughts expressed by them serve is to rationally
   guide action. Rationally guiding action is a vital human
   purpose. When Jones came to believe that Jones was
   wealthy, but not that he* was wealthy, he took work as
   a farmhand. If Jones had continued to believe that he*
   was wealthy, he would have gone back to his opulent former way of life. The purpose of guiding action cannot be
   achieved without beliefs expressed by I*-sentences. No
   propositional attitude lacking a self-concept could move
   Jones to resume his former black-tie-and-champagne life.
   Certainly, his belief that Jones (who was in fact himself)
   was wealthy was impotent to restore Jones to his former
   station.

4. If I*-sentences are not eliminable, then I*-properties are
   not eliminable.
   I*-sentences express I*-propositions that contain
   I*-concepts, and I*-concepts express I*-properties. We

just saw that I*-concepts are not eliminable; so, neither are the I*-properties that I*-concepts express.[10]

5. If I*-properties are neither reducible nor eliminable, then a complete ontology includes I*-properties.

A complete ontology, D, must specify all the individuals and properties that are required for the world to be as it is.[11] That is, D is a complete description of the world if and only if for each individual and each property required for the world to be as it is, either D explicitly mentions it or D entails it. By 1 – 4, I*-properties are neither reducible nor eliminable. It is a conceptual truth that properties that are neither reducible nor eliminable belong in a complete ontology.

∴6. A complete ontology includes I*-properties. (1,3,5 MP)

This completes the linguistic arguments (i) from an I*-concept to an I*-property, and (ii) for the incompleteness of a description of reality lacking I*-properties. Now let's turn to an argument for the ontological incompleteness of a description of reality without I*-properties.

A METAPHYSICAL ARGUMENT AGAINST ONTOLOGICAL NATURALISM

The heart of scientific naturalism is ontological: Science reveals all that genuinely belongs to reality. As the discussion of

---

10. Note that (E) together with the ineliminability of I*-properties does not entail that there are no I*-properties. It entails only that either the (putatively complete) ontology is incomplete, or there are no I*-properties.

11. In Chapter 10, I argue that many properties are temporal: They come into existence by natural selection or by human intervention. If so, we are in no position to speak of a complete ontology *simpliciter*; the complete ontology does not exist until the end of time. However, we can speak of a complete ontology at a time. If an ontology must contain I*-properties to be complete in the twenty-first century, then a complete ontology *simpliciter* must contain I*-person properties.

reductionism and nonreductionism in Chapter 1 showed, there is some controversy about what is to be included as a science. There are narrow (reductive) construals, like David Armstrong's, which hold that "the world contains nothing but the entities recognized by physics." (Armstrong 1980, 149) And there are broader construals, like Hilary Kornblith's and Philip Kitcher's, that include anthropology, sociology, and intentional psychology. (Kitcher 1992; Kornblith 1994) I shall tie down the kind of naturalism at issue here by reference to a standard encyclopedia article, and then broaden the notion to nonreductive naturalism. Frederick Schmitt characterizes ontological naturalism as the view that "only *natural* objects, kinds and properties are real," where "natural" is defined as "what is recognized by natural science."[12] (Schmitt 1995, 343–45)

On this ontological construal of naturalism, a naturalist cannot recognize as real "colours, mental and intentional states, consciousness, the self, linguistic reference and meaning, knowledge and justified belief, moral obligation and goodness, or beauty" unless he can "naturalize" them. On Schmitt's account, we can naturalize a property, say being F, either (i) by giving a functional analysis of the concept *being F* in naturalistic terms, or (ii) by identifying the property, *being F*, with a property recognized by natural science. (Schmitt 1995, 343)

I want to broaden Schmitt's definition in two ways that will make my case against naturalism more difficult: (1) Although Schmitt does not seem to recognize psychology as a natural

---

12. Related to this ontological thesis is a conceptual thesis: An exhaustive description of the world that employs only third-person concepts leaves nothing out. I shall argue that a wholly third-personal description of the world is incomplete. It leaves out first-personal properties that are required for describing and explaining the world. I do not assume that naturalism puts any constraints on concepts themselves.

science, I want to make explicit that "natural science" is to be construed as including the physical, biological, psychological, or social sciences—whether they are reducible to physics or not. (2) Instead of requiring identification of the reduced property F with a single property recognized by natural science, I will take naturalizing F to require only strong supervenience of F on one or more (appropriate)[13] properties recognized by natural science. (This brings Schmitt's second clause in line with my construal of "reductionism" in Chapter 1.)

Let me enter a caveat: In Chapter 2, I construed naturalizing a property as either reducing or eliminating it. Schmitt considers only reduction to be naturalization. To bring my construal into line with Schmitt's, I'll use Schmitt's characterization of naturalizing a property (with the two modifications), and formulate distinct characterizations of naturalizing and eliminating properties:

> A property P is naturalized if and only if (1) the concept associated with P has a functional analysis in terms recognized by natural science, or (2) the property P strongly supervenes on one or more (appropriate)[14] properties recognized by natural science.
>
> A property P is eliminated if and only if a complete account of the world as it is mentions neither P nor a supervenience base for P.

---

13. To require that the subvenient properties be "local" is too strong for externalist nonreductive versions of naturalism; to allow global supervenience would be too weak. I use "appropriate" to rule out these two extremes. Although I doubt that anyone can spell out the limits on "appropriate," I don't think that we need to for the current project.
14. Again, "appropriate" is intended to rule out global supervenience, without restricting the subvenient base to properties intrinsic to the bearer of P.

Now I'll give necessary and sufficient conditions for ontological naturalism, so that the difference between my construal of ontological naturalism and Schmitt's is only terminological:

> Ontological naturalism is true if and only if every apparent property is either naturalized or eliminated from a complete account of the world as it is.

Most of my argument against ontological naturalism is directed against the naturalization of I*-properties. According to this generic account of naturalism, an apparent property is not a genuine property—it is *only* apparent and does not really exist—unless it strongly supervenes on properties that are items recognized by one of the established sciences.

As I have construed it, the notion of reduction is a metaphysical, not an epistemological, idea. So, I do not expect that anyone who makes a claim that a higher-level property is reduced to microphysical properties will be able to specify which microphysical properties are in the supervenience base of the higher-level property. Nevertheless, I do expect that anyone who makes a claim that a higher-level property is reduced to, or supervenes on, lower-level properties will have some justification for the claim—other than, What else can it be? A bare assertion of reduction is just magical thinking. For any higher-level property that is claimed to be reduced, there must be some specific reason to believe that it supervenes on lower-level properties.

Similarly, there should be some justification for a claim that a concept, say, *being F,* has a functional analysis. A mere assertion that a concept has a functional analysis is worthless without some idea of how a functional analysis may be carried out. (Functionalism reminds me of phenomenalism, the view that physical-object sentences are reducible (translatable) into sense-data sentences. No one ever gave such a translation, nor did anyone give any reason to suppose that such a translation was possible. But for decades, perhaps under the sway of inertia, phenomenalism was a significant philosophical position.) As with phenomenalism, the toy examples illustrating functionalism (e.g., To be in pain is to be in a state caused by pinpricks,....) are hardly a start. In any case, for a functional analysis of a first-person concept to be successful—even putting aside the paradox of analysis—the *analysans* obviously must not contain any occurrences of "I" or "I*." As long as the sciences remain wholly impersonal and objective, naturalized properties cannot even covertly be tainted by anything first personal. Here's the argument against naturalizing I*-properties:

Let P be the property of conceiving of oneself as oneself* in the first person. Let the concept associated with P be the first-person concept of oneself as oneself*, or the I*-concept.

(1) If P is a naturalized property, then either (i) the concept associated with P has a functional analysis in terms recognized by natural science, or (ii) the property P strongly supervenes on one or more (appropriate) properties recognized by natural science.

(2) The concept associated with P does not have a functional analysis in naturalistic terms.

(3) The property P does not strongly supervene on any properties recognized by natural science.

∴(4) P is not a naturalized property.

Argument for (1): Recall that Schmitt construed "natural" as "what is recognized by natural science." Functionalizing the concept associated with P in terms recognized by natural science, or showing that the property P strongly supervenes on properties recognized by natural science are (modifications of) the only two ways that Schmitt indicated to show that a property is natural.

Argument for (2): The I*-concept does not seem like a functional concept. It is a nonqualitative concept of a capacity. The I*-concept seems resistant to definition in terms of causes and effects.

But perhaps functionalism could make a different contribution—not in providing an impersonal definition of the I*-concept but in providing a third-person account of the capacity to conceive of oneself as oneself* in the first person. The comparison here would be with computers. Functionalists take belief generally to be definable in terms of functional role, where functional role is determined by the causes and effects of the belief. Although functionalists do not hope to give a complete catalogue of the causes and effects of a particular belief, they do suppose that they can give a higher-level account, an account of the capacity to have beliefs. The capacity to have beliefs is the capacity to have mental representations that combine with other mental representations (desires and other beliefs) to produce action.[15] Perhaps the capacity to have a self-concept can be understood functionally in the third person even if the I*-concept

---

15. I do not think that a functionalist view of belief is adequate. For language users, all conscious beliefs may be linked to verbal behavior: a belief that f = ma, together with a desire to be cooperative and other beliefs may cause the believer when asked, to say, "f = ma." However, many (if not most) of our beliefs are not even connected with causing (nonlinguistic) behavior—all beliefs about the past, many about the present ("There are now seven billion people on Earth"), some about the future ("There will be a lunar eclipse in 2015"), and some that are nontemporal ("f = ma"). Even if we are concerned only with first-person beliefs, their action-causing role is matched in importance with their other roles: being vehicles for conveying information ("I was born in Atlanta"), for correcting misunderstanding ("I was here on time, but the door was locked"), getting to know someone or articulating truths about oneself ("I have a fear of flying"), narratives that make sense of our lives ("I had a happy childhood until I met Frank…"), and so on. So, a functional definition of "belief" (first personal or not) seems to me not to capture the actual concept at issue. And belief would be just a start: we would also need functional definitions of hope, regret, and so on.

itself cannot be understood impersonally. Kornblith and other functionalists have suggested as much.

Kornblith (in conversation) has noted that belief- and desire-like states in a computer may interact and cause behavior, but as Perry argued, only if they contain first-person indexicals. Suppose that a computer program has a special mental representation—"+"—an indexical that is directly connected to action.[16] The symbol "+" plays the role of "I": for example, "+ sees Fs within reach" and "+ wants to get Fs" leads, ceteris paribus, to "+ reaches for Fs." The problem, as I see it, is that the special mental symbol, "+," at best could play the I-role, not the I*-role (even if there were such and we knew what they were).

However, a naturalist like Kornblith may reply: Analogously to the "I" case, there is a different special mental representation for "I*"—say, "#." The inferential role of I*-thoughts, then, may be characterized by the relationship between certain representations containing "#." For example, my belief that I* am a registered voter may be caused by my belief that I* received a notice about the polling place. The "I*" can be eliminated by showing the connection between representations in the "belief box"—between "# received a notice about the polling place" and "# is a registered voter." So, Kornblith may continue, the inferential role of "I*" can be characterized by the relationship between "#" representations.

This seems inadequate for at least four reasons. (i) I*-beliefs are not particularly connected with action as I-beliefs are said to be. I*-thoughts are more typically connected to self-evaluation than to action or perception and hence their causal connections may not issue in any overt action. (See Baker 2011.) Belief is (putatively) functionalized by taking a mental representation in the belief box to be caused by other mental representations, and perceptions, and

16. Just for the record, let me note that I am extremely dubious about representations as physical tokens in the brain.

actions, and to cause actions. But in the I*-case, there are often no observable phenomena causally connected to I*-thoughts. So, there is already a significant disanalogy between the "I" and the "I*" cases.

(ii) The story about "#" is not generalizable. Suppose that I hope that I* will get a such-and-such job, and that one of the causes of my hope is that I believe that I* would make more money in that job; and one of the effects (if I get the job), is that I am glad that I* make more money. Now we have the following connected "#" representations: "# will get such-and-such job," in my hope box, caused by "# would make more money in that job" in my belief box and causing (if I get the job) "# got the job" in my glad box. It is one thing to have inferences among mental representations in one's belief box (if you can swallow the idea/metaphor of a belief box); but it is quite another thing to suppose that there are systematic relations between mental representations in belief-, hope-, glad- and all the other boxes.[17]

(iii) There are too many inferential roles—even too many per person—for I*-thoughts to be characterized in terms of inferential role of mental representations. I*-thoughts are not directly connected to action as simple beliefs and desires are said to be connected to action. The kinds of I*-thoughts (and I*-sentences) are

---

17. Moreover, there is the perennial problem of the semantic interpretation of mental representations. In (Baker 1991), I tried to show that Fodor's view of the semantics of mental representations in terms of "asymmetric dependence" did not work. Philosophers today have just moved on, as if we either had, or did not need, an account of the semantics of "mentalese." I side with those who have given up the notion that we have incommunicable representations in our heads.

However, nothing short of a wholesale reduction of I*-thoughts to, say, semantically interpreted brain states would lend any support to a functional analysis of the capacity of a robust first-person perspective. But as we saw in the discussion of Dennett, even after semantic interpretation we have a first-person residue. Moreover, Dennett's intentional stance does not provide the metaphysically hearty interpretation that we need for reduction. Needless to say, there is no wholesale reduction of I*-thoughts to semantically interpreted brain states in the offing.

too disparate for the capacity to have them to be regimented as functionalism requires.

Someone may suggest that each kind of "I*" thought ("glad that I*," "wish that I*," "sorry that I*," "fear that I*," and so on) has its own functional role. Not only would the same problem of disparateness arise again—this time for each kind of I*-thought—but this suggestion would fragment the account of the robust first-person perspective. Such fragmentation would prevent the robust first-person perspective from playing its important phenomenological role in unifying our lives. Moreover, we still would have no reason to accept an unsupported blanket assertion that each kind of I*-thought has its own functional role—especially in view of the idiosyncratic nature of I*-inferential roles.

(iv) From a functionalist point of view, to conceive of oneself as oneself* in the first person is nothing other than to have "#" mental representations that are causally connected with other mental representations. I*-thoughts are just the "tokening" of mental representations (with wholesale replacement of "I*" by "#" or some other stipulated symbol in mentalese) that causally interact with other mental representations.

So, what it is to think, "I deeply regret that I* misspent the past twenty years," is just a matter of connections between (in my deeply regret box) "# misspent the last twenty years" and other "#" representations. This puts my deep regret (or my profound love) on the same psychological plane as my momentary preference to go to a movie.[18] This does no justice to the phenomenology or moral significance of I*-thoughts. These considerations give us good reason to deny that there is a third-person functional definition of the capacity to have

18. Moreover, this example raises the question of how many boxes we will need: We need to distinguish the deep-regret box from the ordinary (mild) regret box: My regret that I* was a little late for the meeting is not in my deeply regret box.

a robust first-person perspective. What is needed for naturalization of the I*-concept is a third-person characterization of the capacity to conceive of oneself as oneself* in the first person. I have argued that we have no such third-person characterization. So, I take the Argument for (2) to hold.

Argument for (3): In the last section, I argued that a complete description of the world must include I*-properties. If property P supervened on properties recognized by natural science, then natural science would recognize first-person properties. So, as long as science is wholly non-first-personal, it will recognize no properties on which a property that could be identified with a first-person property supervene.

Since the three premises are true and the argument is valid, it follows that P is not a naturalized property. Nor is P eliminated: We just saw that there is no impersonal supervenience base of properties recognized by natural science for P, and we earlier saw that P is a property exemplified by those with robust first-person perspectives. So, an account of the world that does not mention P is incomplete, and P is not eliminated.

Since P is neither eliminated nor reduced to properties recognized by natural science, P is a genuine property that remains outside the purview of natural science. In that case, ontological naturalism is false.

CONCLUSION

I conclude that each of the arguments I gave—the linguistic argument for irreducible and ineliminable first-person properties and the argument against ontological naturalization of first-person properties—has shown ontological naturalism to be an inadequate view of the natural world: First-person properties belong in the ontology.

To review the overall argument: As a preliminary, I argued from the I*-concept to the conclusion that there are first-person properties. Then:

1. There are first-person properties that are neither eliminable nor reducible. (linguistic and ontological arguments)
2. Any property that is neither eliminable nor reducible belongs in the ontology. (conceptual truth)
∴ 3. First-person properties belong in the ontology.
4. If first-person properties belong in the ontology, then ontological naturalism is false. (definition of "ontological naturalism")
∴ 5. Ontological naturalism is false.

The upshot is that the world has an ineliminably personal aspect; it is not wholly impersonal, as ontological naturalism would have it.

Here ends the core argument that I set out to make. Now I want to take a deeper look at the first-person perspective and show how it fits into my own larger view. Although my own larger view is a development of the notion of the first-person perspective, the core argument just completed does not depend on the larger view to come.

PART II

AN ACCOUNT OF THE FIRST-PERSON PERSPECTIVE

Chapter Six

From the Rudimentary to the Robust Stage of the First-Person Perspective

Like the term "naturalism," the term "first-person perspective" is used in multiple ways. The remainder of the book will be a development of the first-person perspective in terms of my own philosophical views. Although the core argument does not depend on the correctness of these views, a fuller background picture in which to locate the core argument deepens the discussion. Other background pictures may do as well, but the one that follows is mine.

Since I use the notion of a first-person perspective to make sense of persons[1]—to show what they have in common with non-human animals, and to show what is unique about them—I shall begin this second part of the book by discussing the trajectory of the first-person perspective of a human person from birth until adulthood.

---

1. On my view, a human person begins life with a rudimentary first-person perspective that typically develops into a robust first-person perspective and is constituted by a human organism. (Baker 2007a)

THE FIRST-PERSON PERSPECTIVE: CONSCIOUSNESS AND SELF-CONSCIOUSNESS

The road that human beings traverse from infancy to maturity runs from consciousness to self-consciousness. It begins with a human newborn, a person, who is conscious, whose waking state is one of awareness, and ends with the same entity who is self-conscious, who can conceive of herself as herself* in the first person. The newborn has no concepts at all, and the mature person has a wealth of concepts, including a self-concept. I shall offer a sketch of this road from (nonconceptual) consciousness to (conceptual) self-consciousness.

Persons, if I am right, essentially have first-person perspectives. It follows that there is no moment that a person (whether infant or adult) exists and lacks a first-person perspective. A first-person perspective is a *perspective* because it is a view on reality from a particular orientation; it is *first personal* because the orientation is from the subject's own point of view. However, a first-person perspective can be manifested in two ways: as rudimentary or as robust. "Rudimentary" and "robust" are two stages of a first-person perspective. I understand mere consciousness in terms of a rudimentary first-person perspective and self-consciousness in terms of a robust first-person perspective. So, I take the trajectory from infancy to maturity to be a road from having a rudimentary first-person perspective to having a robust first-person perspective.

As we saw in Chapter 2, the difference between the two stages of the first-person perspective is the acquisition of a natural language. A creature with only a rudimentary first-person perspective has the capacity to interact—intentionally and consciously—with things in the immediate environment. Lacking language, however, a creature with only a rudimentary first-person perspective (human or not) is unable to refer to herself at all, by means of "I" or a third-person description. Nevertheless, a rudimentary first-person perspective situates an entity in an environment, located at the origin of its perceptions. All the mental activities of a creature with only a rudimentary first-person perspective are, by default, first-personal.

A human infant is a person, and hence has a first-person perspective, but only a rudimentary first-person perspective. As a person matures and learns a language, her rudimentary first-person perspective develops into a robust first-person perspective, the condition of all forms of self-consciousness. Unlike a rudimentary first-person perspective, which does not require having concepts, a robust first-person perspective is a conceptual capacity, which, I shall argue, depends on language. The capacity to understand and use language of a certain complexity is constitutive of having a robust first-person perspective.

A newborn human being, with only a rudimentary first-person perspective, has no self-concept, no idea of oneself (no "me and me again" (Sorabji 2006, 4)) until the middle of the second year. (Lewis 1994, 22) Until the idea of "me" emerges, infants are not capable of generating evaluation of their own actions. (Kagan 1981). A toddler acquires the idea of "me" in her social and linguistic interactions, and finally in learning a language. Learning a language expands one's capacities almost unimaginably. As Dennett remarked, "Putting our brains on the dimly imagined continuum with insect nervous systems at the bottom, and dogs and dolphins and chimps just next to us at the high, complex end, ignores the obvious fact that we're the only species that asks questions!" (Dennett 2009, 28)

Language is the avenue from the rudimentary to the robust first-person perspective. Dennett again: "Language gives our little brains a huge boost in cognitive power denied to all others." (Dennett 2009, 28) And one way language gives us such a boost is by giving us the means to think of ourselves as ourselves* in the first person. In learning to use "I*" constructions (introduced in Chapter 2), we acquire a self-concept that is the vehicle for expressing a robust first-person perspective.

LANGUAGE AND THE ACQUISITION OF CONCEPTS

How does a person progress from a (nonconceptual) rudimentary first-person perspective to the full self-consciousness of a (conceptual) robust first-person perspective? A baby is born with the biological equipment bestowed by natural selection; then culture adds another layer to development. Human infants are born with perceptual systems but must be taught to speak. Learning a language ushers in an explosion of the number and complexity of thoughts that one can entertain. Just as learning a language is part of a natural developmental process, so is the acquisition of a self-concept.[2]

First, note that we persons are social beings. There is empirical support for the social character of beings like us. The psychologist Michael Tomasello gave cognitive tests to two-year-old human beings, and to adult orangutans and chimpanzees, and found that the *only* places in which the human beings outscored the nonhuman primates were on tests that measured social skills: social learning, communicating, and reading the intentions of others.

> Human beings [Tomasello said] have evolved to coordinate complex activities, to gossip and to playact together. It is because they are adapted for such cultural activities—and not because of their cleverness as individuals—that human beings

2. We should not confuse an account of how one comes to acquire a property with what the property is. An account of how one fell in love (first we discussed philosophy, then we had a candlelight dinner with wine, then...) ipso facto provides no account of the state of being in love.

are able to do so many exceptionally complex and impressive things. (Tomasello 2008)

Moreover, a robust first-person perspective is developmentally subsequent to a great deal of social and linguistic interaction. It emerges from a rudimentary first-person perspective along with awareness of others (e.g., caregivers) as conscious beings. It seems to develop from the phenomenon of "shared attention," in which the infant aligns her gaze with her mother's. When infants notice a divergence between their own attention and their mothers', they become aware of their mothers as conscious beings. The activities of shared attention are necessary precursors of learning a language. (Tomasello 1999, Ch. 4) And it is only in a public language that a robust first-person perspective is manifest to others.

Now I want to ratchet up the argument from a mere de facto argument about social and linguistic interaction to a modal argument for the conclusion that the range of thoughts that one can entertain depends on the natural language(s) that one has, and then present some experimental evidence for the same conclusion.

But first, some preliminaries: I take thoughts that we entertain on the inner-speech model, and I use the notion of *concepts* to individuate thoughts, where the word "thoughts" refers to any mental states with propositional content—beliefs, hopes, fears, desires, intentions, and so on. If you don't like this use of "concept," individuate thoughts in some other way, but you'll have to individuate thoughts in a way that distinguishes the thought that snow is white from the thought that the color of a cockatoo is white. The content of a thought is determined by the concepts that are deployed in the "that"-clauses of their attributions.

For example, the thought that grass is green contains the concepts *grass* and *green*. I do not intend the term "concept" to carry theoretical weight. I am simply using the term in order to identify constituents of thoughts, the items that make up the contents of thoughts and determine the identity of thoughts. The concepts contained in canonical attributions of thoughts are concepts that the thinker actually has.

Concepts are individuated by their application conditions in various possible circumstances (or possible worlds, if you prefer).[3] Application conditions determine what falls under the concept. If there is some x such that concept C applies to x and concept C' does not apply to x, then C and C' are distinct concepts. So, application conditions determine the identity of concepts, and the identity of concepts, in turn, determines the identity of thoughts of which the concepts are constituents.

In order to entertain a thought containing a particular concept, one must have the concept in question. To have a particular concept, one must be able to apply it correctly (much of the time). (Even empty concepts like *unicorn* may be applied correctly—in linguistic contexts in which mythical beasts are being considered, or in pictorial contexts of drawings of small horses with horns on their foreheads.) A concept definitely applies to some things and definitely does not apply to other things. And for other things, it may neither definitely apply nor definitely not apply. Complete mastery of application conditions is not required in order to have a concept—just some understanding of the conditions and consequences

---

3. This notion of concept is a philosopher's notion. Cognitive scientists are concerned with the different cognitive processes (e.g., induction, categorization) that may use concepts. Some cognitive scientists go so far as to reject the notion of concepts for science at all; concepts divide into distinct kinds (e.g., prototypes, exemplars, theories), and the different kinds of concepts have little in common and are used in distinct cognitive processes. The different kinds of concepts are too heterogeneous to pick out a natural kind and hence are subject to elimination. (Machery 2010) However, if we individuate concepts in the way that I suggest, we may take prototypes, exemplars, and theories to concern the *implementation* of concepts. If we do this, we may maintain the unity of higher-level concepts along with the heterogeneity of their implementations. (Edwards 2011)

of application. (Burge 1979) Indeed, we have many, many thoughts made up of concepts of which we have only limited understanding: You may believe that there is dark matter, or that the fugue was popular in the eighteenth century without complete mastery of the concept *dark matter* or the concept *fugue*. So, one may have a concept (and hence thoughts containing that concept) without complete mastery of the application conditions of the concept. (Burge 1979) Now, letting "X" range over language users, say:

> *X possesses a concept C* if and only if (i) X is able to apply C correctly in a significant range of cases;[4] and (ii) X has some (perhaps partial) understanding of C's conditions and consequences of application.

As I argued in Baker 2007b and Baker 2007c, I take concept application to be a linguistic and social skill. The mental states of nonhuman animals and human infants are on a less developed part of the cognitive spectrum than those of language users. The errors of nonlanguage users—mistaking foe for friend—should be understood nonconceptually.[5]

In order to entertain a thought that has a concept C as a constituent, one must possess the concept C in this way.[6] In order to apply concept C correctly (and hence in order to possess the concept C), one must learn a language. It is only in learning a language that one can be corrected. In the absence of others to correct a learner, there is no difference between correct and incorrect use

---

4. The vagueness of the "significant range of cases" does not matter for purposes here.
5. For a recent study of the continuities and discontinuities between human and nonhuman minds, see Penn et al. 2008.
6. My notion of having a concept deliberately collapses Peacocke's distinction between attribution conditions and possession conditions of a concept: On my view, an attribution of a concept C to X is correct only if X satisfies its possession conditions of C. (See Peacocke 1992.)

of a word or between correct application and misapplication of a concept. (I find Wittgenstein entirely convincing on this point.) So, in learning a language, one acquires concepts. As one acquires more concepts, there are more and more kinds of thoughts that one can have.[7]

Intuitions about the role of language in conceptual thought are bolstered by experimental evidence. Recently, there has been a significant amount of empirical evidence that language shapes thoughts, and that what and how a person thinks depends on what language one speaks.[8] (Boroditsky 2001; 2011) Studies have shown that people from different linguistic communities think differently about time, about space, and about agency. (Boroditsky 2011) Teach a child new color words and she can make new discriminations. It has long seemed clear that a scientist looking at an electron microscope sees an electron where the child sees a dot. Now there is solid evidence of this phenomenon.

Striking studies show that bilingual people's preferences change depending on which language they are thinking in. Arabic-Hebrew bilinguals, given implicit-association tests, rate Jews more highly when the tests are given in Hebrew than when they are given in Arabic. (Danziger and Ward 2010) In another study of bilinguals that had similar results for English-Spanish bilinguals and French-Arabic bilinguals, the authors concluded

7. Does *every* thought presuppose language? Every thought that one is conscious of having presupposes language. I do not think that much is understood about nonhuman animal thought, but any thought that a thinker can express obviously presupposes language. Malcolm's distinction is useful: A dog may think that the squirrel ran up the tree, but lacking language, the dog does not entertain the thought that the squirrel ran up the tree. (Malcolm 1972)

I disregard the language-of-thought hypothesis since *entertaining* a thought (as opposed to merely thinking that p) is a phenomenon at the level of conscious awareness; it requires a natural language. If there is a language module in the brain for a natural language, it is not at the level of entertaining thoughts but at the level of implementation.

8. The claim is not that language shapes animal thinking. As one researcher put it, "Dogs have dog thoughts." (quoted in Thomas 1993; Grandin 2006, 200)

that the "effects of language on elicited preference were large…, providing evidence that preferences are not merely transmitted through language but also shaped by it." (Ogunnaike, Dunham, and Banaji 2010, 999)

According to Lera Boroditsky, a leader in this area of study at Stanford, "The past decade has seen a host of ingenious demonstrations establishing that language indeed plays a causal role in shaping cognition. Studies have shown that changing how people talk changes how they think." She goes on to say that "there may not be a lot of adult human thinking where language does not play a role." (Boroditsky 2011, 65)

Taking a cue from this line of research, I want to hypothesize more generally that the range of thoughts that one is able to entertain is bounded by the range of concepts expressed by the language(s) one speaks. Even without a language, one can distinguish different states of the immediate environment. As one learns a language, one acquires concepts that enable one to think and reason about anything that one has a concept of. Plasma physicists can have myriads of thoughts that are simply not available to me. To have such thoughts, I would have to learn the language—and hence acquire the concepts—of plasma physics.

HOW TO ACQUIRE A SELF-CONCEPT

To have a robust first-person perspective, one must be able to manifest it. To manifest a robust first-person perspective, one must be able to consciously conceive of oneself as oneself*, to be aware that it is oneself qua oneself that one is conceiving of. That is, one must have a self-concept. The thought that one would express by saying, "I wish that I* were a movie star" contains the concepts, *wish, movie star,* and one's self-concept.

So, in order to be able to think I*-thoughts, and hence to have a robust first-person perspective, one must have a self-concept. How does one acquire a self-concept—a concept denoting oneself conceived as oneself in the first person? The answer is that in learning a language, one acquires indefinitely many empirical concepts—concepts of one's needs and wants (*hungry, milk*), of family members (*mama*), of features of the environment (*bed, car, large*), and so on. As the concepts accumulate, one begins to learn concepts for one's mental states. ("Do you see the dog?") Around the age of two, there's a tipping point and one responds to "Make a wish" by, for example, saying, "I wish that I* had a truck." When one makes such an assertion—not just produce parrotlike sounds—one has the beginnings of a robust first-person perspective.

That one cannot have a self-concept unless one has a battery of empirical concepts is, I think, a conceptual truth. This is so, because a self-concept is a formal concept; it simply signals attribution of a first-person reference to oneself. Attribution of a first-person reference to oneself is not a stand-alone item. An I*-thought has the form, "I ϕ that I* am(were) F," where "ϕ" ranges over psychological and linguistic verbs and "F" ranges over properties. One cannot think an I*-thought unless one has a range of concepts expressing properties with which to fill out the "I*." Thoughts about oneself have as constituents not only self-concepts, but also empirical concepts. Consider the thoughts expressed by "I'm afraid that I'll be alone" or "I wish that I could go to the beach." A thinker of such thoughts must have not only a self-concept, but the concepts of being afraid or wishing and the concepts of being alone or at the beach.

One cannot make a self-attribution unless there is something that one attributes to oneself*, and what one attributes to oneself* is expressed by empirical concepts. So, it is not surprising that the process of acquiring a self-concept presupposes the acquisition of many empirical concepts.

Here is a simple modal argument for the social character of a robust first-person perspective, and hence for a self-concept:

1. Necessarily, one has a robust first-person perspective only if one has self-concept.
2. Necessarily, one has a self-concept only if one has a battery of empirical concepts.
3. Necessarily, one has a battery of empirical concepts only if one has a public language.
4. Necessarily, one has a public language only if one has social and linguistic relations.

∴5. Necessarily, one has a robust first-person perspective only if one has social and linguistic relations.

Since the argument is obviously valid, we need only check to see whether the premises are true.

Premise 1: A self-concept—a concept of onself as oneself* in the first person—is constitutive of a robust first-person perspective. Premise 1 is a conceptual truth that follows from the characterization of a robust first-person perspective. A self-concept is a "formal" (not a qualitative) concept: its role is to self-attribute a first-person reference—in such a way that the user of a self-concept cannot be mistaken about who she is referring to.

Premise 2: A self-concept does not stand alone; it cannot be the only concept in one's conceptual repertoire. One cannot have a self-concept unless one has a store of ordinary empirical, qualitative concepts that one can apply to oneself and others. To engage in self-attribution, one must have a range of qualitative concepts— for example, to self-attribute a wish for an apple, one must have the concept *apple* in order to have the thought, "I wish that I* had an apple." One must have a sizable number of empirical concepts to complement a self-concept.

Premise 3: In order to have a sizable number of empirical concepts, one must have a public language. This is so, because (1) empirical concepts can be both correctly applied and mis-applied to various things, and (2) the difference between correct and incorrect application of an ordinary empirical concept is grounded in public language. As Wittgenstein said, without a public language, there would be no application conditions to ground a difference between using a concept correctly and using it incorrectly.

Suppose that a nonlinguistic Robinson Crusoe finds himself stranded alone on an island and it occurs to him to call the sea creatures he sees "sharks." How could Crusoe's use of the sound "shark" express one concept rather than another? He could not have formed the intention to refer to sharks by "sharks" unless he already has significant parts of a natural language. He could not have formed the intention to refer to the kind of creature that he is seeing by "sharks"; in his languageless state, he could not have acquired the concept of *a kind of creature*.

In the absence of a public language, what would make it the case that any of Crusoe's mental events or vocalizations expressed any concept—*shark* or *fish* or anything else?[9] Crusoe's putative concept does not have an extension that would make his use of what

---

9. There are 350 species of sharks that are radically dissimilar in appearance from one another. Some sharks have anal fins; others don't. Some sharks have flat raylike bodies; others don't; and so on. Sharks range in size from a few centimeters to (perhaps) eighteen meters long. Some sharks with raylike bodies have elongated, sawlike snouts; others with raylike bodies have short, un-sawlike snouts. Some sharks have six or seven gill slits and one dorsal fin; others have five gill slits and two dorsal fins. Some sharks have dorsal fin spines; others have no fin spines. Of the sharks without fin spines, some have mouths behind their eyes, and others have mouths well in front of their eyes. The whale shark (Rhiniodon typus) is the world's largest fish. (John D. Stevens 1987, 18–35) Not only are there many sorts of dissimilar sharks, but also bottlenose dolphins (that are not even fish, but mammals) look a lot like sharks.

sounds like "shark" on a given occasion right or wrong.[10] Any record whatever that Crusoe made of his observations (by, say, marking a tree) and labeled "shark" would be right. Whatever seems right to him is right: "And [as Wittgenstein said] that only means that here we can't talk about 'right.'" (Wittgenstein 1958, par. 258) So, what sounds like "shark" in the mouth of Crusoe does not express a qualitative concept.

What's true of the concept expressed by the English word "shark" is also true of more mundane empirical concepts that are needed for thoughts that contain a self-concept. For example, for my niece to wish that she* had more toys, she would have to have a self-concept and the qualitative concept *toy*. Acquisition of the concept *toy* requires a public language. ("That's not a toy; put it down and be careful with it," her mother would tell my niece if she picked up a fragile vase.)

In short: In order to have a self-concept, one must have a store of empirical concepts whose acquisition depends on a public language—at least for beings like us.

Premise 4: In order to acquire the empirical concepts expressed by a public language, as we just saw, the learner has to stand to be corrected by others; and to stand to be corrected by others is to have social and linguistic relations. So, anyone who has a public language must have social and linguistic relations to others.

Given the argument's validity and the support for its four premises, I think that we should take the argument to be sound and the conclusion to be true.

The upshot is thoroughly non-Cartesian: it is impossible for any entity that is truly alone in the world to have a robust

10. I have been influenced by Kripke here. In virtue of what would a person, considered in isolation, mean addition rather than "quaddition" by "+"? (Kripke 1982)

first-person perspective. And nothing that lacked a robust first-person perspective could have thoughts about herself as herself*. So, Descartes's resolution *to regard himself* as having "no hands, no eyes, no flesh, no blood, no senses" is not a thought that Descartes could have had if it had been true: The very fact that he had that thought (if he could have had it) would guarantee that it was false. Solipsism is a philosopher's fantasy. Individual human beings—persons—are social entities through and through. In the absence of communities, there would be no persons: human organisms, perhaps, but no persons, no individuals who could reflect on themselves as themselves.

So, a first-person perspective—not a substantial self or ego—is what is crucial for the existence of persons and their self-reflection. Without a robust first-person perspective, there would be no inner life at all. Nevertheless, the notion of a robust first-person perspective that I have discussed is clearly non-Cartesian. Entities cannot have robust first-person perspectives unless they have numerous linguistic and social relations by which to acquire a store of ordinary empirical concepts to apply to themselves and to others. Consequently, I suggest that we dissociate the idea of the first-person perspective from the Cartesian ideas of transparency, infallibility, and logical privacy.

In sum, on my account, persons are not solitary selves. Persons are neither solitary, nor do they have parts that are substantial selves or minds. The person herself—embodied and embedded in an environment—essentially has a first-person perspective and is the subject of experience and the agent who is responsible for her deeds. Both these Cartesian errors (as I think of them)— the possibility of solitary thinkers and the need for a substantial self or mind—are closely related to what Descartes was right about, namely, the ineliminable importance of a first-person perspective.

HUMAN PERSONS: WRAP-UP

When human beings are born, they are conscious beings who lack language and concepts. The bridge between infant cognition and adult cognition is natural language. Young children become self-conscious through the acquisition of language. Natural language is not an add-on to psychology; many—perhaps the majority—of our mental states depend on natural language for their existence. The acquisition of language is the acquisition of concepts, including self-concepts. (A self-concept is whatever plays I*-roles; in some languages, what plays those roles may not be a first-person pronoun but some other grammatical device(s).) On acquiring a self-concept, a person becomes self-conscious: she acquires the capacity to conceive of herself as herself* in the first person.

As I said at the beginning of the chapter, I regard this transition from consciousness to self-consciousness as a trajectory from rudimentary to robust first-person perspectives. Persons—not brains, not organisms—undergo this development from being nonconceptual to being conceptual entities. (Brains of organisms, functioning normally and processing environmental stimuli, make this development possible.) One of the merits of this view is that it acknowledges the seamlessness of the animal realm: Since persons are constituted by organisms, persons are part of the animal kingdom. At the same time, this view brings to the fore the uniqueness of persons: Nonhuman animals can have rudimentary first-person perspectives, but only persons have robust first-person perspectives; only persons are self-conscious. (Baker 2003)

The bearers of robust first-person perspectives are embodied—necessarily embodied—human persons. If you grieve for your friend who died, I may see the grief on your face or in your step. The sadness in your eyes is not just caused by your grief; it's an expression of your grief. No part of you—brain or mind—is the subject of your grief; you are. We whole persons are constituted by whole bodies. Brains have a special role in providing the mechanisms that make possible our mental lives. But it is not my brain itself that would like to go on a river cruise; it is not my brain that regrets having offended you. I did it; I regret it. And I am not identical to a brain. Neither brains nor minds are subjects of experience or are rational or moral agents; we persons are.

Although we are essentially embodied, we do not essentially have the bodies that we now have. Our bodies can be made of anything—organic material, silicon, whatever—as long as they provide the mechanisms that support our person-level activities and states. The relation between us and our bodies is constitution—the same relation that a statue has to the piece of bronze that constitutes it. We are constituted by our bodies, and the bodies that constitute us now are organisms. With enough neural implants, brain-machine interfaces, and prosthetic limbs, we may come to be constituted by nonorganic bodies. What is required for our continued existence is the continued exemplification of our first-person perspectives, along with some kind of body that has mechanisms capable of doing what our brains do.

In short: Although human persons are essentially embodied, they are unique in having robust first-person perspectives. Descartes was exactly right about the importance of the first-person point of view. But he was mistaken, I think, to hold that his first-person perspective required that he have a substantial mind or self. However, first-person perspectives are properties that may well have evolved by natural selection. After all, nonhuman animals have rudimentary first-person perspectives. When groups of hominids invented language, and brains evolved to the point of being able to support robust first-person perspectives, a new kind of being came into existence, persons: perhaps not biologically new, but ontologically new—beings with new kinds of causal powers (e.g., causal powers to learn complicated syntax and to form complex organizations to govern the transfer of property). There is simply no need, or even a place, for a self or mind as distinct from a person. To be a person, on my view, *is* already to have a first-person perspective.

Chapter Seven

Is the Idea of the First-Person Perspective Coherent?

There is little doubt that the first stage of a first-person perspective—the rudimentary first-person perspective consisting of consciousness and intentionality, and shared by persons and nonhuman animals—is coherent. After all, it arose by natural selection in nonhuman animals. Questions arise, however, about the robust first-person perspective: What kind of phenomenon is a robust first-person perspective? How can a mere perspective carry the metaphysical load that I have attributed to it?

In this chapter, I shall discuss two sources of doubt about the coherence of the robust first-person perspective. One source of doubt is the role of first-person perspectives as persistence conditions: *you*, a person, continue to exist as long as *your* first-person perspective is exemplified. This seems circular. A second source of doubt concerns the suggestion that the robust first-person perspective turns out to be a substantial object. If it is putatively a substantial object, then it seems to go the way of Johnston's "self": it is a merely intentional object, a notional object, a virtual object—not a real object—and like Santa Claus, it cannot exist except in our own minds.

The first source of doubt concerns the role of a first-person perspective for human persons. A first-person perspective, rudimentary or robust, is an essential property of human persons. When a person comes into existence, her first-person perspective determines her persistence conditions: She exists as long as her first-person perspective is exemplified. When there is only a human organism, its persistence conditions are biological; but when the organism comes to constitute a person, there comes into existence a new entity. And the person's persistence conditions are first personal. How can first-personal conditions support transtemporal identity?

The theory of personal identity over time that I shall offer answers this question. My theory is metaphysical: I am not concerned with what is called "narrative identity," or with how we re-identify a person, or with psychological aspects of personality, or with ascriptions of the word "person." "The problem of personal identity over time," as formulated by Harold Noonan, "is the problem of giving an account of the logically necessary and sufficient conditions for a person identified at one time being the same person as a person identified at another" time.[1] (Noonan 2003, 2)

Standardly, accounts of personal identity over time are classified as being either simple or complex. A simple account takes personal identity to be "an ultimate unanalyzable fact, distinct from everything observable or experienceable that might be evidence for it." (Noonan 2003,16), or a "further fact" that "does not just consist in physical and/or psychological continuity." (Parfit 1984, 210) If personal identity over time is, as Simple Views hold, unanalyzable, then there are no informative or noncircular necessary and sufficient conditions for a person identified at one time to be the same person as a person identified at another time. Complex Views specify informative necessary and sufficient conditions for

---

1. Perhaps it need not be mentioned that "identified" in this context does not imply any act of identifying someone. Unlike "a person at time t," Noonan's wording ("a person identified at time t") avoids the suggestion of temporal parts.

personal identity over time—for example, persistence of body and brain, psychological continuity, and so on. On Complex Views, informative conditions of personal identity can be stated without presupposing the existence of persons over time. Here are my characterizations of "Simple" and "Complex" Views of personal identity:

> An account of personal identity is a Simple View if and only if the account offers no informative necessary and sufficient conditions for a person identified at one time to be the same person as a person identified at another time.
>
> An account of personal identity is a Complex View if and only if the account does offer informative necessary and sufficient conditions for a person identified at one time to be the same person as a person identified at another time.

Most mainstream views (e.g., those of Shoemaker (Shoemaker and Swinburne 1984), Parfit (1971), and Lewis (1983)) are Complex. Complex views (as far as I know) take personal identity to consist in a relation between items—such as mental states or brains or bodies—construed in subpersonal or nonpersonal terms. (That is what makes them informative.) By contrast, Simple Views (e.g., those of Foster (Foster 1991) and Swinburne (Swinburne 1997) and sometimes Chisholm (Chisholm 1991) typically appeal to some kind of immaterialism, according to which a person can exist independently of any body.[2]

Here I shall offer a Simple View, but of a different sort from the views of those who take persons to be immaterial substances. On

---

2. Parfit makes this point by saying that Simple Viewers hold that a person is "a separately existing entity from brain and body." (Parfit 1984, 251) I think that "separately existing entity" is ambiguous: It may mean "not identical to brain and/or body" or it could mean "exists independently of brain and/or body." On my view, we are persons on the first reading but not on the second. (I suspect that many philosophers would not distinguish between the two readings, but there certainly is a conceptual distinction.)

the one hand, I am not a reductionist about persons: I do not believe that personhood can be understood in subpersonal or nonpersonal terms, and hence I do not believe that there are noncircular *informative* necessary and sufficient conditions for a person identified at one time to be the same person as a person identified at a different time. On the other hand, I also reject the view that persons are or have immaterial minds or souls, or are "separately existing entities" that can exist apart from bodies. I reject both standard views and describe a third way. But first, I shall make some general remarks about persons and persistence conditions.

PERSONAL IDENTITY: A FIRST-PERSONAL APPROACH

According to my third way, we are fundamentally persons,[3] who are necessarily embodied, but we do not necessarily have the bodies that we in fact have. I take *person* to be a primary kind. As I have said, on my view, every concrete individual in the natural world is of some primary kind or other. (Baker 2007a, 33–39) An entity x's primary kind F is the answer to the question, What, most fundamentally, is x? Every x is of its primary kind essentially; x could not exist without being of its primary kind.[4] So, to say that a person is a basic entity is to say that *person* is a primary kind, and hence that nothing that had *person* as its primary kind could cease to be a person and continue to exist. An object's primary kind goes hand in hand with its persistence conditions.

3. Throughout this chapter, I am talking about what I call "nonderivative persons." Your body is a person derivatively as long as it constitutes you; but you are a person essentially and nonderivatively. (Baker 2000; 2007a)
4. An object can have a primary-kind property that is not *its* primary-kind property contingently. I spell this out with the idea of "having properties derivatively": A piece of marble can have the property of being a statue derivatively. See Chapter 8 of (Baker 2007a) for details.

Our persistence conditions are determined by the basic kind of being that we are. What makes us the kind of being we are is not what we are made of; rather, what makes us persons is that we have first-person perspectives essentially. What makes us the kind of being that we are is a particular ability: we are of a kind that typically develops a robust first-person perspective—a capacity to conceive of ourselves as ourselves* in the first person, without identifying ourselves by any third-person device—like a name or description or a third-personal pronoun.

For persons, a first-person perspective (first rudimentary, then typically robust) is the essential property that makes the person the fundamental kind of thing she is. Thus, first-person perspectives also furnish persons' persistence conditions: a person persists as long as her first-person perspective (rudimentary or robust) is exemplified.

It follows that persons' persistence conditions are first personal, whereas animals' persistence conditions (including those of the animals that constitute us now) are third-personal, biological properties. Indeed, not only animals, but everything else besides persons—flora and fauna, artifacts, artworks—has third-personal persistence conditions. The reason that persistence conditions of persons, but not of chimpanzees, are first personal is that only persons have robust first-person perspectives, on which all our institutions—artistic, scientific, legal, religious, and so on—depend.

Any view that takes a person's persistence conditions to be biological, or physical, or "somatic" leaves out—*must* leave out—what is distinctive about persons: the robust first-person perspective. This is so because, as Darwin emphasized, the animal kingdom is a seamless whole, and the persistence conditions of organisms are third personal. But persons are of a distinct primary kind that has first-personal persistence conditions. What is unique about a human person is an essential first-person perspective, which I take to be non-Cartesian. (Indeed, my philosophy of mind is externalist through and through. (Baker 2007b; 2007c))

We are necessarily embodied, but we do not necessarily have the bodies that we have. (This is why it is important that a human person's persistence conditions are not biological.) The relation between us and our bodies is constitution—the same relation that a painting has to the canvas and paint that constitutes it. We are constituted by our bodies, and the bodies that constitute us now are organisms. With enough neural implants and prosthetic limbs, however, we may come to be constituted by bodies that are partially or wholly nonorganic. What is required of person-constituting bodies is only that they have the mechanisms to support first-person perspectives.

On my view, human persons are emergent—as are organisms and other constituted things.[5] Your first-person perspective is an exemplification of the property *first-person perspective*, a property whose instances cannot be divided or duplicated.[6] So, a molecule-for-molecule replica of your body would not have your first-person perspective. Hence, fission problems (mercifully!) do not arise. What our robust first-person perspectives give us is the unity that is missing from physical systems.

So, here is my Not-So-Simple Simple View: A person is a being with a first-person perspective essentially, who persists as long as her first-person perspective is exemplified. To allow for the possibility that persons are temporally gappy, I should say: A person exists when and only when her first-person perspective is exemplified. To put this in terms of possible worlds: At any time t and in any possible

5. (Baker 2007a, 237–39). The relation between persons and bodies is not a supervenience relation; nor is it a part-whole relation. Constitution—not supervenience, not mereology—is the glue of the universe.

6. An exemplification of the first-person perspective is like a haecceity, or individual essence. The first-person perspective is not a qualitative property, and my exemplification of it is unique to me.

world w, I exist at t in w if and only if my first-person perspective is exemplified at t in w.[7]

What makes me the particular person that I am is the state of affairs of my exemplifying a first-person perspective. Since I have a first-person perspective essentially, the state of affairs of my exemplifying a first-person perspective is the same state of affairs at all times of my existence. So, here is my simple answer to the standard question of personal identity over time: Person x considered at time t is the same person as Person y considered by time t' if and only if the state of affairs of x's exemplifying a first-person perspective is the same state of affairs as y's exemplifying a first-person perspective.[8]

This condition for personal identity over time is not informative inasmuch as reference to the person is made in the *explicans*: "*her* first-person perspective" or "*my* first-person perspective" or *x's* exemplifying a first-person perspective. However, there is also a necessary condition for exemplifying a first-person perspective: A person must be constituted by something with mechanisms (e.g., neural mechanisms) adequate to support first-person reference to oneself as oneself.[9] (I'll return to the matter of circularity later; now, I just want to point out that this is a Simple View.)

7. Harold Noonan notes that we can take the problem of diachronic personal identity to be "the problem of specifying the relation which body *a* existing at time *t* must bear to body *b* existing at time *t'* if the person *occupying a* at *t* is to be identical with the person occupying *b* at *t'*." (Noonan 2003, 94) Since, on my view, human persons are necessarily embodied, my view may be expressed in Noonan's terms: the person occupying *a* at *t* is identical to the person occupying *b* at *t'* if (and only if) the person occupying *a* at *t* and the person occupying *b* at *t'* have the same first-person perspective.

8. More precisely: If there are times, t and t', such that x exists at t and y exists at t', then x = y if and only if the state of affairs of x's exemplifying a first-person perspective at t is identical to the state of affairs of y's exemplifying a first-person perspective at t'. Since persons have first-person perspectives essentially, the property of having a first-person perspective is not indexed to a time. The state of affairs of x's exemplifying a first-person perspective is the same state of affairs at all times of x's existence.

9. I think that this is close to what Noonan calls "the unoccupied view." (Noonan 2003, 97)

I called my view "not-so-simple." Why? Although the view conforms to the characterization of Simple Accounts that I started with, it differs from other (perhaps more standard) Simple Views. For example, John Foster uses the term "Simple View" to apply to accounts of persons as nonphysical subjects: "Jones and the non-physical subject to which the pain is attributed in the philosophically fundamental account are one and the same." (Foster 1991, 238) My Not-So-Simple Simple View differs from any Simple View that supposes that there are immaterial substances that can exist without bodies in the natural world.

The Not-So-Simple Simple View differs from other Simple Views in other ways as well. Simple Viewers who invoke immaterial substances like souls often take personal identity over time to be determinate at each moment. That is, for any person p and time t, p either definitely exists at t or definitely does not exist at t. For example, Thomas Reid said that when identity is applied to persons, it "admits not of degrees or of more or less." (quoted in Noonan 2003, 16). However, the Not-So-Simple Simple View rejects Reidian determinacy about persons and other ordinary objects. Here is the reason that I reject Reidian determinacy:

Because I take human persons to be natural objects, I take them to come into existence gradually. I think this follows from the empirical fact that no concrete object of any kind—a natural object or an artifact—comes into existence instantaneously or goes out of existence instantaneously. (Our solar system took eons to come into existence. Organisms come into existence gradually.)[10] Hence, we have good reason to believe that human persons do not come into existence instantaneously; like everything else, they come into existence gradually. But if persons, who are essentially

10. A human organism does not come into existence until implantation in a uterus (when a zygote can no longer "twin")—a process that takes up to two weeks. (Anscombe 1985; Baker 2005)

persons, come into existence gradually, there is a time at which their existence is indeterminate. However, as I have argued in *The Metaphysics of Everyday Life*, indeterminate existence (of anything) depends on the determinate existence of that thing. It is indeterminate whether some person p exists at t only if there is some other time, t′, such that it is determinate that p exists at t′. Let me explain by an analogy.

Suppose that you had a house built. Consider the time t at which the foundation was laid and the frame was in place; did your new house exist at t? The answer depends on what happens subsequently: Suppose that your house was completed at t′, at which time it existed determinately. Since your house existed determinately at t′, it existed indeterminately at t when the foundation had been laid and the frame was in place. But if a tornado had torn the structure down right after t, it would not have been the case that there had been a house that existed indeterminately at t. That is, its having existed indeterminately at one time depends on its existing determinately at some other time.

Indeterminacy, so understood, is metaphysical and not just semantic. However, this construal of indeterminacy does not entail that there is indeterminate identity. For any x and y, if x and y are identical, "they" are determinately identical. If x and y have vague temporal and spatial boundaries, x and y are identical only if they are both vague in the same ways to the same degree at the same times. If H is indeterminately a house at t, and H* is determinately a house at t′, then H = H* only if there is a unique x such that x is indeterminately a house at t and x is determinately a house at t′. Identity is determinate, atemporal and necessary; the existence of temporal beings like houses and persons is not. (See subsection on Time and Existence in Baker 2007a.) Identity is all-or-nothing; temporal existence—when an entity is coming into existence, or going out of existence—is not.

Since the first-person perspective depends on the proper functioning of neural mechanisms, and the proper functioning of neural mechanisms is subject to indeterminacies, there are indeterminacies in the coming into existence and going out of existence of persons. (Even if a person does not go out of existence at death, the earthly body—perhaps gradually—ceases to constitute the person.)

However, some philosophers take it to be a merit of standard versions of the Simple View that they are committed to the determinacy of persons. (Noonan 2003, 16) The merit of determinacy is that it seems to avoid the duplication problem. One version of the duplication problem is generated by the "split-brain" thought experiment, where a person's brain is split and one half is put into one body ("Lefty") and the other half is put into another exactly similar body ("Righty").[11] Both successor persons survive after fission, but on pain of contradiction, they cannot be identical to each other. So, which is the original person, Lefty or Righty? Determinacy about persons seems to assure us that there is an answer. But without determinacy, Lefty has no more claim to being the original person than Righty, and vice versa. Although I have little patience with such thought experiments, if there is a puzzle here, it can be solved by my construal of indeterminacy. There are not just two possible answers, but three possible answers to the question: Which is the original person? The answers are either Lefty, Righty, or neither, and the Not-So-Simple Simple View is compatible with all three answers. We may not know which is the correct answer, but the Not-So-Simple Simple View implies

11. Although this thought experiment has gained a lot of traction in the philosophical literature, I believe that Gareth Matthews has shown that we are in no position to judge whether the relationships between the original person and Lefty and the original person and Righty contain anything that interests us in ordinary cases of survival. (Matthews 1977, 58)

that there is a fact of the matter that depends on whether Lefty or Righty or neither has the original person's first-person perspective. So, we do not need Reidian determinacy in order to avoid the duplication problem.[12]

Admittedly, this condition for personal identity over time is not informative inasmuch as reference to the person is made in the *explicans*: "*her* first-person perspective" or "*my* first-person perspective." My reply is that the uninformativeness is inevitable in the nature of the case. Not only do we lack nontrivial necessary and sufficient conditions for transtemporal identity of almost everything, but, on my view of persons, it is impossible to have informative necessary and sufficient conditions for transtemporal personal identity: Persons are basic entities; being a person does not consist in satisfying nonpersonal conditions.[13] So, any correct account of personal identity over time must be uninformative; otherwise it would be reductive.

Peter van Inwagen has complained that I have given no noncircular informative meaning to the words "x and y have the same first-person perspective." (Van Inwagen 2006) What he says is true but hits no target; x's having the same first-person perspective as y is too closely tied to x's being the same person as y (or to x = y) to be characterized noncircularly. Any informative noncircular definition of "x and y have the same first-person perspective" must characterize persons in nonpersonal terms. Since I believe that we are not

---

12. There is still another way that my Not-So-Simple view differs from standard Simple Views. For example, Roderick Chisholm and many other philosophers take the word "simple" to mean "having no parts," where having parts entails conforming to a classical mereological theory of "the part-whole relation." Thus, Chisholm and others take persons to be simple in that they have no parts. I discuss this issue elsewhere. (Baker 2012a) My view is that if we mean ordinary parts (not parts constrained by a formal mereological theory), persons have parts, but if we mean parts as in classical mereology, persons have no (nonderivative) parts; they are mereological simples.

13. So my view qualifies as what Parfit calls a "further fact view." See (Parfit 1984, 211, 225).

reducible to nonpersonal or subpersonal items, of course I cannot give a definition of what makes us persons in nonpersonal terms. Persons are fundamentally different kinds of beings from anything else in the natural world. If this metaphysical claim is correct, then what I say about human persons does not—cannot—amount to a noncircular informative definition.

For persons, exemplification of a first-person perspective is akin to having an individual essence or a haecceity. A person's first-person perspective is dispositional and first personal. (An object x's individual essence, dispositional or not, is a property F such that, necessarily, x has F and nothing else has F (nothing nonidentical to F).)[14] A dispositional essence guarantees that its bearer exists between events that manifest it (e.g., when I am sound asleep). Dispositional essences are no strangers in science (unobservable theoretical entities) or in everyday life (artifacts). "Thermostats, thermometers, axes, spoons, and batteries have dispositional essences." (Mumford 1998, 8) Our first-person perspectives are exemplifications of a first-personal dispositional property that is a necessary condition for perceiving, acting intentionally, or thinking of oneself *as* oneself at all. (See Chapter 8.)

In short, the property of being a person is the property of being an exemplifier of a first-person perspective essentially, where the first-person perspective either is or may become robust. The property of being me is the property of being *this* exemplifier of a first-person perspective. It is being this exemplifier of a first-person perspective that makes me *me*.

So, the first-personal view is a Simple View because it provides no informative criteria of personal identity.[15] The Not-So-Simple Simple View provides no informative criteria of personal identity because

---

14. So individual essences are excluded properties—they cannot be had derivatively. (Baker 2007a, 166–69)

15. Trenton Merricks (1998) argues that there are no criteria of identity over time at all.

it takes personhood to be a basic property, and not susceptible to a nonpersonal or subpersonal account. By a "basic property," I mean one that either was exemplified from the beginning of the universe, or one whose exemplification is emergent. As I have said, new kinds of phenomena, objects, and properties emerge over time—some by means of natural processes and some by means of human ingenuity.

The original property base at the Big Bang is not itself sufficient for all the later emergent items, and hence the emergents are not reducible to the original base. (Plato did not live in a world in which there were properties like being genetically altered corn, or being a stock market crash or being a robot.) A full account of reality would include the original base together with the emergent items. If the first-person perspective is an emergent property, then it cannot be understood in nonpersonal or subpersonal terms, and it belongs in a full account of reality.

It is not surprising, then, if I am right, that there are no informative criteria for diachronic personal identity. To be informative, the criterion of "having the same first-person perspective" at different times would have to be specifiable without using the idea of a person. There seems to be no prospect of doing that. (Baker 2007d)

However, rather than being embarrassed by the absence of informative persistence conditions for persons, we should insist on it. The only alternative is to construe our diachronic personal identity in nonpersonal terms. So, if you agree with me that we are irreducibly persons, then you too will want to avoid informative persistence conditions.

OBJECTIONS AND REPLIES

Since my view of personal identity is not exactly in the mainstream, I would like to consider and respond to three objections.

OBJECTION 1: If persons are not identical to animals, how can they be part of the natural order?

REPLY 1: Biologically speaking, I'm a Darwinian: I believe that there is important continuity between the most primitive organisms and us, that we have animal natures, and that biology can uncover all there is to know about our animal natures. When our biological ancestors developed robust first-person perspectives (along with grammatically complex first-person sentences), entities of a new kind—persons—came into being.[16] My speculation is that grammatically complex first-person language and human persons came into existence together—both in the course of what anthropologists call the period of "cognitive inflation" of human organisms. (Mithen 2004, 164) So, we can certainly imagine how we—with our ability to conceive of ourselves as ourselves* in the first person and hence to enjoy inner lives—could have come about in the natural course of things.

OBJECTION 2: Sure, persons have abilities not shared by other kinds of beings, but why suppose that the difference between persons and other things is ontological?

REPLY 2: Biology can teach us a lot about ourselves, but not everything. A glance at the social sciences indicates that biological knowledge is insufficient for understanding our nature, all things considered. As constituted beings, persons are ontologically unique—irreducible to what constitutes them. It follows from the theory of constitution that if x constitutes y at t, then y is on a higher ontological level than x. When philosophers speak of levels, they

---

16. For example, "I wish that I had more food" or "I believe that I am getting sick" are grammatically complex sentences that indicate a robust first-person perspective.

usually mean levels of description. I do not. I mean levels of reality. (Baker 2007a) On my Constitution View, sums of molecules constitute people, but sums of molecules are fundamentally different kinds of things from people—just as sums of molecules are fundamentally different from fire escapes. So, the difference in level between molecule-talk and people-talk is not just a difference in level of description; it is a difference in what is being talked about. The idea of constitution makes sense of this ontological difference between molecules and people.

OBJECTION 3: Since sameness of first-person perspective cannot be explicated without using the notion of a person, transtemporal personal identity seems to be a matter of primitive persistence: it cannot be explained in nonpersonal terms. Michael Della Rocca has argued, in an article convincing to many, that primitive persistence is incompatible with (PPP), "Parfit's plausible principle."

(PPP) In a case in which there are objects, A, B, and C, $B \neq C$, B and C are equally and significantly causally and qualitatively continuous with A, and there is no other object besides A which exists at the same time as A and which is such that B and C are as causally and qualitatively continuous with it as they are with A, then it cannot be the case that $A = B$ and $A \neq C$ and it cannot be the case that $A \neq B$ and $A = C$. (Della Rocca, 599)

REPLY 3: There is no good reason to accept PPP over primitive persistence. Granted, if PPP is true, then primitive persistence is false. But that just comes down to "one philosopher's modus ponens is another's modus tollens." Moreover, there is not good reason to think that PPP is true at all. The only argument advanced in favor of PPP is that denying it would be arbitrary. OK, but arbitariness concerns what we have reason to believe or claim, not with what is the case. And PPP manifestly is about what is the case, and not about what we have reason to believe or claim.

Indeed, there would be no quarrel with an epistemic version of PPP that had the same antecedent as PPP but that had an epistemic consequent: "we would have no reason to believe that A = B and A ≠ C, and we would have no reason to believe that A ≠ B and A = C." The "arbitrariness" objection supports this epistemic principle as well as it supports PPP.

Moreover, the epistemic version of PPP is quite congenial to primitive persistence. Even in a case of (apparent) fission, on my view there would be a fact of the matter as to which, if any, of a's fission-products is a, but we are in no position to know what the fact is. For all we know, $a = b$ (and $a ≠ c$) or $a = c$ (and $a ≠ b$) or a goes out of existence altogether. So, we are left with no argument that favors PPP over an epistemic version of PPP. Lacking rational support for PPP, we have no bar to rejecting PPP. And rejecting PPP opens the door to accepting primitive persistence. Thus, I do not believe that Della Rocca's argument threatens my view of personal identity.[17]

My account of our identity over time, if correct, shows that we really do endure.[18] Thus, I believe that Rosenberg is mistaken when he says, "There seems to be only one way we make sense of the person whose identity endures over time and over bodily change. This way is by positing a concrete but nonspatial entity with a point of view somewhere behind the eyes and between the ears in the middle of our heads." (Rosenberg 2011b, 16) We (i.e., our identities)

---

17. What I have discussed of Della Rocca's article is really just a subargument. His aim is to show that three-dimensionalism is incoherent, and the only view left standing is four-dimensionalism combined with the principle of the identity of indiscernibles. I believe that his larger argument falls as well. (Baker 2012b)
18. I assume three-dimensionalism, for which I have argued elsewhere. (Baker 2007a, 199–217; 2009)

endure over time with vast bodily changes, without having any nonspatial parts.

This account is distinctive in several ways: First, it is metaphysical: it takes persons as such to be basic entities. It does not regard persons as fundamentally nonpersonal entities (such as organisms or brains) to which we apply a special vocabulary of person-talk. Second, it is ineliminably first personal. Persons—alone among natural entities—have first-personal persistence conditions. (For a different view, see Hershenov 2009.) Third, it does not countenance souls, or "selves": persons do not have immaterial parts—no souls or "selves."

This triad of characteristics—an account that is metaphysical, first personal, and free of anything immaterial—will strike many philosophers as inconsistent. If the account is metaphysical and first personal, then surely it must countenance a soul; alternatively, if the account does not countenance a soul and is metaphysical, then surely it cannot be first personal. I have argued otherwise. This view shows how first-person perspectives—first rudimentary, then robust—can furnish persistence conditions for persons.

Now let us turn to the other source of doubt about the robust first-person perspective, advanced by Mark Johnston (2010).

MARK JOHNSTON ON THE SELF AS ILLUSORY

Johnston has a powerful and subtle argument against first-personal accounts of identity over time. He suggests (or seems to suggest) that my view of the first-person perspective is akin to his own idea of a "self" as a center of an arena of presence. (Johnston 2010, 221) The persistence of one's "arena" depends on one's attending to it. (Johnston 2010, 232–33) On Johnston's view, whether or not some person in the future will be me depends on whether that person makes the backward-looking identification of the arena of presence that she enjoys with the arena of presence that I now enjoy. In virtue of what would the future person's arena of presence be the same as the one that I now enjoy? There is no objective answer—no answer other than what the person says (to which we have a convention of deference). Thus on Johnston's view, my identity over time is an illusion.

Johnston suggests that on my view, a first-person perspective is "not a property but an individual item of some sort." And, he continues, "once we conceive of arenas, consciousnesses, perspectives, and the like as *individual items of some sort or other* then we shall have to face up to their purely intentional status"—like Macbeth's dagger. (Johnston 2010, 221)

Johnston develops his critique in three steps: First, he distinguishes persons from "selves." Then, he argues that what concerns us is tracing selves over time: self-identity, not personal identity. Finally, he argues that selves depend on arenas of presence, but arenas of presence are merely intentional objects that do not exist in reality. Hence, "we selves are creatures of the unreal." (Johnston 2010, 225) After saying a bit more about Johnston's views, I'll argue that it is a mistake to apply his views to my idea of the first-person perspective.

In Step One, Johnston distinguishes selves from persons. Johnston motivates his distinction between persons and selves as a solution to what he calls the "paradox of auto-alienation." This paradox is an inconsistent triad, which I'll formulate from Johnston's point of view: (Johnston 2010, 197)

(1) While knowing that I am Johnston, I can, without semantic incoherence and without ignoring the structure of the fact that I am Johnston, imagine myself existing without Johnston existing.

(2) As a semantic matter, both "I" and "Johnston" rigidly denote what they denote.

(3) The fact that I am Johnston is a fact of identity, namely, this fact: I = Johnston.

Johnston argues that the claim in the inconsistent triad to be rejected is the third one, the one that holds "I = Johnston." Johnston says that he can imagine being Spinoza, and that that feat threatens "the idea that 'I' denotes the likes of Johnston." (Johnston 2010, 198) Rather, he says, "I" picks out a self, "the true or primary subject of thought, something that inhabits a human being." (Johnston 2010, 199) As an inhabitant of a human being, a self on Johnston's view is not identical to a human being or to a person. A number of important philosophers may be attracted to this appeal to selves, as distinct from human beings. (I'm thinking of Thomas Nagel (1983) and Galen Strawson (1997), among others.)

In Step Two, Johnston claims that what we trace over time is self-identity, not personal identity. Perhaps we trace selves "by bringing to bear a salient subjective unity condition." The idea that we trace selves rather than persons fits well with the idea of reincarnation, and it may help make sense of the way in which humanity has had thoughts of an afterlife and thoughts of "coming back as another person." (Johnston 2010, 212)

In Step Three, Johnston argues that a self is a center of an arena of presence—and thus is based on an illusion. The idea of an arena of presence, as Johnston explains, is the idea of "an inclusive mental field, a field comprising the visual, auditory and other sensory fields, the bodily field, and the field of thought and of action experienced from the inside as willed." These fields are quasi-containers that "hold" our sensory presentations. (Johnston 2010, 224)

The fields that make up an arena of presence are organized around an implied center that is a merely intentional object. What kind of container can be organized around a merely intentional object? A merely virtual container, a container that is itself a merely intentional object. (Johnston 2010, 224)

So, an arena of presence, Johnston argues, is merely an intentional object like Macbeth's hallucinated dagger. The identity over time of a "merely intentional object is just a matter of how it actually strikes the subject of the hallucination."[19] (Johnston 2010, 229) We have a convention of deference to the hallucinator, but there is no actual identity over time of intentional objects.

This is to say that the self is defined in terms of a "consciousness or an arena of presence, a 'container' of a stream of consciousness," and such a "container" is merely an intentional object. Johnston concludes, "Given that the identity over time of a merely intentional object is a matter of how things strike the subject, so too is the identity over time of a self!" (Johnston 2010, 231) The upshot is that the identity over time of a self is illusory.[20]

JOHNSTON'S CRITIQUE SIDESTEPPED

Now let's turn to the deployment of Johnston's argument specifically against my view.[21] First, I shall respond to Johnston's critique step-by-step, and then show that there is a mistake in what Johnston assumes makes my view vulnerable to his critique.

19. On my view, to be a subject of hallucination itself requires a first-person perspective.
20. Let me voice my opinion of the oddness of spending a lot of time trying to understand something well enough to deem it illusory.
21. Strangely, Johnston quotes Peter van Inwagen's critique of my view of the first-person perspective at great length, without assessing the criticism. (Johnston 2010, 219) However, I have replied to van Inwagen. (Baker 2011, 55–58)

Step One: I resolve the Paradox of Auto-Alienation differently from the way Johnston does. I deny the first claim, (1). Johnston gives no argument for (1), other than his being "pretty sure" about it and his noting that believers in transmigration must hold something like (1). (1) says that there's no semantic incoherence in imagining myself existing without LB's existing. If (1) is true, then (3) is false: it is not a semantic fact that I = LB. So, Johnston and I can agree that:

> If there's no semantic incoherence in imagining myself existing without LB's existing, then it is not a semantic fact that I = LB.

But whereas Johnston would infer by modus ponens on the conditional that it is not a semantic fact that I = LB, I would infer by modus tollens on the conditional that there is semantic incoherence in imagining myself existing without LB's existing. One philosopher's modus ponens is another's modus tollens.

I am reminded of Kripke's discussion of what you are imagining when you say that you imagine heat's existing without molecular motion's existing: You are not imagining the state of affairs that you think you are imagining. When Johnston says, "I can imagine my existing without Johnston's existing," he is not imagining the state of affairs that he thinks that he is imagining. (A non-Cartesian like me can allow you to be mistaken in what you think that you are imagining.) So, I do not find Johnston's thought-experiment convincing: If I try to imagine being Spinoza, I may imagine being very similar to Spinoza; I may imagine playing Spinoza's role in life, but I do not imagine my being Spinoza. What I am imagining is not that I exist without being LB.

So, I think that we should reject the first claim of the inconsistent triad. If we follow my suggestion of rejecting the first claim, then we undercut Johnston's basis for appealing to a separate self, as well as the need to set up the idea of a self plausibly enough (as a "creature of the unreal") in order to make it worth rejecting. The subject of my thoughts is me, the whole embodied person, not a self that "inhabits a human being." So, I reject the idea of selves as distinct from persons.

Step Two: According to Johnston, the persistence of my "arena" depends on my attending to it.[22] (Johnston 2010, 232–33) Neither this—nor anything like it—is my view, nor does it follow from anything that I say. The persistence of a person (or a self if there were any selves other than persons) does not depend on our attending to (or otherwise doing) anything. In particular, nobody has to be able to track a person or a "self" in order for her to exist over time. My view is that, even if she is thoroughly confused about who she is, a person in the future will be me if and only if she has my first-person perspective. In short, personal identity, and not self-identity, is at issue; and personal identity does not depend on anyone's "tracing" it.

Step Three: A robust first-person perspective is a capacity to entertain many thoughts that we would otherwise be unable to entertain, and a capacity to do many things that we would otherwise be unable to do—like writing memoirs, making vows, swearing to tell the whole truth. It is not a mental "container."

So, when Johnston says that "a perspective is first-personal just when the one that occupies the perspective thinks of herself *as* occupying that perspective," he is not speaking of my conception

---

22. Johnston believes that we can think of "an arena or a consciousness as a persisting thing because our own arenas or consciousnesses have been continually striking *us* as persisting through time." (Johnston 2010, 230, my emphasis) Phenomenologically, I simply disagree: you're in a car wreck and you wake up in the hospital with amnesia; your mental life does not strike you as persisting through time but seems to have a discontinuity.

of a first-person perspective. (Johnston 2010, 221) In the first place, Johnston's container-language is inappropriate for my conception of a first-person perspective: On my view one does not occupy a perspective. To have a first-person perspective is to exemplify a dispositional property—a property that I *have*, and in virtue of having it, I (a person) exist. I do not occupy a property; I exemplify it, and my exemplification of this property is unique. In the second place, I do not first exist and then come to have a first-person perspective. I (the person) cannot exist *without* exemplifying a first-person perspective: I came into existence when the fetus that came to constitute me could support a first-person perspective. In short, the first-person perspective is not thought of as a "center of presence" that can be illusory.

Now, turn to the background assumption that Johnston suggests makes my view vulnerable to his critique. The assumption is that a first-person perspective, on my view, is an "individual item." As I quoted earlier, once we conceive of perspectives and the like "as individual items of some sort or other, then we shall have to face up to their purely intentional status." (Johnston 2010, 221)

Perspectives, as I have said, are dispositional properties. My first-person perspective is a particular exemplification of a dispositional property. Are exemplifications of properties individual items? The terms "exemplification" and "instantiation" are primitive, undefined terms. Although exemplifications do not have full-fledged identity conditions, we can make sense of speaking of *this* exemplification of red (the color of my car at t) as opposed to *that* exemplification of red (the color of my shirt at t′, which matches the color of my car at t).[23]

Similarly, we can make sense of *this* exemplification of a first-person perspective (Jack's exemplification of the person-making property at t) as opposed to *that* exemplification

---

23. And we needn't aver to tropes to make this distinction.

of a first-person perspective (Jill's exemplification of the person-making property at t'). Does this make an exemplification of a first-person perspective an "individual item"? I do not think so. We don't have criteria of identity (synchronic or diachronic) for exemplifications of properties generally. So, understood as I understand it, a first-person perspective is not an "individual item" in the sense that Johnston argues against.[24]

In contrast to Johnston and his distinction between persons and selves, I think that the important distinction is between persons and bodies. I do not think a person/self distinction is called for by Johnston's argument from the paradox of auto-alienation, which relies on the questionable ability to imagine, without semantic incoherence, that you are Spinoza.[25] (Johnston 2010, 197) Moreover, his appeal to selves has infelicitous consequences—namely, that persisting selves are "creatures of the unreal." (Johnston 2010, 225)

On the other hand, the person/body distinction is well motivated by biotechnology. Artificial hearts, robotic limbs and other prosthetic devices, neural implants connected to computers— these and other artifacts already have replaced organic bodies with hybrids, while leaving the person intact. Thus, a person cannot be identified with her body at any time.

The person/body distinction is further motivated by phenomenological considerations. Tony Judt, who died of Lou Gehrig's disease (ALS) in 2010 gradually lost control of his body; he felt increasingly trapped by his body. He, the person, was still

---

24. Johnston urges that "individual 'consciousnesses'" are not to be regarded as "items with determinate conditions of identity over time." (Johnston 2010, 223) I do not disagree. Indeed, I treat consciousness in just the way that Johnston suggests—as "a remarkable ability or capacity that we have, a capacity to become conscious of this or that, to have items in many categories present to us, and so to have them available for demonstration as objects of further thought and talk." (Johnston 2010, 223)

25. And on a technical distinction between de jure rigidity and de facto rigidity. (Johnston 2010, 196–97)

functioning as a journalist even as he lost the ability to write. He dictated pieces for publication. Persons, not "selves," are journalists or historians. If one had a terminal degenerative disease, it seems only natural to think, "My body literally is killing me."

By distinguishing between persons and bodies, I have not disturbed the seamlessness of the animal kingdom. Rather, I have sought to account for the achievements of human beings (i.e., persons) by distinguishing persons from organisms and from other bodies: Only persons have first-personal persistence conditions—conditions that are not just a matter of how things strike one.

To sum up: Johnston's motivation for his distinction between persons and selves (the paradox of auto-alienation) is unconvincing. But even with selves on board, I do not believe that my view of the first-person perspective falls to the criticisms that Johnston offered against selves. A first-person perspective (at either a rudimentary or a robust stage) is not an intentional object; it's not an object at all, but a property whose exemplification is required for us persons to exist. So, my identity over time is not an illusion, after all.

CONCLUSION

I have responded to two sources of doubt about the coherence of the first-person perspective as an essential property giving the persistence conditions of persons. I presented a theory of personal identity that is metaphysical, first personal, and free of immaterialism. And I have argued, pace Johnston, that a first-person perspective is not an "individual item" that is even a candidate for being an intentional object. Hence, I believe that the notion of a two-stage first-person perspective is coherent and that it supplies first-person persistence conditions for persons.

Chapter Eight

A Metaphysical Framework for the First-Person Perspective

Throughout, I have taken the main issue to be one of ontology. Every object or property that is required to make the world as it is must either be mentioned in a complete ontology or strongly supervene on an "appropriate" base of properties mentioned in the ontology.[1] That is, the ontology—the inventory of all that exists—includes all objects and all properties that yield all reality. To put it still another way, ontology includes every object and property needed for a complete description of reality. My argument has been that the first-person perspective is an ineliminable and irreducible property that belongs in ontology.

A first-person perspective, as I have said, is a dispositional property—a property that is exemplified in two stages. The diversity of manifestations at each stage, like the diversity of manifestations of honesty and courage, enormous and unspecifiable. The property of having a first-person perspective is a single property—just as the property of being a cabinetmaker is a single property. Different capacities are exhibited at different stages (for example, rudimentary and robust; apprentice and mastercraftsman). Some entities with first-person perspectives are incapable of reaching a

---

1. I characterize "appropriate" in the relevant sense in Chapter 2.

robust stage, just as some cabinetmakers are incapable of becoming mastercraftsmen. Irreducible person-level properties cannot be comprehended in terms of underlying mechanisms.

At the rudimentary stage, the first-person perspective is the capacity to interact, consciously and intentionally, with the environment from a particular location (the "origin" of the perceptual field); and at the robust stage, which only persons reach, the first-person perspective includes the capacity to conceive of oneself as oneself* in the first person. The second stage of the first-person perspective may be thought of as the first stage enhanced by a natural language and all the abilities that a natural language brings with it. So, the second robust stage subsumes the first.

Before considering the property of being a first-person perspective specifically, let me briefly sketch out a nonstandard metaphysical framework for properties. Start with Chisholm. Taking "exemplifies" to be primitive, Chisholm's definition of the concept of a property is this:

P is a property = $_{df}$ P is possibly such that there is something that exemplifies it.

(Chisholm 1981, 6)

To exemplify a property P is to have the property P. Putting aside mathematical or logical properties, consider properties that are exemplified at times. But what are such properties? Universals? Tropes? I have a hybrid view, according to which properties may be called "temporal universals." Properties may be exemplified by any number of entities; so, they are like universals. But properties on my view are not eternal, and they are not like properties that exist only when exemplified.

If properties are not eternal, then they come into existence at times. Properties come into existence when—by natural selection or intentional activity—they are first exemplified. There was no property of being a nuclear warhead in Plato's time. There was no property of being an organism at the Big Bang. Once exemplified, a property exists from then on. So, although dinosaurs are extinct, the property of being a dinosaur, though unexemplified today, still exists. I would say that a property exists at time t if and only if there is some time t′ (t ≥ t′) at which it is exemplified. (Baker 2010) So, I want to modify Chisholm's definition in two ways: Remove the modality of possibility, and add a reference to time.

P is a property that exists at t =$_{df.}$ There is a time t′ at which something exemplifies P at t′ and (t ≥ t′).[2]

For one who (like me) takes there to be genuine novelty in the world—either by natural selection or by intentional intervention—it is natural to suppose that properties come into existence when they are first exemplified, and then exist thereafter.

Someone may object: "Ontology—and thus ineliminable properties—should be permanent. If there was a time when there were no first-person perspectives, how can there be first-person perspectives now? How can ontology change over time?" To this, I reply: It is only a dogma that ontology must be permanent. Ontology changes when things of new primary kinds come into existence. If you believe in evolution, then you are committed to changes in reality over time: there was a time when bacteria were the only living things; now human beings exist. I suggest that we distinguish between ontology-at-t and ontology-*simpliciter*. Ontology-at-t includes all the objects and properties that have been exemplified before and at t. Ontology-*simpliciter* includes all the objects and properties that there ever will be. (Baker 2007a) Since we are not

2. The temporal asymmetry of properties may be supported by an argument by elimination. Either properties (1) exist eternally (Platonic Forms), or they (2) exist only when they are exemplified, or they (3) exist when they are first exemplified and thereafter, or they (4) exist when they are first exemplified until they are no longer exemplified (for example, the property of being a dinosaur). The most plausible alternative, I think, is (3).

omniscient, we are in no position even to speculate about the extent of ontology-*simpliciter*. But we can be sure that ontology-at-2013 and ontology-*simpliciter* include first-person perspectives.

Now let us turn specifically to the property of the first-person perspective. First, I want to reiterate the point (argued for in Chapter 5) that the property of having a first-person perspective is irreducible and ineliminable, and hence genuinely a first-person property. Second, I shall argue that it is essentially dispositional; and third, I shall suggest that its exemplifications are "haecceitistic."

FIRST-PERSON PROPERTIES

Although Chisholm, like many (almost all) philosophers, holds that all properties are third-person properties (expressible without any first-person pronouns), his definition of properties does not rule out the possibility of there being first-person properties. Nor, of course, does my hybrid view. Moreover, as I argued in Chapter 5, self-concepts—first-person concepts—express first-person properties.

What makes a property a first-person property? Given the way that I have spelled out the rudimentary and robust first-person perspectives, the answer is easy: Property P is a first-person property if either (1) P entails that whatever exemplifies it has the capacity to interact consciously and intentionally with the environment and/or (2) P entails that whatever exemplifies it can conceive of herself as herself* in the first person.[3] That is to say, somewhat uninformatively, that P is a first-personal property if P entails the property of having a robust or a rudimentary first-person perspective.[4]

3. In the introduction, I characterized a first-person property as one expressible by a first-person pronoun. But now we are in a position for a more metaphysical characterization of a first-person property.
4. Property P entails property Q if and only if, necessarily anything that exemplifies P exemplifies Q.

However, I can make the connection between first-personal properties and having a first-person perspective more informative. The rudimentary stage of a first-person perspective is manifested in nonlinguistic animals by intentional behavior that reveals to onlookers the location from which the subject perceives phenomena in the part of reality perceptually available to him. The rudimentary first-person perspective is first-personal in virtue of its providing the perceptually accessible part of reality from a conscious subject's point of view, without referring to the subject.

The robust stage of the first-person perspective is also first personal. In Chapter 5 I argued that an I*-concept expresses an I*-property. Then, I presented both linguistic and ontological arguments to show that I*-properties—first-person properties—are neither reducible nor eliminable, and hence that first-person properties belong in the ontology *simpliciter.*

Since a rudimentary first-person perspective is exemplified only by conscious beings, and a robust first-person perspective is necessary and sufficient for self-consciousness, the first-person perspective, in both stages, is first personal. Anything that is conscious or self-conscious has a first-person perspective. So, to say that the first-person perspective, in both its rudimentary and robust stages is a first-personal property, is not controversial, but not trivial either.

DISPOSITIONAL PROPERTIES

Second, the first-person perspective is dispositional. As I explained, both stages of the first-person perspective are capacities: The rudimentary stage is the capacity to interact consciously and intentionally with one's environment.[5] The robust stage is the capacity to

---

5. I am not talking here about phenomenal consciousness that Chalmers and others take to be categorical. (Chalmers 1996) I am speaking here of consciousness as a capacity, a property that one has even when not manifesting it.

conceive of oneself *as* oneself* in the first person. These first-person capacities are dispositions.

In "What Makes a Capacity a Disposition?" Nancy Cartwright argues that the central criterion for a capacity's being a disposition is its "two-sidedness." (Cartwright 2003) Two-sidedness is there being a distinction between the exemplification of a disposition and its being manifested. Cartwright does not focus on conditions for manifestation of a given disposition, because manifestations of a single disposition may be so various that "no conditional (or set of conditionals) will capture the content of a dispositional ascription." So, capacities like the gravitational capacity "fall into the same family as dispositions, habits, character traits and the like." (Cartwright 2003, 7)

The manifestations of a first-person perspective, rudimentary or robust, are indefinitely various. Indeed, they are wildly disparate. A human infant manifests her rudimentary first-person perspective by any intentional behavior—from reaching for her mother to imitating a psychologist's tongue protrusions. A language-user directly manifests her robust first-person perspective in any utterance or thought of the form, "I believe (regret, hope, said, etc.) that I* am F." And once one has a robust first-person perspective, then any behavior—verbal or otherwise—that she realizes that she* is engaging in manifests her robust first-person perspective. There is no specifiable list of manifestations of the property that is a first-person perspective; manifestations are as various as the whole range of human behavior, feelings, and attitudes.

The second criterion for a capacity to be a disposition is malleability. Cartwright discerns three features of malleability, at least one of which is shared by each other member of the family of dispositions, habits, and character traits: (i) a need for triggering; (ii) the possibility of being enhanced or weakened; (iii) the production of different manifestations, or no manifestations at all if the disposition is interfered with. All capacities and dispositions can be interfered with.[6] One may still have the capacity/disposition even when a triggering does not lead to a manifestation of it. In short, what makes a capacity a disposition is that there is a difference between its existence and its being manifested, between having the capacity and manifesting it.

Both stages of the first-person perspective, rudimentary and robust, satisfy both of Cartwright's criteria for being a disposition. Both stages are two-sided: A person is a conscious being even when she is asleep and is not manifesting consciousness; a language-using person is a self-conscious being even when she is not conceiving of herself and is not manifesting self-consciousness. And both stages are malleable: The manifestations of both share at least one of the three features of malleability: (i) they need triggers; (ii) they can be enhanced or weakened; and (iii) they can be interfered with.

For example, (i) the triggers for behaviors that manifest either consciousness or self-consciousness are as varied as are the behaviors themselves. (ii) Both consciousness and self-consciousness may be enhanced (e.g., by ingesting certain mushrooms) or weakened (e.g., by being inattentive, or by ingesting too many mushrooms). (iii) The manifestations of a first-person perspective can be interfered with. Here are two examples in which first-person perspectives, rudimentary and robust, respectively, are interfered with. (a) The rudimentary first-person perspective: Most of us (including nonhuman animals) have a disposition to come when called; but if someone calls you when you are asleep, you do not respond; yet you retain the disposition to come when called. (b) Similarly, for a robust first-person perspective: If someone asks me, "Where's

6. Nancy Cartwright defends the rider "if nothing interferes" in the absence of a system of rules specifying what counts as an interference. Particular claims—"Aspirins relieve headaches if nothing interferes"—are routinely tested in controlled experiments. (Cartwright 2003, 11)

Lynne?" I am disposed to respond, "Here. I'm Lynne." But if I have amnesia, I do not so respond; yet, even with amnesia, I still have my robust first-person perspective. So, first-person perspectives (rudimentary and robust) satisfy Cartwright's criteria for dispositions.

But what kinds of features do these first-person dispositions have? The literature on dispositions is huge. Some philosophers—for example, Armstrong (Armstrong, Martin, and Place 1996)—believe that dispositional properties are reducible to categorical properties. Others believe that all natural properties have dispositional essences (Bird 2007). Some think that they are causally inert, that the causal work is done by distinct categorical bases (Prior, Pargetter, and Jackson 1982); others think that dispositions themselves are causally relevant (McKitrick 2005). Some think that dispositions (and their causal bases) are intrinsic (Lewis 1997); others that there are extrinsic dispositions (McKitrick 2003). All these concern important features of dispositions, but rather than trying to adjudicate all these controversies, I shall just try to describe the features of dispositional properties that first-person perspectives have.

I want to show that the first-person perspective is not only dispositional but that it is essentially dispositional. I take an essentially dispositional property to be one that is not reducible to categorical properties. The dispositional property that is the first-person perspective is reducible to categorical properties if and only if it strongly supervenes on "appropriate" categorical properties, and ultimately on "appropriate" micro-properties.[7] Let us begin with the rudimentary stage of the property that is the first-person perspective.

The dispositional property that is the first-person perspective in its rudimentary stage entails a combination of consciousness and intentionality. Consider consciousness. The "appropriate"

---

7. Recall the discussion of "appropriate" properties at the beginning of Chapter 2. The reason to introduce the notion of "appropriate" properties is to allow nonreductionists who are externalists to be naturalists.

categorical properties that might be candidates for a subvenient base for consciousness are likely neural properties. Most everyone agrees that your current brain state globally is sufficient for consciousness, but that fact is far from reducing consciousness (much less particular conscious states) to brain states. Perhaps consciousness might have strongly supervened on a particular (specifiable) subset of neural properties ("a neural correlate"), but as of now there is no reason to think that it does. After a great deal of research, no neural correlate has been found that is sufficient for consciousness. (Noë and Thompson 2004) Since a neural correlate sufficient for consciousness is a necessary condition for the reduction of consciousness to categorical properties, we can conclude that consciousness is not reducible to categorical properties; rather, it is essentially dispositional. Further, since consciousness is common to both the rudimentary and robust stages of the first-person perspective, the irreducibility of consciousness to categorical properties suffices for the irreducibility of the first-person perspective in both its stages.

Of course, this scientific situation could change; perhaps a neural correlate sufficient for consciousness is found. What then? First, a neural correlate would not be sufficient for the reduction of consciousness to categorical properties; it would only show an unexpected correlation between consciousness (even when it is not being manifested?) and neural properties. Second, even if (as I strongly doubt) consciousness is reducible, there are still the I*-phenomena of the robust stage of the first-person perspective.

We saw in Chapter 5 that in its robust stage, the first-person perspective is irreducible. My argument in Chapter 5 against functionalization of I*-phenomena applies here. The problem is that the items (putatively) specifying the functional role of I*-phenomena (like "I believe that I* am tall") will themselves be I*-phenomena. My belief that I* am tall is caused in part by other I*-beliefs—what I believe that I* have been told, what I believe that I* saw on the measuring device; in addition my belief that I* am tall causes (in part) other I*-phenomena—my decision that I* should try out for the basketball team, my going to the Tall Girls section of the store, my answering "yes" to a certain question about my height.

As I mentioned in Chapter 5, in the absence of a massive definition that functionalizes all I*-properties at once—a prospect that seems overwhelmingly unlikely—the need for I*-properties stubbornly persists, and the functionalization route to reduction seems blocked. Since I know of no more promising route to reduction of dispositional to categorical properties, I take the argument against functional reducibility of I*-properties to show that at the robust stage, the first-person perspective is an essentially dispositional property.

The extreme diversity of manifestations of a first-person perspective (in rudimentary as well as robust stages) makes it unsurprising that there is not a single categorical property—or even a specifiable disjunction of categorical properties—to which the first-person perspective could be reduced.

In short, I think that the reasonable conclusion is that the first-person perspective—in both its rudimentary and robust stages—does not strongly supervene on "appropriate" categorical properties (and hence is not reducible in the sense discussed in Chapter 5). We do not have to go so far as Ellis and Lierse, who say of dispositional properties generally that they "may supervene on categorical properties, but never on categorical properties alone.... [A] disposition cannot be ontologically dependent only on what is not dispositional." (Ellis and Lierse 1994, 39) Whether or not some dispositional properties are reducible to categorical properties, the first-person dispositional property that is the first-person perspective is not so reducible.

Having argued that the first-person perspective (at both rudimentary and robust stages) is first personal and essentially dispositional, I still need to show how first-person perspectives are related to your being you and my being me. So, let's turn to the third feature of the properties that first-person perspectives are.

HAECCEITISTIC IMPLICATIONS

Someone may object that although I have said what it is to be a person, I have not said what it is to be me (instead of you). The answer to this question is not far to find. Although I cannot say noncircularly what makes me me instead of you, I can put a little flesh on these bones of first-person particularity. (Because these matters concern individual differences between entities of the same primary kind (*person*), I call them "haecceististic implications" of exemplifications of the property that is the first-person perspective.)

> Let F be the dispositional property expressed by "a first-person perspective."

Then, as I have argued,

> Necessarily, x is a person if and only if x exemplifies F essentially.

However, each exemplification of a first-person perspective is a different state of affairs, a different entity's exemplifying F essentially. This observation opens up room for a distinction between being a person and being me. To be a person is to exemplify F essentially. To be me is for there to be a state of affairs, my-exemplifying-F-essentially (or equivalently, LB's-exemplifying-F-essentially).[8] I am a different person from you, in virtue of the fact

---

8. My-exemplifying-F-essentially is the same state of affairs as LB's-exemplifying-F-essentially, because I am identical to LB.

that my-exemplifying-F-essentially is a different state of affairs from your-exemplifying-F-essentially.

If persons are fundamental entities, as I have argued, then neither the property of being a person nor the fact of being me is reducible to anything nonpersonal. In that case, there is no way to avoid the circularity of being me and my-exemplifying-F-essentially; circularity follows from the nature of the case. Again, to be a person is to exemplify F essentially; to be me is for a particular state of affairs, my-exemplifying-F-essentially, to obtain. Again, I am not trying to give an analysis; all that I am trying to do here is to tease out a place to distinguish between being a person and being me.

My discussion of the relation between *being a person* and *being me* may bring to mind medieval and contemporary discussions of haecceity (*haecceitas*). Haecceity, roughly, is "thisness," a nonqualitative property responsible for individuation. I want to modify the notion of an haecceity as a property to take an haecceity to be the state of affairs of someone's exemplifying a property. So, my haecceity is my-exemplifying-F-essentially. Your haecceity is your-exemplifying-F-essentially. Necessarily, person x and person y have the same haecceity if and only if x = y. So, necessarily, I have my haecceity and no one else does. On this (blatantly circular) construal, it is reasonable to say that *being me* (or *being LB*) is my haecceity.[9]

Perhaps an example from the thirteenth century would be helpful: Duns Scotus sought a principle of individuation for singular substances, one that added a further individuating difference than the specific nature of a substance. This individuating difference has come to be called a substance's "thisness" or haecceity. A haecceity does not add to the "whatness" of a thing but distinguishes it from

9. This echoes other construals of haecceities at least faintly. For recent discussion, see, for example, Adams (1979); Wierenga (1989); Chisholm (1976). Note that my construal of an haecceity has no epistemic component; I am simply trying to show how to make the distinctions that we need.

other things of the same kind. Scotus thus broke with the Greek tradition, in which the individual was only incidental; the Greek focus of being and intelligibility was on the specific nature, not on the individual. As Stephen Dumont summed it up, "Perhaps the most significant result of Scotus's doctrine of individuation is that it makes the individual qua individual essentially intelligible, at least in principle, although Scotus denied such knowledge is possible for our intellect in its present state." (Dumont 2002, 361)

Conceding that this brief foray into scholasticism is woefully incomplete, I am not going to wade any further into these deep waters. Suffice it to say that I take the fact that *being me* to be is necessarily tied to there being a state of affairs, my-exemplifying-F-essentially. I take there being such a particular state of affairs to be a haecceitistic implication of the dispositional first-personal property in virtue of which we are persons.

Finally, let us return to the problem raised by Nagel in the Introduction: We are now in a position to understand how my being LB is a fact. The key is that personal identity can be understood in terms of haecceities: x = y if and only if x and y have the same haecceity. "I am LB" expresses a fact if and only if my haecceity is my-exemplifying-F-essentially, and LB's haecceity is also my-exemplifying-F-essentially.

(1) I am a person essentially. (I exemplify F essentially)
(2) LB is a person essentially. (She exemplifies F essentially.)
(3) If x and y share one instance of exemplifying-F-essentially, then x = y. (definition)
(4) LB and I share one instance of exemplifying-F-essentially.
∴(5) I am LB.

Someone may object that (4) is not true unless LB and I are identical and so begs the question. Fair enough, but the argument is not intended to prove that I am LB, but rather to answer the question posed by Nagel—namely, how can there be room in the world for me to be LB? What makes it the case that I am LB? The answer is that what makes me LB is that there is one instance of exemplifying-F-essentially that I share with LB. This straightforwardly shows how I am identical to LB.[10]

CONCLUSION

All properties needed for the world to be as it is belong in the ontology. I have tried to show that first-person perspectives are first personal, essentially dispositional properties with haecceitistic implications. If this is right, it is no surprise that first-person perspectives be must be explicitly mentioned in a complete description of the world.

---

10. I do not share the intuition of Nagel (and other philosophers) that I could have been someone else. (I find his and others' thought experiments for that intuition unconvincing.) On my view, I am identical to LB. I could not have been anything or anyone else, nor could LB have existed without being me.

Chapter Nine

Agents, Artifacts, Moral Responsibility

Some Contributions of the First-Person Perspective

The first-person perspective contributes to reality in a wide variety of ways. The main contribution of the first-person perspective is the existence of persons with their peculiar abilities. In addition, many of the characteristic features of human (and some nonhuman) life presuppose the first-person perspective, in its rudimentary and robust stages. Robust first-person perspectives distinguish the abilities of persons from those of nonhuman animals. The various kinds of agency presuppose a rudimentary or robust first-person perspective. Production of artifacts and artworks requires agency and hence the first-person perspective. The conditions for moral responsibility require a robust first-person perspective. (That's why we do not hold animals, with only rudimentary first-person perspective, morally responsible.) At least one account of moral responsibility presupposes the robust first-person perspective. In surveying such a miscellany of ways that the first-person perspective contributes to reality, I hope to expose its significance to the way things are.

PERSONHOOD

We have already explored one important way that the first-person perspective contributes to reality: As an essential property that determines persons' persistence conditions, the first-person perspective makes it possible for persons to exist. The fact that our first-person perspectives provide our persistence conditions ensures that persons are not just physical systems; they are constituted beings, made unitary by first-person perspectives.

Robust first-person perspectives are implicated in many of the characteristic activities of persons—activities in virtue of which they are memoir-writers, conquering heroes, volunteers, poets, conspirators, benefactors, and all the rest. We could not even have many of the thoughts that we have without robust first-person perspectives. To give just one example, no one could have W. H. Auden's thought in "September 1, 1939" without attributing I* thoughts to others: "For the error bred in the bone/Of each woman and each man/Craves what it cannot have,/Not universal love/But to be loved alone." (Auden 1945, 58–59)

Moreover, much of what we do would be beyond our reach if we lacked robust first-person perspectives. For example, we routinely ascribe mental dispositions to others. As one frequent writer on moral psychology has argued, the ascription of mental dispositions "depends essentially on our empathetic ability, that is, our ability for mental imitation and our capacity to reenact another person's thought processes in our own mind." (Steuber 2009, 258) If this is right, then our ability to ascribe mental dispositions rests on our robust first-person perspectives.

Since I have discussed personhood at some length, I'll turn briefly to some of the many abilities, traits, and activities that distinguish us persons from animals that do not constitute persons. To name a few:

> We share with other species the ability to communicate with conspecifics; but only we human persons have a fully articulated language with necessity and possibility. Only we worry about the paradox of the heap.
>
> We share with other species the trait of having a perspective on our environments; but only we human persons have rich inner lives, filled with counterfactuals. ("...if only I had...")
>
> We share with other species methods of rational inquiry (Where's the bone? I saw it being buried over there. So, I'll look over there); but only we human persons deliberate about what to do and attempt to rank preferences and goals, and try to resolve conflicts among them (and thus be rational agents).
>
> We share with other species activities like self-grooming; but only we human persons have self-narratives.
>
> We share with other species the ability to make things that we need (e.g., nests), but only we human persons make things that we don't need (e.g., enough nuclear warheads to eliminate the human race many times over).
>
> We share with other species the property of having social organization, but only we human persons have war crimes, international courts, and human rights.
>
> We share with other species the property of having a first-person perspective, but only we human persons have a robust first-person perspective that renders us responsible agents.

All these differences between persons and nonhuman animals rest on our having robust first-person perspectives. Robust first-person perspectives bring with them a cascade of new kinds of abilities: We can see ourselves as individuals and as members of communities; we can plan for our futures; we can hold ourselves responsible for what we do; we deceive ourselves; we can write memoirs; we try to reform; we have rich inner lives. And on and on. With respect to the range of what we can do (from trying to control our destinies to daydreaming) and with respect to the moral significance of what we can do (from assessing our goals to confessing our sins), it is obvious that beings with robust first-person perspectives are unique, and thus that the first-person perspective contributes mightily to reality.

So, not only does the first-person perspective, had essentially, contribute persons to reality, but the robust first-person perspective (exclusive to persons) makes possible many of the features characteristic of human life.

VARIETIES OF AGENCY

On Elizabeth Anscombe's influential account, an intentional action[1] is one to which a certain kind of "Why?" question has application— a "Why?" question whose answer gives someone's reason for acting. (Anscombe 1957, 9) The "Why?" question is refused application when the answer is (1) I wasn't aware that I was doing that—for example, a sleeper was disturbed by my loud laughter, or (2) what I did was involuntary (even if I was aware of doing it)—for example, my tremor caused the wine to spill, or (3) I knew that I was doing it, but only because I observed it—for example, my stepping too close to the painting triggered the alarm.

---

1. I use "intentional" to mean any phenomenon that could not occur in a world without intentions.

There are two things to notice: (i) Opting out of the "Why?" question by any of the examples supposes that I have a robust first-person perspective; (ii) Giving a reason for what I did also presupposes that I know what I* did, and hence have a robust first-person perspective. Although I think that Anscombe has accurately diagnosed a standard kind of case of intentional action, I believe that there are more basic kinds of intentional action that require only a rudimentary first-person perspective. However, any agency—no matter how basic or sophisticated—requires a first-person perspective. So, anyone who takes agency to be a part of reality should likewise take first-person perspectives to be genuine properties.

Even if we acknowledge that all agents have first-person perspectives, the relation between agency and first-person perspectives is not straightforward. There are different kinds of agents, and there are different stages of first-person perspectives. On the one hand, all persons are agents, but not all agents (e.g., chimpanzees, dogs) are persons; on the other hand, all rational and moral agents are persons, but not all persons (e.g., human infants) are rational and moral agents.

There are four intertwined matters to explore first: agency, action, intentional explanation, and practical reasoning. Begin with agency: In the most basic sense, an agent is an entity that is able to do things, where the relevant sense of "doing things" is this:

> (DT) An entity x does something [in the sense relevant to agency] if and only if x brings about something that can be adequately explained only by reference to x's beliefs, desires, or intentions.

Anything that has the ability to do things in the sense of (DT) is an agent, including nonhuman animals with rudimentary first-person perspectives. The things that agents do may be characterized correlatively as actions.[2] (Some of the things that we do—e.g., digesting food or growing older—are not explainable by beliefs, desires, and intentions and hence are not actions at all; such things are not relevant to this discussion.) Actions are things that can be done in conformity with (DT), and agents are entities that can do things in conformity with (DT). If someone does something that conforms to (DT), then she does something that is adequately explainable only in terms of her attitudes. I'll call explanations that explain actions in terms of attitudes "intentional explanations."[3]

What connects the agent's attitudes to her actions in intentional explanations is that the agent's attitudes can be used in—perhaps primitive—practical (means-end) reasoning that concludes with the agent's acting. So, we have the following thesis:

(AE) If x brings about something that can be adequately explained only by reference to x's beliefs, desires, or intentions, then x can engage in primitive practical (means/end) reasoning.

From (DT) and (AE), it follows that

(PR) If x does something [in the sense relevant to agency], then x has the ability to engage in (at least) primitive practical (means/end) reasoning.

So, the ability to do things [in the sense relevant to agency] is conceptually tied to the ability to engage in primitive practical

2. Actions are events constituted by other events—your action of reaching for a cup is constituted by your arm's moving. Events (and hence actions) are property-instantiations, not particulars.
3. Although the range of intentional phenomena is much broader than phenomena involving intentional attitudes, I am here restricting the use of "intentional explanations" and later of "intentional causation" to phenomena involving intentional attitudes.

(means/end) reasoning. These coupled abilities make the link between practical reasoning and intentional explanations.

The explanatory power of intentional explanations derives from the fact that intentional explanations capture practical reasoning from the agent's point of view.[4] The practical reasoning that typifies intentional explanations capture may be simple, hardly worth spelling out: I want to get warmer and believe that the best way to get warmer is to move closer to the fire; so I move closer to the fire. Let me make four further points about practical reasoning:

First, practical reasoning is always first personal: The agent reasons about what to do on the basis of her own first-person point of view. It is the agent's first-person point of view that connects her reasoning to what she actually does. Nevertheless, the agent need not have any first-person concept of herself. A dog, say, reasons about her environment from her own point of view.[5] She is at the origin of what she can reason about. She buries a bone at a certain location and later digs it up. Although we do not know exactly what it's like to be a dog, we can approximate the dog's practical reasoning from the dog's point of view: Want bone; bone is buried over there; so, dig over there. The dog is automatically (so to speak) at the center of her world without needing any self-understanding.

Second, as the dog example also illustrates, primitive practical reasoning does not require that the agent have a natural language.

---

4. I'll put aside the possibility of self-deception here for two reasons: (1) Cases of self-deception, in which an agent's practical reasoning is not a reliable guide to the correct intentional explanation of her behavior, are parasitical on the more ordinary and uncontroversial kinds of cases that I discuss. (2) Self-deception is a problem only in a special class of cases, in which the agent has an interest in concealing what she really thinks, and hence can be bracketed.

5. Vonk and Povinelli 2006 argue that chimpanzees' minds are limited to their environments.

Although, as I'll argue later, there is an important difference with respect to agency between entities that have a robust first-person perspective and those with only a rudimentary first-person perspective—theorists and ordinary people alike successfully explain behavior by attributing practical reasoning to creatures that have no natural language. Without assuming that such creatures engage in primitive practical reasoning, we are left with no explanation of their behavior at all.

Third, the practical reasoner—primitive or not—may be unaware that she is reasoning. Even beings like you and me are often unaware of our own reasoning. When I get to the building where the conference is held, I open the door. And I open it intentionally: I want to get inside and believe that the best way to get there is to open the door. Although I do not think about my attitudes or the door, my action is explained by the intentional explanation and the simple practical reasoning that it captures.

Fourth, some actions are accidental or unintended, but insofar as they are actions at all, their explanations invoke attitudes used in practical reasoning. Suppose that a nurse who was to bathe a toddler accidentally scalded the toddler in her care. Suppose that the nurse did not intend to scald the baby but mixed up the hot-water tap and the cold-water tap. Even though she did not do what she intended, her scalding the baby still has an intentional explanation: She wanted to give the baby a bath and believed that turning the hot-water-handle 90 degrees and the cold-water-handle 180 degrees was the best way to give the baby a bath. So, she turned one handle 90 degrees and the other handle 180 degrees. However, since she mixed up the taps, she ended up scalding the baby.[6] So, the scalding—although wholly accidental—needs an intentional explanation that invokes a

---

6. This example derives from one in J. L. Austin 1961, 123–52.

mistaken belief. One cannot do anything by accident unless one can also do things intentionally. In this way, we may also see mistakes as manifestations of agency.

In sum, there are several interrelated concepts—agency, action, practical reasoning, and intentional explanation—that may be characterized as follows:

> an agent $=_{df}$ an entity that is able to do things (as in (DT)) that are adequately explained only in terms of her attitudes
> an action $=_{df}$ something that an agent does (as in (DT))
> practical reasoning $=_{df}$ first-personal reasoning that connects an agent's attitudes to her actions (as in (AE))
> an intentional explanation $=_{df}$ an explanation of an agent's action in terms of the agent's attitudes used in practical (means-end) reasoning (as in (PR))

Agency comes in various degrees. The generic agent as I have just characterized her might be thought of as a minimal agent. So,

> minimal agency $=_{df}$ the ability to do things explainable only by attitudes used in practical (means-end) reasoning.

Some agents are more than minimal agents. A rational agent (as I'll call her) is a minimal agent who has the second-order ability to evaluate her beliefs and desires. She not only has beliefs, desires, and intentions, but also she knows that she has beliefs, desires, and intentions. A rational agent not only reasons about what to do but also can rank preferences and goals, evaluate her beliefs, and try to resolve conflicts among them. She can decide what kind of person she wants to be and make efforts to achieve the character that she wants to have. She can have (second-order) desires about the (first-order) desires that she wants to have.[7] So,

> rational agency $=_{df}$ minimal agency + possession of appropriate second-order attitudes (e.g., desires about one's own desires)

Since rational agency requires second-order attitudes and second-order attitudes require a self-concept, anyone who has a second-order attitude has a robust first-person perspective. So, no being can be a rational agent in this strong sense without having a robust first-person perspective.

Another more-than-minimal agent is a moral agent. To be a moral agent is to be accountable for what one does, to be subject to judgments of praise and blame. Moral agency requires not only that one have second-order attitudes generally, as a rational agent does, but also that one have a very specific second-order attitude: To be a moral agent, one must be able to appreciate the fact that she does things and has done things in the past (as in (DT)).[8] So,

> moral agency $=_{df}$ rational agency + realization that one does things and has done things in the past.

Clearly, again, nothing can be a moral agent without a robust first-person perspective. Since only persons can have robust

---

7. See Frankfurt 1971. An agent who has second-order desires but no interest in which desires motivate her Frankfurt calls a "wanton." I am including wantons as rational agents.

8. I take a moral agent to be subject to praise and blame, and I do not believe that one is subject to praise or blame unless one realizes that he does things and has done things in the past. So, I do not believe that "Swampman," who comes into existence disposed to reason and recognize value, is immediately a moral agent—that is, subject to praise or blame—until he does something.

first-person perspectives, only persons can be rational or moral agents.[9]

If it is possible to have a kind of amnesia in which one does not know that she has done things in the past, although she still has other kinds of second-order thoughts, then a person so afflicted would not be a moral agent.[10]

Now I want to produce some evidence that all persons and some nonpersons are minimal agents. First, consider evidence that human infants (persons with rudimentary first-person perspectives) are minimal agents. Infants as young as two months engage in problem-solving behavior. When an experimenter sets up a light so that an infant can turn it on by moving her head to the left, most infants learn quickly that moving their heads to the left turns on the light. They turn on the light over and over and then the rate of left-head-turning drops dramatically. Then the experimenter changes the contingency to right-head-movement. When the infant turns her head left again, the light fails to come on. Then the infant makes a rapid succession of left-head-turnings. Sooner or later the infant turns her head to the right and the light comes on. This is followed by a high rate of right-head-turnings, which then subside. With changes in the contingencies, an infant can master complex series of movements, such as right-right-left-left.

The infant seems to have little interest in the light itself; she merely glances to see whether it is on, without paying further attention. As one experimenter remarked, "The infant seems to be testing

9. Conversely for rational agents: all beings with robust first-person perspectives are rational agents (in the sense specified). It is not clear to me whether all beings with robust first-person perspectives are moral agents.

10. However, a schizophrenic with a robust first-person perspective and the knowledge that she* had done things in the past would still be a moral agent; but if for everything she did, there was a morally defeating condition, there may be nothing for which she is morally responsible.

hypotheses and trying out sequences of movements in order to discover which one operates at the moment. When the correct sequence is discovered, it is tested a few times and then dropped.... It is quite obvious from the behavior of the infants that the light source is not the motivating factor.... [It] seems that the pleasures of problem solving are sufficient to motivate behavioral and mental activity in young infants." (Bower 1974, 8–9)[11] As problem-solvers, human infants are minimal agents.

Now consider evidence that some nonhuman animals are minimal agents. *Scientific American* 2006 reported on work that showed that bonobos and orangutans not only can use tools to get a fruit treat from a mechanical apparatus, but also they can plan ahead. They were first trained to use a tool to get a fruit treat from a mechanical apparatus. Then, the apes were given tools, some suitable and some unsuitable for the task of getting the fruit; next, they were taken out of the test room into a waiting room and brought back to the test room after an hour. Significantly more often than predicted by chance, the apes took with them a suitable tool for getting the treat and brought it back with them after the waiting period.[12]

So, we have strong evidence that both human infants (persons) and nonhuman higher animals (nonpersons) are agents. From the definitions of "rudimentary first-person perspective" and "minimal agent," together with the thesis (AE), it follows that any entity that has a rudimentary first-person perspective—whether human or not—is a minimal agent.[13] I take the evidence about human infants and chimpanzees to give empirical content to my definitions.

---

11. Thanks to Gareth B. Matthews for showing me this source.
12. The apes "selected, transported, and saved a suitable tool not because they currently needed it, but because they would need it in the future."
13. Here is the argument:
    1. If x has a rudimentary first-person perspective, then x is able to engage in behavior adequately explainable only by attribution of beliefs, desires, and intentions. (by definition of "rudimentary first-person perspective")

In short, entity x is a minimal agent if and only if x has a rudimentary first-person perspective; x is a rational agent only if x has a robust first-person perspective, and x is a moral agent only if x has a robust first-person perspective. Since all rational and moral agents have robust first-person perspectives, all rational and moral agents are persons.

So, all beings with rudimentary first-person perspectives are minimal agents, and all beings with robust first-person perspectives are rational and/or moral agents. All persons are agents, but not all agents (e.g., nonhuman animals) are persons; all rational and moral agents are persons, but not all persons (e.g., human infants) are rational and moral agents.

Although a bit nonstandard, this view of agency remains a broadly causal view. Rejecting the idea that actions are events caused by neural events, I believe that a causal view based on a commonsense notion of causation can accommodate the first-personal aspects of agency. (Here I differ from Anscombe.) The commonsense idea of causation is of ordinary objects' having effects in virtue of bearing certain properties: The cook's adding peanuts to the sauce caused the guest's allergic reaction. There are countless causal verbs whose application entails causal transactions: "attract," "tear apart," "open," "remove," "enlarge," and so on. The root idea of commonsense causation is *making something happen*. To cause is to bring about, to produce, to give rise to something. I'll return to this point in Chapter 10.

2. If x is able to engage in behavior adequately explainable only by attribution of beliefs, desire, and intentions, then x is able to engage in practical (means-end) reasoning. (by PR)
3. If x is able to engage in practical (means-end) reasoning, then x is a minimal agent. (by definition of "minimal agent")
∴4. If x has a rudimentary first-person perspective, then x is a minimal agent. (by 1,2,3: $p \to q$; $q \to r$; $r \to s$; ∴$p \to s$)

All causation is event-causation, but, unlike Davidson, I do not take events to be particulars. As I mentioned earlier, like Kim, I take an event to be an object's having a property at a time: "x's having F at t." But unlike Kim, I take the relation between motivating reasons and action to be causal.

My view of commonsense causation, based on property-constitution, is not Humean, or even nomological. Causation is the exercise of causal powers: It is a relation whereby x's having F at t brings about y's having G at t'. For example, my writing you a good recommendation may bring about your getting a job. This (nonreductive) conception allows intentional phenomena (like someone's writing a recommendation) to have causal efficacy. Upper-level causal events (like someone's writing a recommendation) are not reducible to lower-level causal events (like someone's being in a certain bodily state).

Upper- and lower-level causal events are related by constitution, which is a nonreductive relation. For example, (1) Smith's voting for the school-budget at t had the effect of breaking the tie, (2) Smith's voting for the school budget at t would have had the effect of breaking the tie even if its constituting property-instance (raising his hand) had been different (even if the vote had been taken orally), and (3) Smith's voting for the school-budget at t had conferred causal powers (being a tie-breaker) that could not have been conferred by its constituting property-instance alone (simply raising one's hand does not make one a tie-breaker). (Baker 2007a, Ch. 5)

I join commonsense in supposing that intentional events generally have causal efficacy. For example, A's praising B makes B feels good. (Only a philosopher would doubt such quotidian causal transactions.)[14] If intentional events have causal efficacy, then

---

14. See Chapter 10 for a definition of "independent causal efficacy."

intentional explanations generally are causal explanations; and as I argued earlier, intentional explanations of actions are explanatory in virtue of their connection to an agent's (perhaps primitive) practical reasoning from a first-person perspective. Even a rabbit that sees danger to the left and hops away to the right believes of a certain location that there is danger there, and wants to avoid the danger; and so, hops in the other direction. What connects the rabbit's attitudes to her hopping away is her rudimentary first-person perspective: The danger is believed to be relative to the rabbit's own location (but not conceptualized as such by the rabbit), and the rabbit hops in a direction away from the danger.

In sum, I want to make two claims about ordinary intentional explanations of action: (1) They are causal and (2) they presuppose that agents whose actions they explain have first-person perspectives (rudimentary or robust). The rabbit's belief, coupled with her desire to survive, moves the rabbit to hop in a certain direction; Smith's desire to pass the school budget, coupled with relevant beliefs, motivates her to vote as she does. *Moving* and *motivating* are causal concepts: the attitudes that move and motivate entities have independent causal efficacy. In the second place, both actions presuppose that the agent reasons from a first-person perspective (either rudimentary or robust). An entity with an exclusively third-personal outlook could not be moved or motivated to do anything. The rabbit would not be moved to hop away unless she located the danger relative to her position from her first-person point of view; Smith would not be motivated to vote for the school budget if she* wanted to defeat it. See Perry (1979) and Perry (2002).

Although standard causal theories of action do not capture the first-personal aspects of agency, reasons may yet be causes. In order to explain actions, reasons must be entertained from a first-person point of view. Intentional explanations of action are conceptually tied to practical reasoning, and all practical reasoning is from a first-person perspective. So we need to respect the first-personal role of reasons in a way that allows them to have causal efficacy. On a property-constitution account of causation—one that allows reasons to be constituted by, but not identical to, neural phenomena—reasons may be both first personal and causal. So, the view of agency on offer here is a causal view that automatically includes first-personal aspects of agency.[15]

ARTIFACTS

Artifacts presuppose agency. Since I have discussed artifacts at length elsewhere (Baker 2004; 2007a), here I'll just briefly say that the primary kind of an artifact is determined by what it was intended to do; an artifact has its intended function as an essential property, whether it ever performs its intended function or not. (Often you can just read off the intended function from the name of the kind: polisher, scraper, life preserver.) The intended function is determined by the intentions of the maker, designer, or user of the artifact. I have argued that intentions are not just causally necessary for there to be an artifact, but they are ontologically necessary: the object that is an artifact would not exist if there were no intentions. In the case of manufactured artifacts, this is obvious: There would not be fluorescent lightbulbs in a world without intentions. (If, improbably, a physical duplicate of a fluorescent lightbulb just coalesced in outer space, it would not itself be a fluorescent lightbulb.)

15. There is much more to be said about the exact relation between first-person perspectives and causal explanations, but I can't pursue these further issues here. I thank Gareth B. Matthews for comments on drafts of this chapter.

Designers of a manufacturing process must be aware of what they* are doing—and hence have robust first-person perspectives. Even if an assembly line were fully automated, someone must have intended it to be so and someone must have intentionally designed the robots. Someone must have known what they* were doing, or thought that they knew what they* were doing in order to design an automated assembly line, or in order to design robots that could produce robots that could design an automated assembly line. Hence, robust first-person perspectives are presupposed in manufacturing artifacts.

However, not all artifacts presuppose that there are robust first-person perspectives. Nonhuman animals, with only rudimentary first-person perspectives, also produce artifacts. Here are two obvious examples: birds build nests, and some nonhuman primates insert thin sticks into holes to get out edible insects inside. In the latter case, the natural stick comes to constitute an implement, an artifact, by the intentional use made of it.

The existence of any artifact at all presupposes a maker, designer, or user with a first-person perspective, either rudimentary or robust, who bestowed on it its intended function. Hence first-person perspectives contribute vastly to the world as we know and interact with it—populated with automobiles, computers, air conditioners, condominiums, silverware, sculptures, music synthesizers.

Artifacts are no less "real" than natural objects like pebbles or possums. The fact that we produce them does not diminish their ontological status any more does the fact that mere chemicals produce reproducing organisms diminish the ontological status of organisms that reproduce. We persons are as much a part of reality as chemicals, or microparticles for that matter. Hence, what we produce is fully real. We do not intervene in nature; we can't. We are part of nature, and so are our first-person perspectives. Hence, what is produced with the necessary help of those first-person perspectives is as genuine as what is produced by natural selection. So, part of the contribution of first-person perspectives to reality are artifacts. And in our contemporary world dominated by technology, artifacts are far from insignificant.

MORAL RESPONSIBILITY

Not only do artifacts presuppose agency, but in a different part of the spectrum of reality, so does moral responsibility. Since moral responsibility presupposes agency, and agency requires a first-person perspective, it is easy to conclude that moral responsibility requires a first-person perspective.

Harry Frankfurt, who will provide my starting point, has elaborated on the conditions for moral responsibility. He offers a hierarchical view of the will: We not only have first-order desires; we also have second-order desires. (Frankfurt, 1971) We not only want to do certain things; we also want to want certain things, to be moved by certain desires. A person's will is the desire which actually motivates him: To will X is to have an effective desire to choose or do X, a desire that moves one to choose or to do X. If one has the will that one wants to have (if, that is, one is moved by the desire that one wants to move one), then on Frankfurt's view, one has (compatibilist) free will.[16]

One important feature of Frankfurt's view of the hierarchical will that has gone largely unremarked is that it requires that the agent have a first-person perspective. A person must be able to conceive of her desires *as her own*—in the first person—if she

---

16. Frankfurt himself holds that freedom of the will, although compatible with determinism, is not required for moral responsibility. What is at stake in this discussion, however, are sufficient conditions for moral responsibility.

is to desire to have a certain desire. If Sally wants to be moved by a certain desire, then she wants that she* herself (considered from the first-person) be moved by that desire. To want that someone who is in fact herself be moved by that desire is not enough. If I can make the distinction between wanting that I* (myself) be moved by a certain desire and wanting that S (where "S" is a third-person name for me) be moved by that desire, then I have a robust first-person perspective. See Chapter 2. As we shall see, only beings with robust first-person perspectives can be morally responsible.

On my view, as is obvious by now, a first-person perspective is the defining characteristic of persons.[17] The importance of the first-person perspective for moral responsibility is that it gives us limited control over our desires. Our ancestors, with only rudimentary first-person perspectives, were pushed around by their beliefs and desires. A lion does not consider whether it is a good idea to attack a gazelle. An omnivore (e.g., a hippopotamous) does not decide to become a vegetarian; only people can decide that they* should not eat meat. A first-person perspective makes it possible for us, unlike the other animals, to discover what goals we have, to evaluate them and to try to change them. Animals without robust first-person perspectives do not have this control: they act on their desires, but they cannot set about changing them. But persons can even interfere with biological goals of survival and reproduction. To a significant extent, a person can know what desires she has: She approves of some and is repelled by others. We have partial control, albeit limited by the kinds of people we already are, over our desires. Our partial control is manifest in our (sometimes successful) efforts to change. Yet, such effort—which

---

17. On my view, the first-person perspective is not just a pragmatic feature of language that can be understood just in terms of indexicals. (Baker 2000) It cannot be assimilated to Perry's important work on the essential indexical. (Perry 1979)

is limited by our heredity, environment, experience, even by our insight and imagination—is itself a product of factors beyond our ultimate control.

This partial control over our desires has the consequence that, even if determinism is true, we are not mere conduits for causes beyond our control. Because of our first-person perspectives, we can consider reasons that we have and choose to act on them. We can bring to bear a desire to change our desires to modify our first-order desires that produce our intentions; in this way we can help shape the causes of what we do. We can decide to try to be one kind of person rather than another, to be generous rather than stingy, say. Attention to the robust first-person perspective should make us reject any sharp line between being ultimate originators or mere puppets. We can try to become more like the people that we want to be—even if our wanting to become a certain kind of person, along with the trying itself, is ultimately caused by factors beyond our control.

The first-person perspective cannot be acquired by neural manipulation—any more than a disposition to be honest or to be a good historian or to have any other intentional disposition that requires good judgment. I am supposing that a person at t (when he is not actually reading French) may have the ability to read French without there being anything in his brain at t that makes it the case that a person can read French. I doubt that putting the brain in a given state is ever sufficient for having an intentional disposition. Someone can have a robust first-person perspective only if he has consciousness and has had many kinds of intentional states. Moreover, distinct first-person perspectives may be qualitatively similar.

Frankfurt's conditions for moral responsibility clearly require a first-person perspective: "Suppose that a person has done what he wanted to do, that he did it because he wanted to do it, and that the will by which he was moved when he did it was his will because it was the will he wanted." (Frankfurt 1971, 19) Then, if one "identifies" (Frankfurt's word) oneself with a first-order desire that motivates one to do X, then, at least prima facie, one is responsible for doing X.

Every piece of this account requires a robust first-person perspective. Continuing to use a "*" to mark our attribution to the agent of a robust first-person perspective: S's doing what he* wanted to do, S's doing it because he* wanted to, S's having the will that he* wanted to have, S's identifying himself* (not equivalent to S's identifying S) with a first-order desire that motivated him—all these are manifestations of a robust first-person perspective. So, Frankfurt's conditions for moral responsibility require that the agent have a robust first-person perspective.

Suppose that in addition to satisfying Frankfurt's conditions, the agent endorsed her desires, knowing that they resulted from things that happened before she was born; suppose that she identified herself ("Yeah, that's me, ok") with the factors beyond her control that contributed to her desires and beliefs. More precisely, the condition that I want to add to Frankfurt's conditions is this:

(1) S has the capacity to consider the sources of her* desires.
(2) If (i) S had known that her* wanting to will X had causal antecedents that traced back to factors beyond her* control, and

  (ii) S had known of the causal antecedents that traced back to factors beyond her* control that they were in the causal history of her* wanting to will X and that they were beyond her* control, then:

S still would have: willed X and wanted to will X and willed X because she* wanted to will X.

I shall abbreviate this cumbersome extra twofold condition by this: "S would still have wanted to will X even if she* had known the provenance of her wanting to will X" and label it condition (4) in (RE). Now we have compatibilist conditions for free will, which, I submit, become sufficient conditions for moral responsibility. I'll call this view the Reflective-Endorsement view:

(RE) A person S is morally responsible for a choice or action X if X occurs and:

(1) S wills X,

(2) S wants that she* will X [i.e., S wants to will X],

(3) S wills X because she* wants to will X, and

(4) S would still have wanted to will X even if she had known the provenance of her* wanting to will X.

Conditions (2)—(4) each require that S have a robust first-person perspective. Moreover, these conditions are compatible with the truth of determinism. The causal histories of S's desires and willings may be traceable to factors outside of S's control. Even if S could have done otherwise, she would not have done otherwise. Since "the will that moved her when she acted was her will because she wanted it to be, she cannot claim that her will was forced upon her or that she was a passive bystander to its constitution."[18]

As an illustration of the (RE) or Reflective-Endorsement view, consider the real-life case of Bobby Frank Cherry, who was convicted in the bombing that killed four black Sunday School girls in a church in Birmingham in 1963. Suppose that Cherry (i) willed to participate in the bombing. As a convinced white supremacist (who apparently bragged of his participation), he (ii) wanted to will

18. Frankfurt 1971, 19. I changed the pronouns to feminine in order to make the sentence grammatically parallel to (i)–(iv).

to participate, and he (iii) willed to participate because he wanted to. He (iv) would still be proud of his participation, and would participate again, even though he knew that his wanting to will to participate in the bombing had been caused by his racist upbringing. ("Damn right," he might have said, "and I'm bringing up my boys the same way.") It seems to me obvious that he was morally responsible for his participation in the bombing. He was moved by the desire (to bomb the black church) that he wanted to be moved by. Cherry satisfies (1)—(4) of (RE), and (I believe that) we properly find him morally responsible.

A basic conviction—shared by both libertarian and compatibilist—is that moral responsibility concerns the agent in a deep way. An agent is morally responsible for an action if he *endorses* the beliefs and desires on which he acts: When he affirms them as his own (and makes no factual errors about the circumstances, etc.), he is morally responsible for acting on them. Whereas the libertarian is concerned that a morally responsible agent have (impossible) control over factors that contribute to what he wills, the compatibilist is concerned that a morally responsible agent endorse and align himself* with what he wills. Doing what we want to do, with reflective endorsement, is all the control that we have, and that's enough.

If I can say, "These desires reflect who I am, and this is the kind of person that I want to be," then I am morally responsible for acting on those desires—whether determinism is true or not. I have (nonultimate) control of what I do if, in the absence of psychopathology like kleptomania, I deliberate and make an uncoerced decision to do it.[19] Unlike the libertarian, the compatibilist does not

19. The conditions of the Reflective Endorsement view may be regarded as ways to accommodate Aristotelian defeating conditions of voluntariness: ignorance, compulsion, reduced capacity, and the like. One reason not to focus on Aristotle in the debate over compatibilism is that his view has been claimed by both compatibilists and libertarians.

think that external causes of decisions or actions per se threaten moral responsibility; moral responsibility is precluded only by certain kinds of external causes—those that bypass the agent's own psychological contribution involving his first-person perspective. By focusing on the first-person perspective, a compatibilist can agree with the libertarian to this extent: Being morally responsible has to do with the agent in a deep way, not just with an external series of causes. Reflective Endorsement offers a *via media* between a (physically dubious) libertarianism, and a (morally hopeless) hard determinism.[20]

CONCLUSION

After arguing in earlier chapters that first-person properties are neither reducible nor eliminable, in this chapter I have surveyed an assortment of ways that the first-person perspective actually contributes to reality. Some of the contributions concern only the robust first-person perspective and hence are specific to persons. These include differences between persons and animals, presuppositions of rational and moral agency, requirements for artifacts, and conditions for moral responsibility.

As William James famously said, "The trail of the human serpent is over everything." (James 1948/1907, 150) The trail that the human serpent leaves is largely the fruit of the robust first-person perspective.

---

20. Derk Pereboom (2001) has offered an influential slippery-slope argument against compatibilism, which I try to rebut in Baker (2006).

Chapter Ten

Natural Reality

Naturalism gave us a handle on natural reality. Natural reality includes entities and properties that came into being through the purposeless processes of nature or that came into being through the purposeful intentions of human beings.[1] So, one might ask at this point, if scientific naturalism cannot accommodate the first-person perspective, how should we regard natural reality? In this chapter, I try to answer this question by removing some of the a priori (and otherwise unsupported) principles that have blocked development of a more credible view than scientific naturalism.

NEAR-NATURALISM

The view that I shall outline and tentatively endorse may be called "near-naturalism": It is naturalistic in the weak sense of bracketing questions about anything supernatural. (If God created the world, he created it to be intelligible to human beings on its own terms.)

---

1. By speaking of "natural reality" this way, I definitely intend to include artifacts and artworks—which would not exist in a world without entities with first-person perspectives—within the scope of natural reality. (Baker 2004)

However, the important differences between my near-naturalism and scientific naturalism are several:

(1) Scientific naturalism is a metaphysical view that takes what I'm calling "natural reality" to be the whole of reality; near-naturalism is a metaphysical view limited to natural reality and is quiet about anything transcendent. So, the domains of scientific naturalism and of near-naturalism are the same, (i.e., natural reality). However, scientific naturalism imposes a closure principle on natural reality, while near-naturalism does not. My view leaves open the question of whether natural reality is all that there is. (Scientific naturalists, like the old cartoon character, cheerfully tip their hats and say, "That's all, folks!")

(2) Unlike scientific naturalism, near-naturalism incorporates the first-person perspective as ineliminable and irreducible, and thus as part of fundamental reality; it is a (dispositional) property belonging in ontology.

(3) Near-naturalism is a form of practical realism (Baker 2000; 2007a). Practical realism takes the world of medium-sized objects—persons, animals, and artifacts—to be basic entities, as genuine as electrons. While accepting science,[2] near-naturalism does not take science to be the exclusive arbiter of reality. It aims to be a metaphysics of the commonsense world that we all encounter and interact with everyday.

Since naturalism, with no room for the first-person perspective, is incomplete, we will have to modify naturalism in order to allow it to accommodate the first-person perspective. We must acknowledge

---

2. To say that I accept science is to say that I take any established claim of any of the sciences to be either true or to be subject to further investigation. It is not to say that I am beholden to any particular philosophical interpretation of such claims.

the first-person perspective in the ontology. But I think that we should do more. I am going to argue for an expansive view of natural reality, which, I believe, De Caro and Voltolini could easily fold into their liberal naturalism if they were so inclined. (De Caro and Voltolini 2010)

PROPERTY-CONSTITUTION AND CAUSATION

My aim here is to use a notion of property-constitution to sketch a picture that allows irreducible higher-level properties to be causally efficacious. First, a couple of caveats: (1) I call this "an account" because others—for example, Derk Pereboom (2011)— has a somewhat different account of property-constitution. (2) Although I say "property-constitution," it is not literally properties themselves that are constituted, but property-instances. A property-instance is a thing's exemplifying having a property at a time. I do not take a white thing (e.g., the Taj Mahal) to be a property-instance of whiteness. (So I do not follow van Inwagen's usage. (Van Inwagen 2005, 121) I take property-instances to be property-exemplifications, schematically, " x's having F at t."[3] Property-constitution is a time-indexed relation between property-exemplifications. (I follow Kim and not Davidson on events: An event is an object's having a property at a time; an event is not a particular.) Property-constitution of contingent properties is a contingent relation: If x's having F at t constitutes x's having G at t, then it is possible that x could have F at t and not constitute x's having G at t. Whether or not constitution obtains depends in large measure on the circumstances. For example, in some

---

3. Property-constitution is analogous to the idea that I developed in Baker (2000) for understanding material objects in terms of what I simply called "constitution."

circumstances, raising one's hand to one's forehead constitutes a salute, and in other circumstances it does not.

Let me begin with some commonsensical ideas that I have worked out more rigorously elsewhere. (Baker 2007a) First, we have a notion of different levels of reality. Whether there is a fundamental level or not, subatomic particles are at a lower level than atoms, which are at a lower level than molecules, and so on. Although there is no single ordering of levels, we can be confident that a bodily motion is at a lower level than an intentional action. I'll return to this point in a later section; for now, I'll take it for granted that there are different levels of reality.[4]

Property-constitution is the relation between property-instances at different levels: In certain circumstances, a mereological sum of water molecules constitutes (but is not identical to) a tidal wave at time t. Constitution obtains only in certain circumstances; the very same mereological sum of water molecules scattered all over the world would not constitute a tidal wave. The mereological sum of water molecules exists as long as those very water molecules exist, but there is a tidal wave only in circumstances of rapidly moving water molecules. The tidal wave is on a higher level than the sum of water molecules that constitutes it at t.

To take another example, before the days of electric turn-indicators in cars, one signaled that one was going to turn left by extending one's arm straight out the left window. In certain circumstances, my extending my arm out the left window at t constitutes my signaling that I am going to turn left at t. In other circumstances when, say, I am driving a visitor past my favorite barn, my extending my arm at t constitutes my pointing at t. In still other circumstances, when I'm driving alone on a country road idly moving

---

4. Unlike Chalmers and many others, I take levels to be ontological, not just different levels of description or abstraction. (Chalmers 1996, 179)

my arm out the left window, my extending my arm at t constitutes nothing at t. The phenomenon of property-constitution is heavily dependent on the circumstances.[5]

I call the circumstances in which an instance of F can constitute an instance of G "G-favorable circumstances." For example, in circumstances in which someone is aiming a loaded, well-functioning pistol with the safety off at an intruder, his pulling the trigger constitutes a shooting. In other circumstances (e.g., the safety is on), pulling the trigger is not a shooting. The addition of an appropriate F (pulling the trigger) to G-favorable circumstances (aiming a loaded, well-functioning gun with the safety off at an intruder) guarantees that there is an instance of G (a shooting). A siren in certain circumstances constitutes an all-clear signal. An arm motion in certain circumstances constitutes a salute.

Property-instances are individuated in such a way that the same property-instance could have occurred in different circumstances. Suppose that x's shooting a target at t is constituted by x's pulling the trigger at t in appropriate circumstances, and suppose that x pulls the trigger with her middle finger. Now consider a slightly different situation in which all the circumstances remain the same and the gun is aimed in the same way, but x pulls the trigger with her forefinger and the gun still hits its target in the same place. In this alternative case, there would have been the same shooting at t, but it would have been constituted by a different trigger-pulling. Any G-instance (a shooting) must be in G-favorable circumstances, but if a G-instance (x's shooting at t) is constituted by a different F-instance (x's pulling the trigger at t), the exact same shooting

5. For a definition and a more rigorous discussion of the relation of property-constitution, see Baker (2007a, 113–14). When I use the term "the property-constitution view," I refer to my version of a property-constitution view. Others, for example, Derk Pereboom, have equal claim to the label, but his and my views differ; my nonreductivism is more robust than his, but his physicalism is more robust than mine. See Baker (forthcoming.)

would have a different constituter. (This is analogous to the notion of token-constitution, where a single token event may be constituted by various lower-level events, defended in Pereboom and Kornblith (1991).)

The relation of property-constitution has an important consequence: if x's having F at t constitutes x's having G at t, then x's having G at t cannot be reduced to x's having F at t. The constituted event is irreducible to the constituting event. Why? Because constitution obtains only when certain relevant circumstances obtain. Batting a ball over a fence constitutes a home run only in the context of a baseball game. Lying constitutes perjury only when the liar is under oath. The motion of a piece of paper into an opening constitutes putting a $20 bill in a slot only in certain circumstances (e.g., the opening is a slot in a machine), and putting a $20 bill in a slot constitutes buying a Metro ticket only in certain further circumstances (e.g., the machine is a Metro machine that accepts $20 bills).

In each case, there is no constitution in the absence of the relevant circumstances. It follows that the mere occurrence of a lower-level event does not necessitate any higher-level event. The emphasis on circumstances of constitution prevents reduction of a constituted event to its constituter. It further follows that higher-level constituted events are irreducible to their constituting events.

Now the question is, Are higher-level irreducible constituted events causally efficacious? I think that we must answer in the affirmative, if we are to make sense of the world that we interact with. Hitting a home run changes the score; committing perjury often results in a felony charge; buying a Metro ticket allows you to ride on the Metro.

I'll make the point about the causal efficacy of constituted events in greater detail by an example to show that (1) irreducible constituted events have causal powers, and (2) the causal powers of irreducible constituted events exceed the causal powers of their constituters.[6]

Suppose that one evening Jones pays his electric bill. Jones's paying his electric bill has certain causal powers—for example, it preserves his credit rating. Jones's fingers moving in a certain way also has causal powers—for example, the power to bring on arthritis pain whether Jones was paying his bill or not. If Jones's fingers had moved in the way that they did in other circumstances not conducive to paying electric bills (say, plonking on a piano), their moving would not have had the effect of preserving Jones's credit rating. And conversely, if Jones had paid his electric bill in some other way than by moving his fingers as he did, Jones's paying the bill still would have preserved his credit rating. Jones's paying the bill would have preserved his credit rating—no matter how he paid the bill (by mail, online, in person with a debit card, or some other way). In short, the causal efficacy of constituted property-instances (Jones's paying his electric bill) does not depend on which event constituted Jones's paying his electric bill. The property-constitution view thus shows how irreducible higher-level properties make a causal contribution to what happens.[7] Let's look more closely:

Let: V be Jones's paying his electric bill at t.

P be Jones's fingers moving in a certain way at t.

---

6. Some other nonreductionists (Fodor 1974; Kornblith 1994; Clapp 2001; Pereboom 2002) have a less hearty view of causal powers from mine. Mild reductionists take all causal powers to emanate from a micro-level. I do not endorse this "the trickle-up theory" of causation.

7. The property-constitution view also shows how constituted objects differ in their nonderivative causal powers from their constituters. As we have just seen, Jones's paying his electric bill is constituted by Jones's fingers moving in a certain way. Jones has the property of paying his bill nonderivatively; the motion of his fingers, which constitutes his paying his bill, is at best a derivative cause: the finger motion has the effect of giving Jones relief only because it constitutes his paying his bill. So, Jones has different nonderivative causal powers (e.g., paying a bill) from Jones's body, which can only

V* be Jones's relief as he finishes at t'.

P* be Jones's neural state at t'.

C be circumstances that obtain for paying bills at t.

Suppose that V is constituted by P at t and that V* is constituted by P* at t'. We already know that V is causally efficacious; so suppose that V causes V*. We also already know that P is causally efficacious (it can cause arthritis pain). We also know that P is not sufficient for V since in piano-playing circumstances, P would not constitute V. V could not occur in the absence of the circumstances surrounding paying electric bills, but P could occur in all manner of circumstances, including many in which P would not constitute anything. V would result in preserving Jones's credit rating no matter what constituted it. So, the causal powers of V cannot be reduced to those of P. Therefore, not only do irreducible higher-level properties have causal powers, but also they have causal powers that cannot be accounted for by the causal powers of their constituters.

The potential constituters of an instance of G may have nothing in common, other than their suitability to constitute an instance of G in various circumstances.[8] For example, a single instance of the property of accepting a job offer may be constituted by sending an email, making a phone call, sending a letter by snail-mail, or yelling "yes" at the boss, or something else.[9] There is no general answer to the question of how much latitude there is among potential lower-level property-instances that may constitute a single higher-level

derivatively pay bills in virtue of constituting something that nonderivatively pays bills. I discuss the idea of having properties (non)derivatively in detail in Baker (2007a).

8. This feature distinguishes my idea of property-constitution from ideas of constitution found in Pereboom (2002) and in Clapp (2001).

9. For a defense of this claim, see Pereboom and Kornblith (1991). Suppose that a particular thought of yours at t was constituted by a particular brain state; if you had earlier eaten something that in the course of things ended up in your brain as part of the constituting brain state, it would be wrong to say that, in that case, you would have had a different thought "token."

property-instance. My only point is that there is some latitude: A constituted property-instance may have any of a variety of different kinds of nonintentional constituters, and there may be no physical similarities among the potential constituters.[10]

Some nonreductionists (e.g., Kornblith, personal communication) may object that, despite the physical heterogeneity of the constituters of Jones's bill-paying, the potential constituters all have a property in common which accounts for the causal-efficacy of Jones's bill-paying; and in that case, Jones's bill-paying does not have independent causal efficacy after all. Well, what might the constituters' common property be? Given the wide range of events that could constitute Jones's bill-paying, the only property that I can think of that the constituters might share is the property picked out by "causes relief" or "causes relief in the circumstances." But a constituting property picked out by "causes relief in the circumstances" is wholly uninformative ("E is caused by the event that caused E") and ad hoc.

If our best efforts to find a shared property among the potential constituters yield no more than a property expressible only as a tautology, then there is no reason to think that the range of events of would-be constituters of Jones's paying his bill must have anything at all in common that would account for Jones's relief. Recall how

---

10. This is a point that distinguishes my view of constitution from other views. For example, my view differs from Pereboom's in Pereboom (2002) in several important ways. Most significantly, (1) Pereboom suggests that causal powers are instances of intrinsic properties (Pereboom 2011, 128) (2) Pereboom takes the relation between levels to be realization, where a realizer is nomologically sufficient for the realized property. (3) Pereboom takes the causal powers of the realized property to be determined by ("constituted by") those of the realizer. I differ on all scores: (1') Assuming that causal powers derive from properties in virtue of which something has an effect, I take almost all intentional causal powers to be relational. (2') I take the relation between levels to be constitution, where a constituter is *not* nomologically sufficient for the constituted property, and (3') I take the causal efficacy of intention-dependent properties *not* to be determined by their constituters. For an explanation of intention-dependence, see Baker (2007a, 11–13).

disparate are the events in the range of the would-be constituters. To suppose that there *must* be something common to the disparate properties that would account for Jones's relief seems tantamount to postulating a ghost in the machine. So, the heterogeneity of the would-be constituters of Jones's paying his bill gives us reason to suppose that they have no property in common that accounts for the effect of the causal event. Hence, we should not suppose that the would-be constituters have in common some elusive constituting property—much less a constituting physical property—that accounts for the effect of giving Jones relief.

We can summarize this discussion of the causal efficacy of irreducible higher-level properties by setting out a principle of Independent Causal Efficacy.

(ICE) An irreducible higher-level property-instance (x's having F at t) has independent causal efficacy if and only if

(1) x's having F at t has an effect e, and

(2) x's having F at t would have had the effect e even if its constituting property-instance had been different, and

(3) x's having F at t confers causal powers that could not have been conferred by its constituting property-instance alone.

If constituted properties-instances have independent causal efficacy, then they do not inherit their causal powers from their constituters. Any property whose instances have independent causal efficacy is a genuine causal property.

Let me conclude this section with a brief contrast between Jaegwon Kim's view of causation and mine. On his view, higher-level properties must be reducible to have causal efficacy. (Kim 2000a; 2005) Consider first Kim's Causal Inheritance Principle, according to which higher-level property-instances. inherit their causal powers from low-level property-instances (Kim 1993, 326) I suggest replacing the Causal Inheritance Principle with my principle of Independent Causal Efficacy. On my view, constituted property-instances confer causal powers that are "over and above" the causal powers of their constituters. The advantage of ICE over Kim's Causal Inheritance Principle is that ICE allows irreducible higher-level properties to be causally efficacious—just as they seem to be.

Another of Kim's principles that my view may be thought to violate is the Causal-Closure Principle.[11] The Causal-Closure Principle says, roughly, that any physical event that has a cause at t has a complete physical cause at t. On my view, all property-instances are physical in this respect: any property-instance is either identical to or ultimately *constituted by* microphysical property-instances.[12] Higher-level properties—even mental properties—thus are physical properties. So, the causal efficacy of higher-level properties does not violate the Causal-Closure Principle.

Someone may object that higher-level properties as I have construed them are not really physical properties that conform to the Causal-Closure Thesis: the only physical properties are microphysical or "micro-based properties" that are just aggregates of micro-physical properties. (Kim 2000a, 114) Even so, the property-constitution view would not violate the Causal-Closure Principle.

Consider a case of basic action: Suppose that Ms. Smith is being introduced to the Queen. Smith wills[13] to curtsy (M) and she

---

11. I have detailed rebuttals of Kim's Causal-Closure argument elsewhere (Baker 2007a, 2009). Here I just want to show the benefits of using the notion of property-constitution instead of supervenience for the relation between properties at different levels.

12. If there is no fundamental level, then property-instances have no *ultimate* constituters at all. Here I am assuming that we will still count a microphysical cause as a *complete* cause, even if, in the absence of a fundamental level, there is no *ultimate* cause.

13. I am using "will" as an all-purpose term that covers choosing, deciding, forming an intention for the immediate future. "Will" carries no metaphysical weight here.

curtsies (M*). Curtsying may seem far afield from science, but not if you include sociology as a science; in any case, since I am trying to show that near-naturalism that does not violate the Causal-Closure Thesis, I am entitled to appeal to sociology.

Suppose that Smith's willing to curtsy causes her to curtsy. Let MP be the microphysical constituter of Smith's willing to curtsy and let MP* be the microphysical constituter of Smith's curtsying. (Note that the relations between MP and M, on the one hand, and MP* and M*, on the other hand, are instances of my constitution relation, not of Kim's realization relation, which is a supervenience relation.)

On the property-constitution view, the microphysical *constituter* of Smith's willing to curtsy (MP) is not a complete cause of the microphysical constituter of Smith's curtsying (MP*). To see that (MP) is not nomologically sufficient for (MP*), consider a world with the same laws as ours in which Smith's brain is in a vat in the same microphysical state that it is in the example. In that world, (MP) would not cause (MP*), because in that world Smith doesn't have legs to bend. Hence, (MP) is not nomologically sufficient for (MP*). Moreover, since curtsying is a social action, no microphysical state of a person's brain could be the complete cause of her curtsying: For something to be a curtsy, various social conditions must be satisfied.

So, there are multiple reasons for denying that (MP) is a complete cause of (MP*). Still, there is no violation of the Causal-Closure Principle.[14] The Causal-Closure Principle requires only that MP* *have* a complete microphysical cause, not that MP *be* that complete cause of MP*.

On the property-constitution view, the relation between M and MP is not supervenience, but constitution. At best, MP is

---

14. I am not endorsing the Causal-Closure Principle; I'm only pointing out that my view of property-constitution does not contravene it.

only a proper part of a larger collection of microproperties that is nomologically sufficient for MP*.[15] There is no difficulty for the property-constitution view in saying: (1) Smith's willing to curtsy is constituted by MP; (2) Smith's curtsying is constituted by MP*; (3) Smith's willing to curtsy causes her to curtsy; but (4) MP does not cause MP*. So, one can deny that the micro-constituter of a willing to curtsy (MP) completely causes the micro-constituter of a curtsying (MP*) without violating the Causal-Closure Principle.

If the microphysical state of one sizable spatiotemporal region that ends at the time of Smith's willing causes the microphysical state of a slightly later sizable region that begins at the time of Smith's curtsying, then the Causal-Closure Principle is honored.[16] But note that there is no "global constitution" analogous to global supervenience, nor does constitution (unlike supervenience) invite worries about overdetermination. The point here is this: Although the property-constitution view does not require MP to be causally sufficient for MP*, the property-constitution view nevertheless does not violate the Causal-Closure Principle.[17]

One last question about the property-constitution view of near-naturalism: What is the relation between constitution and supervenience? Although constitution is not itself a supervenience relation, constitution is compatible with global, or near-global, supervenience. Although a constituted property-instance does not supervene on its constituting property-instances, it may supervene ultimately on its subatomic constituters *together with* the

---

15. Compare Noordhof (1999); Segal and Sober (1991); Lowe (1993).
16. There is much more to be said about the Causal Closure Principle. Kim holds that physicalism "need not be, and should not be, identified with micro-physicalism." In that case, if we disentangle the Causal Closure Principle from the thesis of mereological supervenience, my near-naturalism satisfies the Causal-Closure Principle. See Kim (2000a, 117).
17. We may still have a harmless kind of overdetermination. But note that the overdetermination is generated by the whole supervenience base, not by the constituter.

microphysical supervenience base of all the circumstances in which the instance of the constitution relation obtains.[18] The supervenience base will be very broad—too broad to be specified or to be useful in explanation—but it may be metaphysically sufficient for the constituted property-instance. So, there is no logical conflict between global supervenience and the property-constitution view.[19]

Thus the notion of property-constitution, as I construe it, provides a version of near-naturalism that does not violate the causal-closure thesis, despite the fact that the causal efficacy of higher-level property-instances cannot be reduced to the causal efficacy of their constituters. Moreover, if near-naturalism is correct, then the relation between properties at different levels is constitution and not supervenience. Property-constitution does not have the disastrous causal consequences of strong supervenience.

EMERGENTISM AND DOWNWARD CAUSATION

I endorse two (more?) unpopular views: ontological emergence and downward causation. I am committed to there being causally efficacious emergent properties that are not reducible to a single fundamental level of microphysics. These causally efficacious properties generate "downward causation," causation from higher to lower levels. Nonreductionism, emergence, and downward causation are a package, against which reductionists argue. (Kim 2000b)

18. Constitution is contingent and highly context-dependent; supervenience is necessary and independent of context.
19. Even if near-global supervenience is correct, I suspect that we will never come close to specifying even one supervenience base for any higher-level property. And hence, we will never come close to specifying a complete microphysical cause for any higher-level event. I take global supervenience to be explanatorily irrelevant.

There are two questions for a nonreductivist of my stripe: (1) Are emergence and downward causation objectionable? (2) Am I committed to them? I'll argue that reductivism of my stripe is committed to a certain conception of emergence and downward causation, but my conception steers clear of Kim's arguments against ontological emergence and downward-causation.

There are two recognized forms of emergence: ontological and epistemological. The ontological variety holds that emergent properties are not just surprising or unpredictable, are not entailed by local lower-level properties. Ontological emergence is to be something "objective in the world, not a phenomenon that has to do with our cognitive resources and powers." (Kim 2009, 62) (I should point out that I do not equate what is "objective in the world" with mind-independence; artifacts, which could not exist in a world without minds, are as "objective in the world" as natural objects (Baker 1995, 233–34; 2007a, 18–20).) It is ontological emergence, not epistemological emergence, which countenances unpredictable phenomena, that is at stake here.

Kim has an argument against ontological emergence. Emergent properties are supposed to be irreducible higher-level properties. First, I shall characterize levels as Kim does, and then formulate Kim's argument against a classical construal of emergence. Although I think that—given his construal of emergence—Kim's argument is successful, I shall offer a different construal of levels that supports ontological emergence. I shall proceed in three stages: Kim on Ontological Levels, Kim's Argument against Classical Emergentism, and A Way around Kim's Anti-Emergence Argument.

Kim on Ontological Levels: To show what makes one property on a higher level than another, a proponent of emergent properties (and of nonreductionism) must appeal to the notion of ontological levels. To retreat to descriptive or conceptual levels will not be enough for ontological emergence. (Kim 2000b, 320) The standard way to construe ontological levels is in terms of mereology. At the bottom level (if there is one), objects have no physically significant proper parts (Kim 2000a, 15).[20] On Kim's view, except for the bottom level (if there is one), objects at level L are mereological sums of objects at level L-1.

On a mereological-supervenient conception of levels, according to which objects at every level (above the bottom if there is one) are mereological sums of objects at preceding levels, a sum and its parts are on the same ontological level. If D is the sum of A,B, and C, then D is on the same level as A,B, and C. As Kim says,

> The series of supervenient properties, one mereologically supervenient on the next, when we go deeper and deeper into the micro, remains at the same level in the micro-macro hierarchy. (Kim 2000a, 86)

If levels are related by mereological-supervenience, then phenomena at the ostensibly lower levels entail phenomena at the ostensibly higher levels, and ostensibly higher-level properties are reducible to (ostensibly) lower-level properties. Properties reducible to level L "must belong to level L." (Kim 2000b, 319) So the hierarchy collapses. On Kim's view, there is but one ontological level.

Kim's argument against classical emergentism: The classical version that is the target of Kim's anti-emergentist argument was first formulated by the classical ontological emergentists, C. Lloyd Morgan (1923) and C.D. Broad (1925). Morgan and Broad held that a condition on emergence was supervenience. What distinguishes emergence from reduction is that an emergent property is not entailed by its subvenient base: Property F is an emergent

---

20. If there is no bottom level, there will be levels where objects have no physically significant parts.

property if and only if there are base-level conditions B, such that (i) F supervenes on B, and (ii) B does not entail F.

But now there is a problem. To put it roughly, either the supervenience base includes "bridge laws" connecting base-level phenomena to higher-level phenomena or it does not. If the base does include bridge laws, then F is deducible from (entailed by) the base-level conditions—and hence not emergent; if the base does not include bridge laws, then F does not supervene on (is not determined by) the base-level conditions—and hence, is not emergent. In neither case is F emergent in the sense of being supervenient on, but not entailed by, the base-level conditions. So, it seems that ontological emergence on this classical construal is incoherent.[21] Although Kim (2009) has a much richer argument for the same conclusion, I think that this truncated version is enough to show that Kim decisively defeats this classical version of ontological levels and with it, a certain version of emergence.

A Way around Kim's Anti-Emergence Argument: Nevertheless, the argument tells against emergence and the distinctness of ontological levels only if emergence is construed as nonentailment-plus-supervenience. We have just seen that there is an alternative to supervenience as the relation between higher- and lower-level properties: property-constitution, which can be defined without appeal to levels. (Baker 2007a, 161) The idea of constitution can now be used to give a principled (nonmereological) account of ontological levels, and of emergence.

On my view, the relation between, say, your cat and the particles that make it up at t is not identity, but constitution.[22] The property of being a cat and the property of being a certain sum of

---

21. Kim (2009) has a much richer argument for the same conclusion.
22. I have written voluminously elsewhere on my ideas of constitution. See, for example Baker (2004; 2007a; 2008). Here I want to deploy those ideas in defense of nonreductionism.

particles are fundamentally different *kinds* of properties. Neither is reducible to the other. Suppose that your cat is constituted by a certain sum of particles at t; let "S" designate that sum. Then, at t', your cat loses a few hairs; so, at t' your cat—the very same one—exists but is no longer constituted by S at t'. Constitution, unlike identity (as we have seen), is time-indexed. If x constitutes y at t, then the relation between x and y (at t) is contingent.

Integral to my idea of constitution is the notion of primary kinds. Every material object is of some primary kind essentially: An object could not come into being or continue to exist without having its primary-kind property. *Dog* is a primary kind; *mascot* is not a primary kind: Uga, the University of Georgia's mascot, could cease to be a mascot and still exist; but *dog* is Uga's primary kind: Uga could not cease to be a dog without ceasing to exist altogether. Every object has its primary-kind property esssentially. An object's primary-kind property determines what sorts of changes it can undergo and still exist, and what sorts of changes would result in its ceasing to exist altogether; that is, an object's primary-kind property determines its *de re* persistence conditions.

The basic idea of constitution is this: When things of a certain primary kind (e.g., two wooden blocks) are in certain circumstances (e.g., cylindrically shaped of unequal length, attached in a certain way), a thing of a different primary kind (a mallet)—a new object, with different persistence conditions and different causal powers—comes to exist. The mallet and the blocks are of different primary kinds, and the mallet has causal powers (e.g., the causal power to drive a nail) that the blocks do not have. If x constitutes y at t, then x and y have different primary-kind properties and y's primary-kind property is on an ontologically higher level than x's. (Baker 2007a, 236)

Because constitution depends so heavily on circumstances, the mere existence of the (sum of) the two wooden blocks is not sufficient for existence of the mallet; nor is exemplification of x's primary-kind property, *being a wooden block*, sufficient for exemplification of y's primary-kind property, *being a mallet*. Apart from the circumstances, the sum of the blocks does not constitute the mallet; apart from the circumstances, x is not sufficient for the exemplification of y's primary-kind property. Hence, x does not necessitate y.[23]

Once we have primary-kind properties and the relation of constitution on hand, we have a partial ordering of ontological levels.[24] If x constitutes y at t, then y is on an ontologically higher level than x; and y has causal powers that x does not have. If we add to this constitutional account of ontological levels the plausible hypothesis that higher-level primary kinds come into being over time, we get an ontologically robust sort of emergence. When objects of new kinds come to be constituted (by natural processes or by intentional invention), there is a new and higher level of reality. Constitution is an engine of novelty. If there is ontological novelty in the world, then there is ontological emergence of entities with new causal powers.

For example, organisms, which evolved over eons, have causal powers (e.g., ability to replicate) different from the causal powers of the sums of hydrogen, carbon, and nitrogen, oxygen, and sulfur atoms that make them up. The property of being an organism confers on its bearer causal powers that exceed those of the constituting property of being a sum of carbon, and other, atoms. The organism seeks a mate; the sum of atoms does not.

Artifacts too have causal powers beyond those of the sums of particles that make them up. For another example, a manufactured fire escape may make the difference between life and death. The fire escape has a causal power beyond that of sums of particles even

---

23. I disagree with Pereboom both on this point and on his commitment to internalism. Pereboom holds that if x constitutes y, then x necessitates y. His nonreductionism rests on his denying that y necessitates x, on account of multiple realizability of y. (Pereboom 2011) On my view of constitution, there is no necessity either way.

24. Note that I am not assuming that there is a "single monolithic and all-inclusive hierarchy of levels." (Kim 2002, 20)

though the fire escape has an intentional necessary condition for its existence. The fire escape (as opposed to a tree branch next to a window that could be used to escape a fire) had to be designed, manufactured, and/or used for a particular purpose. (Baker 2007a, 166–69)

Someone may object that the sum of particles that constitute the fire escape at t has the same causal powers that the fire escape has at t. But that is not so: The bearer of causal powers of the fire escape is the fire escape itself, but the bearer of relevant causal powers of the sum of particles that constitutes the fire escape at t can *not* be the sum itself; what may have the relevant causal power is a sum only of particles-arranged-in-a-certain-way. Particles-arranged-in-a-certain-way is a complex state of affairs, not a sum. The sum is the constituter, and the sum exists no matter how the particles are arranged. Being arranged-in-a-certain-way is not a part of the constituter, but part of the circumstances under which a sum of particles constitutes a fire escape.

Moreover, there is a further difference between the constituting sum of particles and the constituted fire escape. The fire escape has the power to save a life at t nonderivatively; the sum of the particles has that power at t only derivatively, only in virtue of the fact that their sum constitutes a fire escape at t. (Recall that to have a property only derivatively is to have it at t only in virtue of constituting or being constituted by something that has the property nonderivatively at t—by something that has the property on its own, so to speak.) The same sum (i.e., the same particles) that is in fact the constituter could exist scattered around the world; if the sum were scattered, it (the same sum) would not be the constituter of the fire escape and would not have the power to save a life.[25] But the same fire escape,

---

25. x is the same sum as y if and only if x and y have all and only the same parts. An arrangement of parts is not itself a part. I am like a mereological universalist who takes sums to be free riders. For my view, see Baker (2007a, 191–94).

constituted by a different sum of particles, would still have the power to save a life.

The fire escape's power to save a life does not depend on its constitution relations. The fire escape would have that causal power no matter what constituted it. A very different sum of particles would have constituted it if the fire escape had been made of pieces of metal, wood, or rope or something else. So, the fire escape has the power to save a life, because it is a fire escape, not because of what constituted it. Thus, the fire escape has the power to save a life at t nonderivatively, and the sum of particles has the power to save a life at t only derivatively. The nonderivative power to save a life is a higher causal power than the derivative causal power to save a life at t. A fire escape has nonderivative causal powers at t that its constituter would not have had derivatively at t if it had not constituted a fire escape at t.

To sum up: If x constitutes y at t, then y is on an ontologically higher level than x, and y has higher-level causal powers than x at t. And y's primary-kind property is on an ontologically higher level than x's primary-kind property. And since y has higher-level causal powers than x, and since y is not necessitated by x at t, y's primary-kind property is an ontologically emergent property. So, there are ontologically emergent properties. Over time, genuinely new kinds of objects come into existence—by natural selection and by human invention—and these new kinds with novel causal powers make for ontological novelty.

So, a constitutional account of levels avoids the reductionist's argument against emergence. A nonmereological account of levels allows distinct ontological levels, with emergent objects that have emergent primary-kind properties and new kinds of causal powers. This view seems the natural one to hold if one believes that the universe evolved from the Big Bang, and that species evolved from single-cell organisms.

Associated with the idea of emergence is the idea of downward causation, which as Kim pointed out, "is central to emergentism, for the obvious reason that for emergent properties to play any causal/explanatory role they must be capable of causally influencing processes at lower levels." (Kim 2000b, 305) In numerous articles, Kim has shown his skepticism about downward causation by arguing that "higher-level properties can serve as causes in downward causal relations only if they are reducible to lower-level properties." He adds that if they are reducible, they are not really "higher level." (Kim 2000b, 319) His argument against downward causation depends on a number of a priori principles that I regard as dubious. (Baker 2007a, 116–19) In particular, we should reject Kim's "principle of downward causation," which is supported by Kim's mereological view of levels:

> To cause any property (except those at the very bottom level) to be instantiated, you must cause the base conditions from which that property arises (either as an emergent or as a resultant). (Kim 2000b, 310)

This principle, Kim says, "shows downward causation to be essential to all higher-level causation; without it, no higher-level properties can be causally effective." (Kim 2000b, 310) Kim takes the principle of downward causation to show that there are no causally effective higher-level properties. He asks, "How is it possible for the whole to causally affect its constituent parts on which its very existence and nature depend?" (Kim 2000b, 314) And he answers, "It cannot."

My response is twofold: (1) The very existence and nature of a whole does not always depend on its constituent parts. Consider a US dollar bill; its existence and nature depend on whether its manufacture was properly authorized, not on its constituent parts. If the

United States started printing dollar bills on sheets of plastic, dollar bills would have different material parts, but still be US dollar bills. Or consider a human heart; its existence and nature depend on its evolutionary history and its function, not on its constituent parts. So, the question—"How is it possible for the whole to causally affect its constituent parts on which its very existence and nature depend?"—has a false presupposition: It is not the case that the existence and nature of a whole always depend on its constituent parts.

(2) The false presupposition rests on a mereological account of levels to which I have already given an alternative. On my constitutional account of levels, a higher-level cause is only constituted by a lower-level cause and the higher-level cause has effects without bringing about their base conditions. Think of Jones's paying his electric bill; Jones's paying his bill does not cause his resulting relief by bringing about his neural state.

Perhaps Kim's view would fit Jones's case if Jones, on finding no relief after paying his bill, then drank a glass of champagne, thereby altering his neural state. But that's not the example that we were using. Moreover, the modified example seems like a straightforward case of downward causation without reduction—unless the truth of reductionism is already assumed.

Suppose that I am right and that the principle of downward causation is false. Perhaps Kim would not care. His aim is not to defend the principle but to show that there are two putative kinds of downward causation: synchronic and diachronic. It is only synchronic downward causation that is incoherent; synchronic downward causation is a matter of there being a time at which a whole has one proper part that causes a change at another proper part. I agree that this is incoherent.

The other kind of downward causation, diachronic causation, Kim says, gives rise to no metaphysical difficulties, because the downward causation in the diachronic case does not involve emergent properties. The properties of the whole (e.g., the motion of a bird) are of the same kind as the properties of the parts (e.g., the motion of the bird's tail). There is no mystery about the whole bird's being at location$_1$ at time$_1$ and the bird's tail being at location$_2$ at time$_2$. (Kim 2000b, 317) But both these types of downward causation presuppose Kim's mereological view of levels, about which I have said enough. Constitution gives us a different (and better) way to understand ontological levels.

Even if he were right, Kim says that we may still have a use for the idea of downward causation, but not a use that involves ontological levels. Kim suggests that we "define 'higher' and 'lower' not for properties but instead for predicates and concepts." (Kim 2002, 19) If we do that, then even though two predicates may designate the same property, one of the predicates may be higher than the other. Downward causation, then, may be salvaged as a conceptual (nonontological) affair. "That is, we interpret the hierarchical levels as levels of concepts and descriptions, or levels within our representational apparatus, rather than levels of properties and phenomena in the world." (Kim 1999, 33) Then, we can speak of downward causation when a cause is described in higher-level language than its effect.

However, if your interest concerns reality and not just what we are allowed to say about it, as mine does, you will not be happy with Kim's suggestion. And I have tried to show how we can avoid the suggestion.

Let's take stock. We have seen an alternative to Kim's arguments in terms of property-constitution and a rejection of Kim's mereological-supervenient view of levels; but is there any positive argument to accept the causal efficacy of irreducible upper-level property-instances? Yes, and it lies at the heart of naturalism. For a naturalist, the trump card is empirical evidence, and there is ample empirical evidence that supports downward causation and hence the causal efficacy of irreducible upper-level property-instances.

"Our perceptual faculties are extraordinarily well suited to providing us with an accurate picture of the world around us." Our perceptual equipment "alerts us to certain features of standard environments" and enables us "to recognize the environment for what it is, both quickly and accurately." (Kornblith 1994, 44) This claim is not just an epistemic claim, but an ontological one: We not only form a picture of the world around us, but we form an *accurate* picture of our world. I do not believe that a disenchanted naturalist could agree; an accurate picture of the world for a disenchanted naturalist would be a world of bosons and fermions, not of food and friends.

Not only do we have general considerations for nonreductionism like those discussed, but there are actual empirical studies that support downward causation. Here are three: (1) When people learn to juggle, the motor and visual areas of the brain get larger. In a recent study, twelve healthy young adults were trained to juggle for six weeks, after which the jugglers could perform at least two continuous cycles of the classic three-ball cascade. Both the jugglers (12) and the control group (12) were scanned using diffusion MRI both before and after the training. According to the scientists at Oxford University, and reported in the journal *Nature Neuroscience*, there was a 5 percent increase in white matter in the area of the jugglers' brains that contain nerves that react to our reaching and grasping objects in our peripheral vision (the intraparietal sulcus). One of the investigators commented, "It is extremely exciting to see evidence that training changes human white matter connections." (Anon. 2009) (2) A study of taxi drivers in London showed that the more time taxi drivers spent on the job, the larger the hippocampus grew. The leader of the research team said, "The hippocampus has changed its structure to accommodate their huge amount of navigating experience." (Anon. 2000) (3) *Scientific American* reported on a study by the National Academy of Sciences that found a link between psychological stress and telomere shortening. (Telomeres are chromosomal caps that promote genetic stability; they naturally shorten with age.) The team leader said, "The new findings suggest a cellular mechanism for how chronic stress may cause premature onset of disease. Chronic stress appears to have the potential to shorten the life of the cells, at least immune cells." (Graham 2004)

These are just a few of the results that strongly suggest the causal efficacy of upper-level properties. To deny that these examples are cases of downward causation by giving a reductive interpretation of upper-level properties seems like a "work-around," especially in light of the fact that no one has an inkling of what a reduction of, say, learning our way around London might be or of how to go about finding it.

But what, you may ask, does this have to do with the first-person perspective? I take the discussion to be an example of a near-naturalistic general view that can accommodate the first-person perspective. The examples that I gave of the causal efficacy of upper-level properties were the simplest ones I could think of. Examples of first-person cases tend to be more complicated. Here is one:

Suppose that Jay is considering his* future—a typical first-person case—and that he is afraid that he* will not have enough money to retire; so, he decides that he* will become a consultant. I take there to be a causal connection between Jay's fear that he* won't have enough money to retire, and his decision that he* will become a consultant. Almost nothing is known about what physical states may constitute his fear and his decision except this: Physical states that constitute I*-phenomena themselves are not themselves I*-phenomena; nor—and this is the advantage of constitution over supervenience—is there any entailment relation between constituting physical states and the upper-level phenomena that they constitute; in particular, constituting physical states (whatever they may be) do not entail I*-phenomena. The causal power of I*-thoughts surpasses the causal power of their constituting physical states in the same way that the causal power of Jones's paying his electric bill surpasses the causal power of Jones's moving his fingers in a certain way.

The causal connection between Jay's fear and his decision need not be mirrored by a causal connection between the physical constituters of his fear and his decision. Here is the main point: Whether or not there is a causal connection between the physical constituters of his fear and his decision, the upper-level causal connection between his fear and his decision is the one that is explanatory. (This is the advantage of ICE over any kind of Causal Inheritance Principle.) So, near-naturalism can easily accommodate commonsense causal transactions, including those requiring a first-person perspective.

HOW NATURALISTIC IS NEAR-NATURALISM?

Near-naturalism is naturalistic in an old-fashioned way. Although it is consistent with the known laws of nature, it is not guided by or derived from science.[26] Although it leaves room for inquiry into reality beyond what is natural, there is no appeal to anything supernatural. The world pictured by near-naturalism is notably humane and expansive.

I have tried to clear the path for near-naturalism by removing a priori barriers—supported by notions like supervenience and

---

26. Some philosophers (Kim 1999; 2000b) suspect that downward causation would violate microphysical laws. I doubt that enough is known about microphysical laws and their connection with our macrophysical interactions with the world to have any confidence in such conjectures. In general, I would defer to empirical results over abstract or a priori principles.

mereology—that serve to constrict the world rather than to illuminate it. The near-naturalism that remains gives onto a generous reality, with ontological room for us and our first-person perspectives. From the point of view of near-naturalism, the everyday world—the world of getting and spending and of laying waste our powers—is as real as it gets. This capacious world—more English garden than desert landscape—is natural enough.

BIBLIOGRAPHY

Adams, Robert Merrihew. 1979. "Primitive Thisness and Primitive Identity." *Journal of Philosophy* 76 (1): 5–26.

Almeder, Robert. 1998. *Harmless Naturalism.* Chicago: Open Court.

Anon. 2000. *Taxi Drivers' Brains "Grow" on the Job.* Internet report. BBC News. http://news.bbc.co.uk/2/hi/677048.stm.

———. 2009. *Juggling Increases Brain Power.* Internet report. BBC News. http://news.bbc.co.uk/2/hi/8297764.stm.

Anscombe, G.E.M. 1957. *Intention.* Oxford: Basil Blackwell.

———. 1981. "The First Person." *Metaphysics and the Philosophy of Mind: Collected Papers, Vol. II,* 21–36. Minneapolis: University of Minnesota Press.

———. 1985. "Were You a Zygote?" In *Philosophy and Practice,* ed. A. Phillips Griffiths, 111–15. Cambridge: Cambridge University Press.

Armstrong, David M. 1980. "Naturalism, Materialism, and First Philosophy." In *The Nature of Mind and Other Essays,* 149–65. St. Lucia: University of Queensland Press.

Armstrong, David M., Charles B. Martin, and Ullin T. Place. 1996. *Dispositions: A Debate.* London: Routledge.

Auden, W.H. 1945. *The Collected Poetry of W.H. Auden.* New York: Random House.

Austin, J.L. 1961. "A Plea for Excuses." *Philosophical Papers,* 123–52. Oxford: Clarendon Press.

Baker, Lynne Rudder. 1981. "Why Computers Can't Act." *American Philosophical Quarterly* 18: 157–63.

———. 1991. "Has Content Been Naturalized?" In *Meaning in Mind: Fodor and His Critics,* ed. Barry Loewer and Georges Rey, 17–32. Oxford: Blackwell.

———. 1995. *Explaining Attitudes: A Practical Approach to the Mind*. Cambridge: Cambridge University Press.

———. 1998. "The First-Person Perspective: A Test for Naturalism." *American Philosophical Quarterly* 35: 327–48.

———. 2000. *Persons and Bodies: A Constitution View*. Cambridge: Cambridge University Press.

———. 2003. "The Difference That Self-Consciousness Makes." In *On Human Persons*, ed. Klaus Petrus, 23–40. Frankfurt: Ontos Verlag.

———. 2004. "The Ontology of Artifacts." *Philosophical Explorations* 7: 99–111.

———. 2005. "When Does a Person Begin?" *Social Philosophy and Policy* 22 (2): 25–48.

———. 2006. "Moral Responsibility without Libertarianism." *Noûs* 40: 307–30.

———. 2007a. *The Metaphysics of Everyday Life: An Essay in Practical Realism*. Cambridge, Cambridge University Press.

———. 2007b. "Social Externalism and the First-Person Perspective." *Erkenntnis* 67: 287–300.

———. 2007c. "First-Person Externalism." *The Modern Schoolman* 84: 155–70.

———. 2007d. "Naturalism and the First-Person Perspective." In *How Successful Is Naturalism?* ed. Georg Gasser, 203–27. Frankfurt: Ontos-Verlag.

———. 2008. "A Metaphysics of Ordinary Things and Why We Need It." *Philosophy* 83 (1): 5–24.

———. 2009a. "Identity across Time: A Defense of Three-Dimensionalism." In *Unity and Time in Metaphysics*, ed. Ludger Honnefelder, Edmund Runggaldier, and Benedikt Schick, 1–14. Berlin: Walter de Gruyter.

———. 2009b. "Nonreductive Materialism." In *The Oxford Handbook of Philosophy of Mind*, ed. Brian P. McLaughlin, Ansgar Beckermann, and Sven Walter, 109–127. Oxford: Clarendon Press.

———. 2010. "Temporal Reality." In *Time and Identity*, ed. Joseph Keim Campbell, Michael O'Rourke, and Harry S. Silverstein, 27–47. Cambridge MA: MIT Press.

———. 2011a. "First-Personal Aspects of Agency." *Metaphilosophy* 42 (1–2): 1–16.

———. 2011b. "How to Have Self-Directed Attitudes." In *Self-Evaluation: Affective and Social Grounds of Intentionality*, ed. Anita Konzelmann Ziv, Keith Lehrer, and Hans Bernard Schmid, 33–43. Dordrecht: Springer.

———. 2011c. "Christian Materialism in an Age of Science." *International Journal for the Philosophy of Religion* 70: 47–59.

———. 2012a. "A Not-So-Simple Simple View." In *Personal Identity: Complex or Simple?* ed. Matthias Stephan and Georg Gasser, 179–191. Cambridge: Cambridge University Press.

———. 2012b. "Three-Dimensionalism Rescued: A Brief Reply to Michael Della Rocca." typescript.

————. forthcoming. "Pereboom's Robust Nonreductive Physicalism." *Philosophy and Phenomenological Research.*

Beilby, James. 2002. *Naturalism Defeated? Essays on Plantinga's Evolutionary Argument against Naturalism.* Ithaca, NY: Cornell University Press.

Bird, Alexander. 2007. *Nature's Metaphysics: Laws and Properties.* Oxford: Oxford University Press.

Block, Ned. 1995. "On a Confusion about a Function of Consciousness." *Behavioral and Brain Sciences* 18: 227–47.

Boroditsky, Lera. 2001. "Does Language Shape Thought? Mandarin and English Speakers' Conceptions of Time." *Cognitive Psychology* 43: 1–22. doi:10.1006/cogp.2001.0748.

————. 2011. "How Language Shapes Thought." *Scientific American* (February): 63–65.

Bower, T.G.R. 1974. *Development in Infancy.* San Francisco: W.H. Freeman.

Boyd, Richard. 1980. "Materialism without Reductionism: What Physicalism Does Not Entail." In *Readings in the Philosophy of Psychology,* ed. Ned Block, 67–106. Cambridge MA: Harvard University Press.

Braddon-Mitchell, David, and Robert Nola, eds. 2009. *Conceptual Analysis and Philosophical Naturalism.* Cambridge, MA: MIT Press.

Bratman, Michael E. 2001. "Two Problems about Human Agency." *Proceedings of the Aristotelian Society* 101 (3): 309–26.

Broad, C.D. 1925. *The Mind and its Place in Nature.* New York, Harcourt Brace and Company.

Burge, Tyler. 1979. "Individualism and the Mental." In *Studies in Metaphysics, Midwest in Philosophy IV,* ed. Peter A. French, Theodore E. Uehling, Jr., and Howard K. Wettstein, 73–121. Minneapolis, University of Minnesota Press.

————. 2010. *Origins of Objectivity.* Oxford: Clarendon Press.

De Caro, Mario, and David Macarthur. 2010. "Science, Naturalism and the Problem of Normativity." In *Naturalism and Normativity,* 3–19. New York: Columbia University Press.

De Caro, Mario, and Alberto Voltolini. 2010. "Is Liberal Naturalism Possible?" In *Naturalism and Normativity,* ed. Mario De Caro and David Macarthur, 69–86. New York: Columbia University Press.

Carruthers, Peter. 2009. "How We Know Our Own Minds: The Relationship between Mindreading and Metacognition." *Behavioral and Brain Sciences* 32 (1): 121–82.

————. 2010. "Introspection: Divided and Partly Eliminated." *Philosophy and Phenomenological Research* 80 (1): 76–111.

————. 2011. *The Opacity of Mind: An Integrative Theory of Self-Knowledge.* Oxford: Oxford University Press.

Cartwright, Nancy. 2003. "What Makes a Capacity a Disposition?" Centre for Philosophy of Natural and Social Science. http://personal.lse.ac.uk/cartwrig/PapersGeneral/what%20makes%20a%20capacity%20a%20disposition.pdf.

Castañeda, Hector-Neri. 1966. "He: A Study in the Logic of Self-Consciousness." *Ratio* 8: 130–57.

———. 1967. "Indicators and Quasi-Indicators." *American Philosophical Quarterly* 4: 85–100.

Chalmers, David. 1996. *The Conscious Mind*. New York: Oxford University Press.

Chalmers, David J. 1991. "First-Person Methods in the Science of Consciousness." http://consc.net/papers/firstperson.html.

———. 1995. "Facing Up to the Problem of Consciousness." *Journal of Consciousness Studies* 2 (3): 200–19.

Chisholm, Roderick. 1976. *Person and Object*. LaSalle, IL: Open Court.

———. 1981. *The First Person: An Essay on Reference and Intentionality*. Minneapolis: University of Minnesota Press.

———. 1991. "On the Simplicity of the Soul." In *Philosophical Perspectives: 5 Philosophy of Religion*, 5:167–81. Philosophical Perspectives. Atascadero, CA: Ridgeview.

Churchland, Patricia Smith. 1988. *Neurophilosophy: Toward a Unified Science of the Mind/Brain*. Cambridge MA: MIT Press.

Clapp, Lenny. 2001. "Disjunctive Properties: Multiple Realization." *Journal of Philosophy* 98: 111–36.

Danziger, Shai, and Robert Ward. 2010. "Language Shapes Implicit Associations between Ethnic Groups and Evaluation in Bilinguals." *Psychological Science* 21 (6): 799–800.

Della Rocca, Michael. "Primitive Persistence and the Impasse between Three-Dimensionalism and Four-Dimensionalism." *Journal of Philosophy* 108 (11).

Dennett, Daniel C. 1991. *Consciousness Explained*. Boston: Little, Brown.

———. 1993. *Content and Consciousness*. London: Routledge.

———. 2001. "The Fantasy of a First-Person Science." http://ase.tufts.edu/cog-stud/papers/chalmersdeb3dft.htm.

———. 2009a. "Daniel Dennett." In *Mind and Consciousness: 5 Questions*, ed. Patrick Grim, 25–30. 5 Questions. Automatic Press/VIP.

———. 2009b. "Intentional Systems Theory." In *Oxford Handbook of Philosophy of Mind*, ed. Brian P. McLauglin, Ansgar Beckermann, and Sven Walter, 339–50. Oxford: Clarendon Press.

Dumont, Stephen D. 2002. "John Duns Scotus." In *A Companion to Philosophy in the Middle Ages*, ed. Jorge J.E. Garcia and Timothy B. Noone, 253–369. Oxford: Blackwell.

Edwards, Kevan. 2011. "Higher-Level Concepts and Their Heterogeneous Implementations." *Philosophical Psychology* 24 (1) (February): 119–33.

Ellis, Brian, and Caroline Lierse. 1994. "Dispositional Essentialism." *Australasian Journal of Philosophy* 72 (1): 27–45.

Fodor, Jerry. 1974. "Special Sciences or: The Disunity of Science as a Working Hypothesis." *Synthese* 28 (2): 97–115.

Fodor, Jerry A. 1987. *Psychosemantics: The Problem of Meaning in the Philosophy of Mind*. Cambridge, MA: MIT Press.

Foster, John. 1991. *The Immaterial Self: A Defense of the Cartesian Conception of the Mind*. London: Routledge.

Frankfurt, Harry. 1971. "Freedom of the Will and the Concept of a Person." *Journal of Philosophy* 68: 5–20.

Frankish, Keith, and Jonathan St. B.T. Evans. 2009. "The Duality of Mind: An Historical Perspective." In *In Two Minds: Dual Processes and Beyond*, ed. Keith Frankish and Jonathan St. B.T. Evans, 1–29. Oxford: Oxford University Press.

Gallup, Gordon, Jr. 1977. "Self-Recognition in Primates: A Comparative Approach to Bidirectional Properties of Consciousness." *American Psychologist* 32: 329–38.

Geach, Peter. 1957. *Mental Acts*. London: Routledge and Kegan Paul.

Goldman, Alvin I. 1997. "Science, Publicity and Consciousness." *Philosophy of Science* 64 (4): 525–45.

Graham, Sarah. 2004. "Cellular Aging." *Scientific American*, November 30. www.scientificamerican.com/article.cfm?id=high-stress-levels-linked.

Grandin, Temple. 2006. *Thinking in Pictures: My Life with Autism*. 2nd ed. New York: Vintage Books.

Hershenov, David B. 2009. "Problems with a Constitution Account of Persons." *Dialogue* 48 (2): 291–312.

Huebner, Bryce, and Daniel C. Dennett. 2009. "Banishing 'I' and 'We' from Accounts of Metacognition." *Behavioral and Brain Sciences* 32: 148–49.

Jackson, Frank. 1998. *From Metaphysics to Ethics*. Oxford: Clarendon Press.

James, William. 1948/1907. What Pragmatism Means. In Essays in Pragmatism, ed. Alburey Castell, 141–158. New York: Hafner Publishing Compary

Johnston, Mark. 2010. *Surviving Death*. Princeton, NJ: Princeton University Press.

Kagan, Jerome. 1981. *The 2nd Year: The Emergence of Self-Awareness*. Cambridge MA: Harvard University Press.

Kahneman, Daniel. 2011. *Thinking, Fast and Slow*. New York: Farrar, Straus and Giroux.

Kaplan, David. 1989. "Demonstratives." In *Themes from Kaplan*, ed. Joseph Almog, John Perry, and Howard K. Wettstein, 481–564. New York: Oxford University Press.

Kim, Jaegwon. 1993a. "Multiple Realization and the Metaphysics of Reduction." In *Supervenience and Mind: Selected Philosophical Essays*, 309–35. Cambridge: Cambridge University Press.

———. 1993b. "'Strong' and 'Global' Supervenience Revisited." In *Supervenience and Mind: Selected Philosophical Essays*, 79–91. Cambridge: Cambridge University Press.

————. 1993c. *Supervenience and Mind: Selected Philosophical Essays*. Cambridge: Cambridge University Press.

————. 1999. "Making Sense of Emergence." *Philosophical Studies* 95: 3–36.

————. 2000a. *Mind in a Physical World*. Cambridge MA: MIT Press.

————. 2000b. "Making Sense of Downward Causation." In *Downward Causation*, ed. Peter Bogh Andersen, Claus Emmeche, and Peder Peder Voetmann Christiansen, 305–21. Aarhus, Denmark: Aarhus University Press.

————. 2002. "The Layered Model: Metaphysical Considerations." *Philosophical Explorations* 5: 2–20.

————. 2005. *Physicalism, or Something Near Enough*. Princeton: Princeton University Press.

————. 2009. "'Supervenient and Yet Not Deducible': Is There a Coherent Concept of Ontological Emergence?" In *Reduction: Between the Mind and the Brain*, ed. Alexander Hieke and Hannes Leitgeb, 53–72. Frankfurt: Ontos Verlag.

Kitcher, Philip. 1992. "The Naturalists Return." *Philosophical Review* 101 (1): 53–114.

————. 2011a. "Challenges for Secularism." In *The Joy of Secularism*, ed. George Levine, 24–56. Princeton, NJ: Princeton University Press.

————. 2011b. *The Ethical Project*. Cambridge, MA: Harvard University Press.

Kornblith, Hilary. 1994. "Naturalism: Both Metaphysical and Epistemological." In *Philosophical Naturalism*, ed. Peter A. French, Theodore E. Uehling, and Howard K. Wettstein, *Vol. 19*, 39–52. Midwest Studies in Philosophy. Notre Dame: Notre Dame Press.

————. 2012. *On Reflection*. Oxford: Oxford University Press.

Kripke, Saul. 2011. "The First Person." In *Philosophical Troubles: Collected Papers, Vol. 1*, 292–321. Oxford: Oxford University Press.

————. 1982. *Wittgenstein on Rules and Natural Language*. Cambridge, MA: Harvard University Press.

Lewis, David. 1979. "Attitudes De Dicto and De Se." *Philosophical Review* 88: 513–43.

————. 1983a. "An Argument for the Identity Theory." In *Philosophical Papers, Vol. 1*, 99–107. New York: Oxford University Press.

————. 1983b. "Survival and Identity." In *Philosophical Papers, Vol. 1*, 55–77. New York: Oxford University Press.

————. 1986. *Philosophical Papers, Vol. II*. New York: Oxford University Press.

————. 1997. "Finkish Dispositions." *Philosophical Quarterly* 47: 143–58.

————. 1999. "Reduction of Mind." In *Papers in Metaphysics and Epistemology*, 291–324. Cambridge Studies in Philosophy. Cambridge: Cambridge University Press.

Lewis, Michael. 1994. "Myself and Me." In *Self-Awareness in Animals and Humans*, ed. Sue Taylor Parker, Robert W. Mitchell, and Maria L. Boccia. Cambridge: Cambridge University Press.

Lowe, E.J. 1993. "The Causal Autonomy of the Mental." *Mind* 102: 629–44.

Mach, Ernst. 1949. *The Analysis of Sensations*. Trans. C.M. Williams and S. Waterlow. Chicago: Open Court.

Machery, Edouard. 2010. "Precis of Doing without Concepts." *Philosophical Studies* 149 (3): 401–10. doi:10.1007s11098-010-9527-y.

Malcolm, Norman. 1972. "Thoughtless Brutes." *Proceedings and Addresses of the American Philosophical Association* 46 (1) (March): 5–20.

Matthews, Gareth B. 1977. "Surviving As." *Analysis* 37 (2): 53–58.

———. 1992. *Thought's Ego in Augustine and Descartes*. Ithaca, NY: Cornell University Press.

———. 2009. "The Euthyphro Problem." typescript.

McKitrick, Jennifer. 2003. "A Case for Extrinsic Dispositions." *Australasian Journal of Philosophy* 81 (2): 155–74.

———. 2005. "Are Dispositions Causally Relevant?" *Synthese* 144 (3): 357–71.

Merricks, Trenton. 1998. "There Are No Criteria of Identity over Time." *Nôus* 32 (1): 106–24.

Metzinger, Thomas. 2003a. *Being No One: The Self-Model of Subjectivity*. Cambridge MA: MIT Press.

———. 2003b. "Phenomenal Transparency and Cognitive Self-Reference." *Phenomenology and the Cognitive Sciences* 2: 353–93.

Mithen, S. 2004. "Review Symposium of Andy Clark's Natural-Born Cyborgs." *Metascience* 13 (2): 163–69.

Moore, G.E. 1903. "The Refutation of Idealism." *Mind* 12: 433–53.

Morgan, C. Lloyd. 1923. *Emergent Evolution*. London, Williams and Norgate.

Mumford, Stephen. 1998. *Dispositions*. Oxford: Clarendon Press.

Nagel, Ernest. 1961. *The Structure of Science*. New York: Harcourt, Brace & World.

Nagel, Thomas. 1983. "The Objective Self." In *Knowledge and Mind: Philosophical Essays*, ed. Carl Ginet and Sydney Shoemaker, 213–32. New York: Oxford University Press.

———. 1986. *The View from Nowhere*. Oxford: Oxford University Press.

———. 2005. "Secular Philosophy and the Religious Temperament". Pdf. http://records.viu.ca/www/ipp/2pdf.

———. 2010. "Secular Philosophy and the Religious Temperament." In *Secularism and the Religious Temperament: Essays 2002–2008*, 3–17. Oxford: Oxford University Press.

Nisbett, Richard, and Lee Ross. 1980. "The Lay Scientist Self-Examined." In *Inductive Inference: Strategies and Shortcomings of Social Judgment*, 195–227. Englewood Cliffs, NJ: Prentice-Hall.

Noë, Alva, and Evan Thompson. 2004. "Are There Neural Correlates of Consciousness?" *Journal of Consciousness Studies* 11 (1): 3–28.

Noonan, Harold W. 2003. *Personal Identity*. 2nd ed. London: Routledge.

Noordhof, Paul. 1999. "Causation by Content?" *Mind & Language* 14: 291–320.

O'Brien, Lucy. 2007. *Self-Knowing Agents*. Oxford: Oxford University Press.

Ogunnaike, Oludamini, Yarrow Dunham, and Mahzarin R. Banaji. 2010. "The Language of Implicit Preferences." *Journal of Experimental Social Psychology* 46 (6): 999–1003.

Parfit, Derek. 1971. "Personal Identity." *Philosophical Review* 80: 3–27.

———. 1984. *Reasons and Persons*. Oxford: Clarendon Press.

Peacocke, Christopher. 1992. *A Study of Concepts*. Cambridge MA: MIT Press/ Bradford.

Penn, Derek C., Keith J. Holyoak, and Daniel J. Povinelli. 2008. "Darwin's Mistake: Explaining the Discontinuity between Human and Nonhuman Minds." *Behavioral and Brain Sciences* 31: 109–78.

Pereboom, Derk. 2001. *Living without Free Will*. Cambridge Studies in Philosophy. Cambridge: Cambridge University Press.

———. 2002. "Robust Nonreductive Materialism." *Journal of Philosophy* 99: 499–531.

———. 2011. *Consciousness and the Prospects of Physicalism*. Oxford: Oxford University Press.

Pereboom, Derk, and Hilary Kornblith. 1991. "The Metaphysics of Irreducibility." *Philosophical Studies* 63: 125–46.

Perry, John. 1979. "The Problem of the Essential Indexical." *Noûs* 13: 3–21.

———. 2002a. *Identity, Personal Identity, and the Self*. Indianapolis: Hackett.

———. 2002b. "The Self, Self-Knowledge, and Self-Notions." In *Identity, Personal Identity, and the Self*, 189–213. Indianapolis: Hackett.

Pinker, Steven. 1997. *How the Mind Works*. New York: W. W. Norton.

Plantinga, Alvin. 2011. *Where the Conflict Really Lies: Science, Religion & Naturalism*. New York: Oxford University Press.

Povinelli, Daniel. 2004. "Behind the Ape's Appearance: Escaping Anthropocentrism in the Study of Other Minds." *Daedalus* (Winter): 29–41.

Povinelli, Daniel, and Jennifer Vonk. 2004. "We Don't Need a Microscope to Explore the Chimpanzee Mind." *Mind and Language* 19: 1–28.

Prior, Elizabeth, Robert Pargetter, and Frank Jackson. 1982. "Three Theses about Dispositions." *American Philosophical Quarterly* 19 (3): 251–57.

Putnam, Hilary. 1975. "The Nature of Mental States." In *Philosophical Papers* 2: 429–40. Cambridge, MA: Harvard University Press.

Quine, W.V.O. 1969a. "Speaking of Objects." In *Ontological Relativity and Other Essays*, 1–25. New York: Columbia University Press.

———. 1969b. "Epistemology Naturalized." In *Ontological Relativity and Other Essays*, 69–90. New York: Columbia University Press.

———. 1995. "Naturalism: Or, Living within One's Means." *Dialectica* 49: 251–62.

Rea, Michael C. 2002. *World without Design*. Oxford: Clarendon Press.

Rosenberg, Alex. 2009. "The Disenchanted Naturalist's Guide to Reality." *On the Human*. http://onthehuman.org/2009/11/the-disenchanted-naturalists-guide-to-reality/.

———. 2011a. *The Atheist's Guide to Reality: Enjoying Life without Illusions*. New York: W.W. Norton.

———. 2013. "Disenchanted Naturalism." In *The Metaphysics of Evolutionary Contemporary Philosophical Naturalism and its Implications*, eds. Bana Bashour and Hans D. Muller. New York: Routledge.

Russell, Bertrand. 1945. *A History of Western Philosophy*. New York: Simon & Schuster.

Schaffer, Jonathan. 2003. "Is There a Fundamental Level?" *Nôus* 37: 498–517.

Schlick, Moritz. 1949. "Meaning and Verification." In *Readings in Philosophical Analysis*, ed. Herbert Feigl and Wilfrid Sellars, 146–70. New York: Appleton-Century-Crofts.

Schmitt, Frederick F. 1995. "Naturalism." In *A Companion to Metaphysics*, ed. Jaegwon Kim and Ernest Sosa, 342–345. Oxford: Blackwell.

Searle, John R. 1992. *The Rediscovery of the Mind*. Cambridge MA: MIT Press.

———. 2000. "Consciousness." *Annual Review of Neuroscience* 23: 557–78.

Segal, Gabriel, and Elliott Sober. 1991. "The Causal Efficacy of Content." *Philosophical Studies* 63: 1–30.

Sellars, Wilfrid. 1963. "Empiricism and the Philosophy of Mind." In *Science, Perception and Reality*, 127–96. London: Routledge and Kegan Paul.

Shoemaker, Sydney, and Richard Swinburne. 1984. *Personal Identity*. Oxford: Blackwell.

Shook, John R., and Paul Kurtz, eds. 2009. *The Future of Naturalism*. Amherst, NY: Humanity Books.

Sorabji, Richard. 2006. *Self: Ancient and Modern Insights about Individuality, Life, and Death*. Chicago: University of Chicago Press.

Sorenson, Roy A. 1992. *Thought Experiments*. New York: Oxford University Press.

Steuber, Karston. 2009. "Empathy, Mental Dispositions and the Physicalist Challenge." In *Debating Dispositions: Issues in Metaphysics, Epistemology, and Philosophy of Mind*, ed. Gregor Damschen, Robert Schnepf, and Karston R. Stueber, 257–77. Berlin: Walter de Gruyter.

Stevens, John D. 1987. *Sharks*. New York: Facts on File.

Strawson, Galen. 1997. "The Self." *Journal of Consciousness Studies* 4 (5/6): 405–28.

Swinburne, Richard. 1997. *The Evolution of the Soul*. Oxford: Clarendon Press.

Thomas, E.M. 1993. *The Hidden Life of Dogs*. Boston: Houghton Mifflin.

Tomasello, Michael. 1999. *The Cultural Origins of Human Cognition*. Cambridge, MA: Harvard University Press.

———. 2008. "How Are Humans Unique?" *New York Times*, May 25. www.nytimes.com/2008/05/25/magazine/25wwln-essay-t.html?8br.

Van Inwagen, Peter. 2005. "The Self: The Incredulous Stare Articulated." In *The Self?* ed. Galen Strawson, 110–24. Malden, MA: Blackwell.

———. 2006. "I Look for the Resurrection of the Dead and the Life of the World to Come." Unpublished—Online Word doc. http://philosophy.nd.edu/people/all/profiles/van-inwagen-peter/documents/Resurrection.doc.

Velleman, J. David. 1992. "What Happens When Someone Acts?" *Mind* 101: 461–81.

Vonk, Jennifer, and Povinelli, Daniel. 2006. "Similarity and Difference in the Conceptual Systems of Primates: The Unobservability Hypothesis." In *Comparative Cognition*, ed. T. Zentall and E.A. Wasserman, 363–87. Oxford. Oxford University Press.

Wierenga, Edward R. 1989. *The Nature of God: An Inquiry into Divine Attributes.* Ithaca, NY: Cornell University Press.

Williams, Bernard. 1978. *Descartes: The Project of Pure Inquiry.* Atlantic Highlands, NJ: Humanities Press.

Wittgenstein, Ludwig. 1921. *Tractatus Logico-Philosophicus.* Trans. D.F. Pears and B.F. McGuiness. London: Routledge and Kegan Paul.

———. 1958. *Philosophical Investigations.* Third. New York: Macmillan.

Zahavi, Dan. 2005. *Subjectivity and Selfhood: Investigating the First-Person Perspective.* Cambridge MA: MIT Press.

INDEX